The Revolution Will Be Improvised

The Revolution Will Be Improvised

The Intimacy of Cultural Activism

Elizabeth Rodriguez Fielder

University of Michigan Press
Ann Arbor

Copyright © 2024 by Elizabeth Rodriguez Fielder

This work is licensed under a Creative Commons Attribution-NonCommercial 4.0 International License. *Note to users*: A Creative Commons license is only valid when it is applied by the person or entity that holds rights to the licensed work. Works may contain components (e.g., photographs, illustrations, or quotations) to which the rightsholder in the work cannot apply the license. It is ultimately your responsibility to independently evaluate the copyright status of any work or component part of a work you use, in light of your intended use. To view a copy of this license, visit http://creativecommons.org/licenses/by-nc/4.0/

For questions or permissions, please contact um.press.perms@umich.edu

Published in the United States of America by the
University of Michigan Press
Manufactured in the United States of America
Printed on acid-free paper
First published October 2024

A CIP catalog record for this book is available from the British Library.

Library of Congress Cataloging-in-Publication Data

Names: Fielder, Elizabeth Rodriguez., author. | Michigan Publishing
   (University of Michigan), publisher.
Title: The revolution will be improvised : the intimacy of cultural activism / Elizabeth
   Rodriguez Fielder.
Description: Ann Arbor : University of Michigan Press, [2024] | Includes bibliographical
   references (pages 195–203) and index.
Identifiers: LCCN 2024024465 (print) | LCCN 2024024466 (ebook) |
   ISBN 9780472077045 (hardcover) | ISBN 9780472057047 (paperback) |
   ISBN 9780472904662 (ebook other)
Subjects: LCSH: Activism—Social aspects. | Student Nonviolent Coordinating Committee
   (U.S.) | Civil rights workers—Social aspects. | Protest movements—Social aspects. |
   Social change—Political aspects. | Politics and culture—Social aspects. | Minorities—
   Civil rights—Social aspects. | Intimacy (Psychology)—Political aspects.
Classification: LCC HN17.5 .F53 2024 (print) | LCC HN17.5 (ebook) |
   DDC 303.48/4--dc23/eng/20240628
LC record available at https://lccn.loc.gov/2024024465
LC ebook record available at https://lccn.loc.gov/2024024466

DOI: https://doi.org/10.3998/mpub.12849979

The University of Michigan Press's open access publishing program is made possible thanks to additional funding from the University of Michigan Office of the Provost and the generous support of contributing libraries.

*In memory of John O'Neal and Doris Derby
and all those who dedicated their lives to the Movement.*

And to Stephanie Kubick.

Contents

List of Illustrations	ix
Acknowledgments	xi
Preface	xv
Introduction: The Role of Art in the Process of Social Change	1
1 The Free Southern Theater and Visual Jazz Performance	26
2 Creative Labor: Spiritual Activism, El Teatro Campesino, and the Farmworkers' March	55
3 A New Lesson for Activism: Art Education and Performance	79
4 The Fabric of Social Change: Liberty House and Craft-Making Cooperatives	101
5 Art/Work: The Independent Media Archives of the South	126
Conclusion: The Open Channel of Cultural Activism	153
Notes	175
Bibliography	195
Index	205

Digital materials related to this title can be found on the Fulcrum platform via the following citable URL: https://doi.org/10.3998/mpub.12849979

Illustrations

Figure 1. Urban Bush Women performance, New Orleans, 2013 — xvi

Figure 2. The Free Southern Theater's *Waiting for Godot*, 1964 — 41

Figure 3. The Free Southern Theater's *Slave Ship*, 1970 — 47

Figure 4. El Teatro Campesino's *Governor Brown*, 1966 — 69

Figure 5. El Teatro Campesino's *La quinta temporada*, 1968 — 72

Figure 6. The Free Southern Theater's production of *The Lesson*, 1967 — 80

Figure 7. El Teatro Campesino's production of *Las dos caras del patroncito, 1968* — 87

Figure 8. The Free Southern Theater's production of *Does Man Help Man*, 1966 — 92

Figure 9. The Free Southern Theater's production of *The Rifles of Señora Carrar*, 1965 — 95

Figure 10. Head Start workshop, *gele* wrapping — 114

Figure 11. Cooperative women sewing — 119

Figure 12. Filmstrip of Poor People's Corporation's cooperative meeting in Mississippi — 120

Figure 13. Image of okra from *Something of Our Own* — 128

Figure 14. Farm machinery from *Something of Our Own* — 136

Figure 15. Child jumping from *Farm Worker's Strike* — 138

Acknowledgments

I would first and foremost like to thank Maria Varela for reading and commenting on so much of this manuscript and for her dedication to the ongoing project of the civil rights movement. Thank you to Maude Bruce at the DJB Foundation for permission to use Doris Derby's images and encouragement that I've been on the right path to honoring her work. Thank you to the archivists and librarians who have helped with this work, those at the Stuart A. Rose Special Collections at Emory University and the El Teatro Campesino archive at UC Santa Barbara, but especially Lisa Moore at the Amistad Research Center, who has been a calm presence on the other end of my frantic phone calls. It is truly a privilege to be able to research and I'm grateful for the work of archivists, librarians, and student workers for doing the heavy lifting and scanning, so that I might have the time to think and write.

Thank you to Sara Cohen at the University of Michigan Press for her support and feedback as well as the faculty executive board and the two anonymous reviewers of my manuscript for their generosity and honesty. Thank you to copy editor John Raymond for the attention to detail. And thank you to Daniel Fischlin who encouraged me toward the press and for his support for this project. I extend gratitude to all the administrators and deans who have funded this project: the Monroe Fellowship at the Center for the Study of the Gulf South, the Office for the Vice President of Research at the University of Iowa for subvention funds, the University of Iowa, the Humanities Center and the Department of English at the University of Pittsburgh, and a grant from the Stuart A. Rose Special Collections at Emory University.

I want to thank my various department chairs who have supported me, advocated for me, and guided me in my career: Blaine Greteman, Loren Glass, Claire Fox, Gayle Rogers, Don Bialostosky, and Ivo Kamps. And where would any of us be without our mentors? Thank you to Jen Buckley, Kim Marra, Naomi Greyser, Harry Stecopoulos, James Smethurst, Jaime Harker, and especially Leigh Anne Duck, who has continued to read my work and mentor me long after grad school.

The fact that I know personally so many of the people that I cite proves that scholarship exists because of community. And I want to thank all the communities that have shaped me as a scholar. All the people at the University of Iowa who have sat around my dining room table and read parts of this work to help me move ideas forward: Allison Rowe, David Gooblar, Megan McVancel, Kristy Nabhan-Warren, and Doris Witt. The people of the Obermann Center's Performance Studies group and the people of the Imagining Latinidades Summer Seminar: Lina-Maria Murillo, Thelma Trujillo, and our facilitators, Naomi Greyser and Aimee Carillo-Rowe. A special shout-out to Eric Vasquez, who has sat by my side in so many ways, and to Asha Bhandary, who is a generous reader of my work, a Zumba inspiration, and a sister to me.

Thanks to my University of Pittsburgh intellectual community for writing and friendship: Imani Owens, Jules Gil-Petersen, Peter Campbell, Paul Johnson, and Caitlin Bruce. And my friends who showed me how powerful women of color scholars can be: Yodit Betru, Matiangai Sirleaf, Jaime Booth, Toya Jones, and Gina Garcia. Thank you to the wonderful intellectual community at the University of Copenhagen, especially Martyn Bone and Dave Struthers. I cannot forget my Columbia University American Studies crowd that introduced me to the concept of the colleague who is also a friend, especially Mina Nikolopoulou. The Society for the Study of Southern Literature community—with all its sweet tea drama—has been a home for me and I thank all of you who have been transforming that community for the better, y'all know who you are! Finally, I want to thank all the people who offered me informal support in terms of references and ideas and conversations about my work, such as Katie DeVries, Johanna Kasimow, Dorian Dean, Michelle Bright, Jane Meek, Ben Hassman, and especially clay scofield, who kept me laughing during late night writing sessions, cheering me on to the finish line. To any I've forgotten, I send you my gratitude and apologies. Thank you to the amazing creative community of artists and parents who keep Iowa City such a cool place to live.

A special thank you to two family members who were such strong supporters of my work, John Kolk and Patricia Mercurio Montalvo, who passed away during the final stage of this book, but whose memory kept me going. Thank you to my family: my parents Martha Rodriguez and Robert Fielder, my cousins Veronica, Donna, Gabriela, Matt, Mike, and Austin, all their fabulous partners and my tias, tios, and all the myriad people I am somehow related

Acknowledgments · xiii

to who are with me in spirit. To Avi and Marta, who watched my kiddos so I could keep writing while becoming a new mother, and especially to Will Rhodes, an exemplar of co-parenting and supporter of me in so many ways.

To my longest friend, Jillian Egan, for always believing in me, and to Carla Hung, my inspiration both when we were kids at punk shows in Queens and as adults in academia. To my therapist, Janel, for guiding me through the storm. A special thank you to Ryan Charlton who read and reread every line of this book, fixing my English, being my editor and dear friend.

And to my children, Adrian and Marcelo, thank you endlessly for bringing me back to my own humanity.

Preface

In 2013, I attended the fiftieth anniversary celebration of the Free Southern Theater, a theater group founded at Tougaloo College in Mississippi during the civil rights movement. Activists, artists, and scholars gathered in New Orleans for a weekend of reflection and action at the Ashé Cultural Arts Center, where I listened to a panel of former members—Doris Derby, John O'Neal, Chakula cha Jua—reflect on the legacy of their mission. Influential figures such as Gil Moses and Tom Dent had passed on, but those in attendance reflected on the legacy of the Free Southern Theater and how they had achieved their impossible vision of an integrated activist theater group in 1960s Mississippi, a place that at the time was the symbol of racial oppression in the United States.

Then, unexpectedly, the conference leaders organized us into breakout groups called Story Circles where I was expected to share *who I was* in relationship to my work. I had to discuss my investment in art and activism, not as a researcher/observer, but as a participant in dialogue with others. I could not just sit in the back taking notes; I had to put the pen down and get involved. At the Ashé Cultural Arts Center, the organizers created an alternative definition of a conference, one where I and the other handful of scholars joined in as meaning-makers, an act that demanded vulnerability. As a Latina and a woman in academia, vulnerability is uncomfortable, yet the Story Circle drew me into a greater intimacy with the people around me and to the work that eventually became this book. To the writing of this book, I bring my embodied experience as a performer, a woman of color, a daughter and granddaughter of union people, and recognize how that matters to my scholarship.

After the Story Circles, we boarded a yellow school bus and toured New Orleans. At each site, dancers from Urban Bush Women performed interpre-

Figure 1. Urban Bush Women performance, New Orleans, 2013. Photograph by author, 2013.

tations of the place, such as the railroad tracks where in 1892 Homer Plessy (of *Plessy v. Ferguson*) boarded a "whites only" car. At a later stop, outside a locked-up school building, dancers climbed a chain-link fence and performed a dance of rage and pain at Katrina's effects on the infrastructure of the city. The young Black dancers were dressed in collared dresses evocative of the images of Elizabeth Ekford as she entered Little Rock Central High School in 1957. In appearance, they collapsed time between the civil rights movement and the aftermath of Katrina. The strength of their movements (that I thought any minute would surely break down the fence) created a performance that expressed both frustration and the potential for liberation. Their bodies improvised a relationship between sound, the visuality of the school, and each other. They told a story through embodiment across temporal and geographic registers, giving me more insight into the meaning of cultural activism than all the folders and boxes in the archive. In that moment, drawing on my identity as a dancer, I understood how the multiplicity of meaning communicated in performance opens up time and space, calling on us to rearrange the social order.

Later that evening, at an exhibit of Doris Derby's photographs, the former Free Southern Theater members reflected on a production of Amiri Baraka's *Slave Ship* in West Point, Mississippi, recalling the names of actors and reminiscing on the emotional impact of the performance. Even though the walls were covered with images of the past, Derby used the platform to emphasize her recent work and the work of her students. It fit the theme of the whole conference: *Here is what we did, but here is what we are doing now.* The civil rights movement was never far from discussions about post-Katrina New Orleans, teaching me that civil-rights-era cultural activism has always been relational to contemporary arts and performance collectives.

People in the Movement vocalized their political commitment set to the tune of "We Shall Overcome," while at the same time they asked difficult questions and worked out their contradictions through collective and collaborative art-making. The *Revolution Will Be Improvised* tells this story through the performances, improvisations, teachings, and artistic experimentations of activists and local people during the civil rights movement. Despite the era's commitment to manifestos, pledges, proclamations, and ten-point programs, the creative expressions made by activists forged a space to question ideology and political commitment. Too often institutional stability is a sign of success; however, because these arts organizations continued to evolve based on what communities needed, they have lasted in an alternative genealogy, which I discuss further in the conclusion. The Movement lives on as a method of communication: a way of storytelling, where activists continue a conversation they inherited from the previous generation. The civil rights movement never really died, it seems, it just continued to evolve into a generational approach to social change, where the revolving door of organization names and leaders are a testament to a necessary flexibility in social movement organizing.

At the Ashé Cultural Center in New Orleans, I absorbed a different timeline and narrative of the American civil rights movement where Martin Luther King Jr. and Malcolm X carry less relevance than Gilbert Moses and Bob Moses. Here, the Movement was not relegated to history; it was a living series of familial networks and what Robin D. G. Kelley calls freedom dreams, "the alternative visions and dreams that inspire new generations to continue to struggle for change."[1] Years later, when reading adrienne maree brown's *Emergent Strategy*, I understood how inspiration and dreamwork could move across time as she weaves together past and present, bringing in the voices of revolutionary thinkers, such as Grace Lee Boggs and Ella Baker. She quotes Baker in the epigraph, "This may only be a dream of mine, but I think it can be made real," and writes into the space between the possible and impossible in her books on activism and how both dreamwork and cultural work move across time.[2] In *Holding Change*, brown claims, "When we are facilitating a space and we remember that time can bend, we focus not on time scarcity, but on the people in the room, the presence, and the work that can be done."[3] Philosophers of activism then and now have committed to describing the intangible and making scalar moves between the smallest interactions and multigenerational ideas. Their work has inspired my own methodological approach to the Movement, in which I witness intimate interactions in the archive of civil rights art activism and connect them to the broader goal of social change.

Introduction

The Role of Art in the Process of Social Change

———

There is an unfettered, unyielding nature to the civil rights movement that's difficult to capture in any linear or disciplinary fashion. Analysis of the Movement evades fixed ideological frameworks or single-issue approaches because its participants—especially the unfamous majority of them—worked with fluidity between organizations, campaigns, and philosophies. This is why, over half a century later, we are still fascinated with the civil rights movement. Not because of its tangible material outcomes, which are still being debated on the basis of the continuity of overt and systemic racism in the United States. Rather, because it calls on us to see social movements beyond the binary of success and failure and to bear witness to the complexity of social justice. The civil rights movement was a time of experimentation limited only by the violent atmosphere in which activists and local people worked. The line between activist and "local person" overlapped and blurred, just as did the line between farmworker and performer, or poet and organizer. In the relational network of the civil rights movement, I use the term *cultural activist* or *cultural worker* interchangeably to refer to someone seeking to make social change through collaborative art-making practices. They kept dialogue open across different channels and methods of organizing, ready with a poem, a performance, a projector, or an economic strategy in hand.

The improvisational and multifaceted approach of cultural activism places the civil rights movement in an unexpected place: as a transformative locus within American experimental art. Cultural workers improvised with each other to not only disrupt society but to do the work of world-building that demanded creativity as a human right. They used whatever tools and resources they could to build relationships with local people—an unquantifiable process of becoming more intimate with their communities. Traces of their intentions exist in an archive of theater productions and improvised performances, collaboratively made filmstrip media, fabrics and photographs, DIY (do-it-yourself) pamphlets and poetry collections, and dozens of unfinished, imagined projects. This book gathers these art objects together to craft a narrative about artistic expression and experimentation during the civil rights movement and how this work impacts performance, independent media, education, and labor. I begin with theater, specifically the Free Southern Theater and El Teatro Campesino, and trace how performance moves into other experimentations with media and crafting. Rather than stay within the bounds of artistic disciplines, I argue that activists and local people crossed boundaries of genre and form, improvising in response to their limited resources and their desire for experimentation.

Activists also invested in physical spaces for cultural work, such as the Free Southern Theater's building on Dryades Street in New Orleans and the Poor People's Corporation Training Center in Edwards, Mississippi, which trained people for skills in craft-making, business, and marketing. These spaces became cultural hubs that infused future generations of artists and activists within a civil rights movement paradigm. At one such location, the Liberty House in Harlem, world-renounced Black Arts poet Nikki Giovanni remembers hearing Gil Scott Heron recite his poem "The Revolution Will Not Be Televised" for the first time.[1] The store was an extension of the Liberty House in Jackson, Mississippi, which marketed and sold crafts made by cooperatives of the Poor People's Corporation. Filled with the craftwork of Black women from Mississippi, Heron and others read their poetry in Liberty House, inspiring Giovanni and whoever else was in the room that night. The anticommercialist theme of Heron's poem—one of the most famous poems of the Black liberation struggle—resonated with the economic revolution the cooperatives sought. At the least, they wanted autonomy to better their lives, and those organizing poetry readings at Liberty House wanted the revolution to be Black owned and operated. My title derives from Heron's poem and this book underscores his point—that the people making the revolution must be the ones responsible for its narrative.

"The Revolution Will Not Be Televised" acts as a vector to understand cultural activism as a method of autonomous community narration. The poem refuses modes of communication predicated on whiteness and advertisement, selling Coke or diet programs; in the poem's penultimate stanza, even the weather report is white. Heron envisions a world where the media is no longer a distraction and Black people are no longer being sold to—a future where Black people are "in the street looking for a brighter day" and "in the driver's seat." Ultimately, the poem's final line, "The revolution will be live," calls on participants to improvise their own future, beyond the ad-laden scripts of the mainstream media. The poem communicates this message through words and music, specifically the improvisation of Hubert Law's flute playing as it weaves through Heron's voice. "The Revolution Will Not Be Televised" reflects the collaborative process of cultural activists, and the desire of the poem's content—to imagine a revolution of communication—comes through the liveness of jazz.

As Heron warned, the cultural memory of the civil rights movement has been overdetermined by an archive of images controlled by the white media gaze and what they considered acceptable and sensational.[2] The grand-scale images of the March on Washington and the burden of representation of police brutality in 1963 Birmingham oppose the images in this book, for example, of farmers in West Batesville, Mississippi, teaching others how to grow okra and form a cooperative. So many narratives of the civil rights movement celebrate the everyday life of activism and the glimpses of joy found in the process of organizing. Cultural activism centers people telling their own story of social change, often in experimental ways, such as through ephemeral, mostly unrecorded performances and media missing from the archive. The stories of the civil rights movement invite a dialogue across time between how people felt about the world then and how we exist in it now. What we imagine from these stories and fragments reveals more about our contemporary moment than it does the 1960s. To those invested in culture and the arts as a necessary component of social change, the methods and processes of these improvisational experiments direct us toward the creative potential of collaboration.

Jazz musician and writer Ajay Heble defines Sun Ra's improvisation as a "manifestation of the possible" and simultaneously "performing the impos-sible."[3] In this paradox, Heble captures the spirit of the civil rights movement and its archive of cultural activism, which manifests the freedom dream of social equality into the realm of possibility through art practices. Heble begins with "such performance practices that cannot readily be scripted, predicted, or compelled into orthodoxy" and argues that improvisation "encourage[s] new, socially responsive forms of community building across national, cul-tural, and artistic boundaries."[4] Sun Ra manifested a reality unimaginable to most people (except to those who shared his vision), and he reminds us of the multiplicity of modes of communication and interpretation available to humans. Improvisation inspires us to witness the intentionality of civil-rights-era art activism as a great surrender to community. It makes space for the makeshift and unmade in our discussion of the avant-garde, a conversation that too often ignores places like the South and people like farmworkers. These expressions do not necessarily locate cultural production as promising the real story of the Movement; rather, they reflect how activists felt about public images that did not represent their lived experiences. In Sharon Monteith's analysis of SNCC's (Student Nonviolent Coordinating Committee) literary culture, she argues that we "learn more about the interior dynamics of a social movement through sustained attention to how it forged its narrative and consciously curated a range of storytelling practices."[5] Artistic expression offers people a way to say the unsayable. Cultural activists could produce work at odds with the politics of the Movement or any other specific ideology.

Robin D. G. Kelley, via poet Askia Touré, recognizes the role of art for the civil rights movement: "For Toure, the 'movement' was more than sit-ins at lunch counters, voter registration campaigns, and freedom rides; it was about self-transformation, changing the way we think, live, love, and handle pain."[6] In her writing on visual art, bell hooks expands Kelley's and Touré's ideas to the wider scope of Black liberation and calls on Black people to reenvision "black revolution in such a way that we create collective awareness of the radical place that art occupies within the freedom struggle and of the way in which experiencing art can enhance our understanding of what it means to live as free subjects in an unfree world."[7] Kelley and hooks join the many voices who scoff at the idea that art would be frivolous to the revolution.

One of the great practitioners and generators of cultural activism, Toni Cade Bambara, famously claimed, "As a cultural worker who belongs to an oppressed people my job is to make the revolution irresistible."[8] Her editor and close friend, Toni Morrison, remembers Bambara laughing at the "fake debate" between art and politics:

> Any hint that art was over there and politics was over here would break her up into tears of laughter, or elicit a look so withering it made silence the only intelligent response. More often she met the art/politics fake debate with a slight wave-away of the fingers on her beautiful hand, like the dismissal of a mindless, desperate fly who had maybe two little hours of life left.[9]

Bambara makes clear through the waving of her hand that there was no separation between art and social movement activism: all of it was cultural work. As Toni Morrison says, "There was no division in her [Bambara's] mind between optimism and ruthless vigilance; between obligatory aesthetics and the *aesthetics of obligation*."[10] Defining what Morrison meant by the aesthetics of obligation is the main impulse of this book, as I navigate the terrain of cultural activism: as a method of creativity and a system that could connect people and make them intimate with one another through a spectrum of obligation, care, and love. Within Bambara's aesthetics of obligation, creative labor should always be beholden to the community in which it is created, and the community holds the right to self-expression.

The aesthetics of obligation intersect with terms and ideas describing socially engaged art, such as "artistic citizenship," a term created by David J. Elliott, Marissa Silverman, and Wayne D. Bowman that describes art as "action dedicated to personal and collective flourishing, grounded in commitments to transform and enrich people's everyday lives."[11] Aspects of artistic citizenship appear within cultural activism, especially when racism made civic citizenship so difficult to obtain. Rúben A. Gaztambide-Fernández makes a similar case in his discussion of the role of "the arts" in education, claiming that what he calls cultural production "seeks to account for the patterns of interaction that evolve in different contexts and under particular material and symbolic conditions."[12] In other words, cultural production reveals the relationships and circumstances from which it emerges. As cultural workers practiced participatory democracy, they enacted a form of citizenship in art-making that they sought to manifest politically. Nato Thompson gathers these concepts in a handful of terms applicable to contemporary art: social aesthetics, Nicolas Bourriaud's "relational aesthetics," social practice, the Critical Art Ensemble's "tactical media," and others describing "new forms of interpersonal, immediate art."[13] Far from the resources and ability to imagine themselves as a radical art collective, cultural workers of the civil rights movement came together organically to form new aesthetics emerging from their relationships to their communities. The collectives in this book remain firmly tethered to the organizations from which they emerged and to communities they serve as activists. In some ways, obligation can be a temporal marker that describes the moment of emergence from activist interaction with local people and the need for cultural workers to communicate about social movements on their own terms. For a social movement as encompassing as the civil rights movement, art reveals how people expressed their obligations to one another, which I refer to as intimacy-making.

As an art-making process, *intimacy-making* describes the carework of sustaining community. Intimacy entails being close enough to understand and care about the lives and experiences of others, to see and be seen. Within activist theater of the civil rights movement, a style of performance emerged that offered an introspective, improvisational space, placing communities in dialogue with *themselves* rather than with the white supremacist progenitors of violence. This introspection looks beyond a vision of the civil rights movement's strategy as reactive to the dominant oppressive structure and turns inward toward the transformative possibilities explored within theater, performance, and other cultural expressions that sought to redefine how people relate to themselves and one another. Lauren Berlant moves the concept of intimacy across public and private spheres, claiming that it "poses a question of scale that links the instability of individual lives to the trajectories of the collective."[14] Following Berlant's line of thinking, the projected impact of cultural work becomes the transformative process of becoming deeply invested in another's well-being.

English lacks a verb that describes this process of becoming invested in another, as the kenning intimacy-making draws attention to. Elliott, Silverman, and Bowman's definition of praxis comes close as a term describing "a multidimensional concept that includes active reflection and critically reflective action guided by an informed ethical disposition to act rightly, with continuous concern for protecting and advancing the well-being of others."[15] Praxis gives language to the depth of belonging so essential in cultural activism, but intimacy-making acts as a more specific antonym to the Marxist term *estrangement*, meaning alienation from self and the world because of oppressive industrial labor. Intimacy-making is the more accurate—if clunky and imperfect—word opposing estrangement. The fact that there is no easy antonym to estrangement (the word "appropriation" really falls flat) speaks volumes about the attention paid to the process of falling apart rather than of coming together. We can imagine how an unjust world and a capitalist society can make us estranged from our labor and our lives, but how can we theorize intimacy-making between self and labor? Or self and other, self and community, self and self?

The scalar model of self-to-community centralizes intimacy and interpersonal relationships as reflective of larger social relationships. In her book on social movement activism, *Emergent Strategy*, adrienne maree brown describes relationality as a fractal. She claims that "what we practice at the small scale sets the pattern for the whole system," which she models both from years of participating in activism and her observations of the natural world.[16] The "structural echo" of the fractal can be observed in the fern plant as it can be in electoral politics because "the patterns of the universe repeat at scale" and organizations are, in fact, part of the universe.[17] Articulated by her mentor, the civil rights activist and philosopher Grace Lee Boggs, brown embraces the adage "*Transform yourself to transform the world.*"[18] Her philosophy of social movements speaks across time to the grassroots work of the civil rights movement. *Emergent Strategy* is in itself a fractal that follows a pattern of the feminist philosophies of people of color that extends through brown's dialogues with Grace Lee Boggs, bell hooks, Ella Baker, and so many others. The book, and its extensive citations of activists and cultural workers, witnesses a network of theory proximate to the praxis of carework and community. What sets the pattern is the *being with* in conversation; as Diana Taylor argues, "The way we do this is the way we do everything."[19] For Taylor, conversation "means going to meet people in their own spaces, on their own terms, not to study or observe them but to listen and learn from their actions, words, and epistemic systems."[20] The art objects of cultural activism evidence how activists placed small-scale intimacy and dialogue as central to social change.

Cultural workers, especially within a Black feminist tradition, locate love as essential to genuine, lasting social change. As Alice Lovelace remembers, Bambara defined community organizing as "strategic thinking grounded in love," with a focus on observation, listening, and living in the place in order to understand both what the community needs and also *what they want to say.*[21] Jennifer Nash argues for love's "radical potentiality" within the history of Black feminist thought, because love "operates as a principle of vulnerability and accountability, of solidarity and transformation, that has organized and undergirded black feminist practice."[22] Activist love makes a clear distinction between listening to the needs of the community and the paternalistic version of organizing in which the goals of a larger organization dictate the methods and practices applied to a local level. Yet there is a limit to love's potentiality during the contentious moment of civil-rights-era interracial, class-crossing organizing. The archive reveals moments of real misunderstanding and lack of communication across these barriers.[23] Intimacy-making makes space for obligation and care without needing to embrace one another in love. Through resource-sharing, activists and local people built relationships with one another and obligations to each other as building blocks toward autonomy. Feminist philosopher Asha Bhandary articulates social systems of care that focus on "the labor of caregiving, not caring in the affective sense," so that we can witness activists working to create a system of social obligation that makes space for love, but does not demand it in order to thrive and accommodates uncomfortable and challenging situations.[24] For cultural workers, collaborative storytelling did the work of intimacy-making in the

Movement. Not only was collaborative storytelling part of a project of labor, but it also claims space as a civil right—the right to tell one's own story—for a community so often spoken for (and against) by others.

As I shift focus from high-profile protests to smaller, more intimate interactions, I follow a question Grace Lee Boggs poses: "what [would] our movements would look like if we focused on critical connections instead of critical mass."[25] Boggs and brown call on us to place the numbers, statistics, and material gains aside, even momentarily, to concentrate on the way people relate to one another, "shifting from 'mile wide inch deep' movements to 'inch wide mile deep' movements that schism the existing paradigm."[26] The same could be said for analyses of the civil rights movement that seek to encompass its entirety. This book takes an inch-wide mile-deep approach to readings of cultural production, going vertical by meditating on a selection of works of collaborative art.

Locating Cultural Activism in Civil Rights Movement History

"The Role of Art in the Process of Social Change," which is the title of this introduction, comes from a poster for the last performance of the Free Southern Theater that took place November 1985, called *The Role of Art in the Process of Social Change: A Valediction Without Mourning for the Free Southern Theater 1963–1980*. The phrase promises an answer, but in reality represents an ongoing question: What does art do to make the world better? The Free Southern Theater was driven by this question until their final performance, which was a second line funeral process that marched across New Orleans. The performance illustrated how the theater died, but also transformed into other arts organizations, many of which attended the funeral and conference. In this way, the performance represents the process through which activist art coalesces, moves, and transforms within social movements. Even though the funeral happened on a specific date in 1985, the process was much longer and more fluid, reflecting the temporality of the civil rights movement, which is much more flexible than is often represented in scholarship and public history.

Debates on when the Movement "happened" and when it became the Black Power or Black Arts Movement overlook ways in which the civil rights movement brings together many independent organizations with their own timelines and evolutions. We see this in the "long movement" debate in which Sundiata Cha-Jua and Clarence Lang argue that the disintegration of the temporal, geographic, and ideological boundaries of the civil rights movement takes on "vampiric traits" of undead wanderings around time and space. Cha-Jua and Lang take a more nuanced approach that takes into consideration the civil rights movement's specificities and locations. With cultural activism, scholarship brackets artistic work into the Black Arts Movement, which has an overlapping timeline with the civil rights movement and follows a variety of timelines across the United States, especially in the South. As James Smethurst notes, the Black Arts Movement in the South "peaked later and survived longer than in other areas."[27] Temporally, much of what I locate during the civil right era, scholars such as Smethurst and Margo Natalie Crawford would term the Black Arts Movement, or the beginning of the Chicanx movement. However, organizations such as SNCC envisioned themselves as part of the civil rights movement. Additionally, the early work of El Teatro Campesino was part of the National Farm Workers Association, and the farmworkers' strike filmstrips emerged from the SNCC photography and communication unit. A broader term, such as cultural activism, has a flexibility reflective of the Movement and can move between the different registers of terminology. My archive remains mostly within the mid-1960s and in SNCC's network, which extended to California and has linked the southern Black freedom struggle with the farmworkers' strike.[28] Yet, like the Movement itself, the archive of this book does not always stay within clear boundaries, making space for those activist-artists operating adjacent to the SNCC network, who nonetheless created collaborative work within the framework of cultural activism. Thus, a transformative moment such as the 1985 funeral-performance of the Free Southern Theater transcends debate over its temporality, as it adheres to the civil rights movement, to the Black Arts Movement, and to the broader term, *cultural activism*.

To give a brief history of the civil rights movement risks reducing all this richness into an easy narrative, yet to make a map of all the political organizations in which cultural workers were involved would take attention away from the focus on the art they produced. Among this cross-section of activist organizations, projects, and initiatives, almost everyone discussed in this book was involved with SNCC, a widespread political organization that emerged from the sit-in movement. SNCC formed in 1960 in Raleigh, North Carolina and attracted young people, mostly students, to the civil rights cause. Despite its reputation as a youth organization, all kinds of people were connected to SNCC, including Ella Baker, an activist who grew up in North Carolina and graduated from Shaw University in Raleigh, and who was involved in so many aspects of organizing. In 1960 she returned to Shaw to help organize SNCC and developed a philosophical groundwork that came to be known as "participatory democracy," a nonhierarchical approach to leadership. Baker's biographer, Barbara Ransby, defines participatory democracy as a "new type of inclusive, consensus-oriented democracy, which opened organizational doors to women, young people, and those outside the cadre of educational elites."[29] While this definition opens a larger purview, smaller communities such as the Free Southern Theater or a quilting cooperative could put participatory democracy in practice in their daily interactions. Participatory democracy shaped how activists showed up in their art-making, and so few of the art objects discussed in this book could be attributed to a single person. As SNCC and other organizations did their best to avoid dominating leadership, spaces of creativity became an open door to manifest participatory democracy through collectively produced arts. In her study of activist documentary, Angela Aguayo extends the concept of participatory democracy to consider "participatory media culture(s)" and "participatory commons" that use the "collective social practices of creating, remixing, and sharing documentary recordings as a means of engaging publics."[30] The drive for autonomy, both economically and artistically, tangled together action and aesthetics, enabling art to function as a set of instructions for revolutionary activity and vice versa.

Even though the farmworkers' movement has its own timeline and historical trajectory, there were spiritual connections with the civil rights movement through its processes and values. When migratory labor between the lands known today as Mexico and the United States became formalized through the Bracero Program in 1953, the U.S. government institutionalized a cycle of cheap, exploitable labor with a disregard to the consequences and its impact on people's lives. Even after the program was officially terminated in 1964, migratory pathways continued and working conditions continued to deteriorate, leading to a robust labor movement and a 1965 strike organized by Larry Itliong and Ben Gines of the Agricultural Workers Organizing Committee. They invited a fledgling labor organization, the National Farm Workers Association, cofounded by Cesar Chavez and Dolores Huerta, to join the strike, which they did. As they organized strikes, boycotts, and marches, activists from the Bay Area flocked to Delano to help, many of whom were involved with SNCC and other civil rights organizations. The influence of the southern Black freedom struggle is palpable in their campaign and their ethos of nonviolence. Both movements envisioned themselves as creating social change beyond legal and civic improvements. This is not to diminish the real ways they fought for those changes, but to augment their ability to see revolution as a fractal that should touch every aspect of a person's life.

Introduction · 11

The version of the civil rights movement in this book focuses on the experimentation and improvisation of grassroots cultural work and how that work created dialogue between activists and local people. Therefore, the historiography in which I engage focuses on uncovering a more grassroots version of the civil rights movement along with a proliferation of primary source collections, oral histories, and biographies of less recognized figures, such as women in SNCC and the farmworkers' union.[31] This scholarship argues that the civil rights movement was more ideologically diverse, more feminist, and more intersectional than cultural memory dictates. Scholars have reframed voter registration, desegregation, and union status as just some of the many platforms for change taken up by activists. For example, Greta de Jong's work focuses on the economic side of grassroots organizing and makes the argument that voter registration did not have a universal appeal to local people, many of whom needed to improve their economic situation first.[32] This is best summarized by the Alabamian activist Ezra Cunningham, who said, "You can't eat freedom and a ballot is not to be confused with a dollar bill." Cunningham also introduces a major problem that de Jong argues is underrepresented in cultural memory of civil rights movement voter registration: the job losses suffered by activists for their involvement and the toll on their physical and mental health. Activists, especially those remaining in the South after Freedom Summer, devoted resources to the economic aftermath of political strategy. The civil rights movement, therefore, was also a campaign to reimagine labor and livelihood for marginalized people in the U.S.

As activists reimagined what a revolution could be, they sought creative ways to interact with communities. In Mississippi in 1963, Doris Derby claimed to Gil Moses and John O'Neal, "Well, if theater means anything anywhere, it certainly ought to mean something here," asking them, "Why don't we make a theater?" The Free Southern Theater was formed in Mississippi, but soon moved to New Orleans where it became a cultural powerhouse for the Black Arts Movement in the South, even though it continued to tour rural communities of the Deep South throughout the 1960s. Their theater was contemporaneous with El Teatro Campesino, yet they have different origins and historic trajectories. El Teatro Campesino began to meet the needs of a unique picket line, which took place in a widespread agricultural area. Striking farmworkers stood on the backs of pickup trucks, shouting to communicate to those out in the fields and from there they evolved into a theater of necessity for the farmworkers' March to Sacramento. These theaters grew separately, but the Black freedom struggle in the South and the farmworkers' movement out West were interconnected. In California, the strike found inspiration in what was happening in the South and pledged to nonviolence as a civil rights tactic. They were also connected through SNCC, whose San Francisco headquarters printed *The Movement*, a newspaper that covered both the South and the strike.

Popular celebrations of the civil rights movement honors the people who came down from the North for the Freedom Rides and Freedom Summer, where droves of young students risked their lives for integration and voter registration. The high-profile murders of three of those civil rights workers, James Chaney, Michael Schwerner, and Andrew Goodman, exposed to the world the danger faced by activists trying to make a difference for a year, or a summer. For many, involvement in the civil rights movement in the South was temporary, even though it was impactful. For others, it was the decision that forever shaped their lives. Cultural activism tells the story of people who stayed long enough to engage deeply in their communities, such as Doris Derby, John O'Neal, Gil Moses, Maria Varela, Jane Stembridge, and Charlie Cobb, to name a few. The activists who stayed beyond Freedom Summer have been immortalized through fictional characters, such as Alice Walker's titular character in *Meridian* and Velma in Bambara's *The Salt Eaters*. Their real-life counterparts became part of an ongoing, and *never-ending*, effort to create new ways for people to live better lives through cultural organizations, theaters, workshops, artisan and farm cooperatives, and so much more.

In this timeline, the Movement does not die. Alice Walker frames it as a contrast between media perceptions of its failures versus her lived experience in her breakthrough 1967 essay, "The Civil Rights Movement: What Good Was It?" She critiques a vision of the civil rights movement as something that could be measured by material gains:

> Still, white liberals and deserting civil rights sponsors are quick to justify their disaffection from the movement by claiming that it is all over. "And since it is over," they will ask, "would someone kindly tell me what has been gained by it?" They then list statistics supposedly showing how much more advanced segregation is now than ten years ago—in schools, housing, jobs. They point to a gain in conservative politicians during the last few years. They speak of ghetto riots and of the recent survey that shows that most policemen are admittedly too anti-Negro to do their jobs in ghetto areas fairly and effectively. They speak of every area that has been touched by the civil rights movement as somehow or other going to pieces.[33]

Walker offers another path when she concludes, "If the civil rights movement is 'dead,' and if it gave us nothing else, *it gave us each other forever*.... Because we live, it can never die."[34] Walker redirects the purpose of the Movement away from its material gains and toward the intimacy fostered between its participants, the giving of each other. The critical connection approach brown takes echoes both Walker and bell hooks, who writes, "The absence of a sustained focus on love in progressive circles arises from a collective failure to acknowledge the needs of the spirit and an overdetermined emphasis on material concerns."[35] Even if a march, protest, or campaign did not result in the long-lasting, quantitative social change we might consider success, that does not mean it failed. If a social movement creates the kind of intimacy and consciousness-raising that Walker desires, then it matters regardless of material gain, and calls on us to imagine better discourse on activism's impact.

Locating American Experimental Art through Jazz

This book starts from the premise that activist art is worthy of critical analysis, and, like Toni Cade Bambara, waves away any notion that creative expression produced from a social movement is not true art. "This notion is not just misleading," Elliott, Silverman, and Bowman argue, "it is implausible and irresponsible, leading us to trivialize or marginalize some of art's most powerful contributions to our shared humanity."[36] The ongoing debates between art and politics have too often excluded and marginalized works of art created within and in response to social movements. Nato Thompson attempts to rectify this by recounting a history of art activism in *Seeing Power: Art and Activism in the 21st Century*. Thompson presents a common version of art activism that exists in cultural memory, even though it is debatable historically. For one, Thompson's narrative, like many other accounts, is invested in the 1960s as something powerful, but short-lived, and locates art of "social aesthetics" as emerging in the mid-1990s.[37] The intellectual history of art activism, according to Thompson, begins with the rise of Marxism and traces the philosophies of Antonio Gramsci, Theodor Adorno, and Max Horkheimer. No doubt, these philosophers are essential in the ongoing discussion of how art functions politically and culturally. What makes cultural activism unique in this conversation is how artistic production emerges spontaneously from within activist organizations and their interactions with the communities they serve. Groups such as Thompson's own Creative Time, N55, and the Critical Art Ensemble form independently in order to respond to and support social issues, yet collectives such as the Free Southern Theater, El Teatro Campesino, and the SNCC photography and communications unit evidence how social movements can and will organically produce groups focused on artistic expression. The artistic collectives of the civil rights movement and their purchase on the avant-garde—their search for new forms and methods—calls for a reevaluation of art activism's trajectory and whether this offers a usable past or accurate future for approaching the cultural activism of the civil rights movement.

Listening to the words and sounds of cultural workers, I place cultural activism within a history of American avant-gardism via jazz cultures and methodologies, which exists just outside of the standard narrative that Fred Moten calls the "a-side" of the avant-garde. Jazz has been a counterhistory of the avant-garde partially because of Adorno's notorious dismissal of jazz, which Fumi Okiji processes and reconciles in *Jazz as Critique: Adorno and Black Expression Revisited*. Okiji addresses the racist abnegation of blackness in "key texts chronicling the malevolent underbelly of modernity—such as Adorno's," and yet stays with Adorno's critique in order to prove the compatibility between jazz and Adorno's insights into the "emotional shocks of aesthetic experience" that hold potential for liberation.[38] Okiji riffs on Adorno to navigate the place of jazz in avant-garde history, yet Moten explores the potential for another side of the story. In *In the Break*, Moten claims that "interest in the history and theory of the avant-garde in black performance demands that one be more concerned with the b-side than the a-side of this now standard recording."[39] As I explore the b-side (and the c-side of unfinished, unmade artifacts), I approach nonmusical media within a jazz paradigm, reflecting how jazz extends outward into other cultural forms, and also because cultural activism holds an unruliness at the same time that it connects across various forms and expressions, which Amiri Baraka describes as "the changing same" in *Blues People*.[40] SNCC used a variety of methods such as the "tell it like it is"[41] approach and the "'just do it' philosophy . . . that did not wait for approval or direction," that opened them to an immediacy and willingness to experiment.[42]

Activists in the 1960s operated within a version of the avant-garde with its own histories that predate civil-rights-era organizations. For example, in the South, Highlander Folk School, now Highlander Research and Education Center, acted as both an arts center and a place for activist education in which Rosa Parks and Martin Luther King Jr. received a political education. In the West, the tradition of *carpa* theater and *pastorelas* in the borderlands have been sites of resistance against social norms for centuries. And on a national scale, the Federal Theater Project—part of the New Deal that extended government support to artists—emphasized the performing arts in areas beyond New York City and to marginalized people with little previous access to theater. From these roots, the 1960s exploded the idea of what theater could be and integrated performance into the burgeoning revolutionary politics of the day, what James Harding and Cindy Rosenthal call the American avant-garde.[43]

Scholars such as Harding, Rosenthal, and Mike Sell have recognized the unique way the 1960s seemed to spontaneously produce avant-garde forms of cultural production, "not of *derivative*, but of *independent* parallels."[44] Harding's point is valid: each moment and place have their own way of producing art specific to that community, even if they share aesthetic techniques. For example, El Teatro Campesino used stock characters—a character representing "The Union" or "The Boss"—the same way Bertolt Brecht would hang signs around the neck of actors that spelled out their role for the audience. We could trace influence from European theater to California, or we could trace influence from the medieval form of drama that has existed along the U.S.-Mexico borderlands since colonization; however, no lineage of influence really answers the question of what stock characters meant for striking farmworkers in California. My inch-wide-mile-deep approach slows down to consider the meaning-making potential of this work and its impact on how people related to one another.

As Lorenzo Thomas argues, too close a focus on process, influence, and technique misses the point. In an essay describing the Lower East Side in the 1960s, Thomas reflects with reverence for this "remarkable period" and playfully attributes its creative energy to the fact that "there was so much jazz in the air."[45] Thomas elevates the relationships between artists across disciplines, and opposes this to "historians [who] like to fix and x-ray avant-garde movements and analyze them in terms of process or product." Yet those who were involved, he argues, "know that the avant-garde is less about change in the arts than it is about genuine experimentation in social relations."[46] The avant-garde 1960s of the South and in California cannot share the proximity of the Lower East Side, but Thomas's description of social relations transposes well. Avant-garde experimentation in the civil rights movement began with social relations first, followed by the unique demands of more rural areas. By bringing jazz forward as an analytic for reading artistic experimentation, "jazz in the air" becomes more than just poetic description, but a theoretical framework for reading avant-garde art.

Improvisation between Worlds:
Jazz Methodology and the Contrafact

Improvisation invites us to suspend an analysis of social movement activism based on models of success determined by material gains or capitalist and colonialist notions of progress. It invites us to improvise calls on participants to let go of a specific intended outcome and focus on each other. Following SNCC's commitment to participatory democracy, methods of improvisation engaged activists in the politics they wanted to practice, and I connect these experiments within a jazz methodology that one Free Southern Theater member called a "new idiom" for the theater.[47] If activists and local people could improvise together, they could "prepare themselves for the inevitable conflicts, ruptures, obstacles, and disappointments that occur in human interactions," as David Fischlin, Ajay Heble, and George Lipsitz describe, "yet remain committed to working things through with others and solving problems together."[48] They could also do the creative labor to imagine freedom dreams, while nurturing the flexibility required to stay committed to each other across differences. In contrast, Dan DiPiero argues that improvisation has too readily come to signify the open and possible as a progressive platform without regard to how it reflects everyday life in all its iterations. DiPiero states, "I take seriously the possibility that musical improvisation and everyday life are structurally identical" and that it is "the *people* who make improvisation into something compelling."[49] Like in music, improvisation has a relationship to rigorous training, and expresses a connection over shared knowledge and expectation. I bring these approaches together in my definition of improvisation for cultural activism: the everyday work of manifesting the impossible by moving between the praxis for participatory democracy and the dreamwork of social change.

Bambara's novel *The Salt Eaters*, though fictional, theorizes on how jazz extends beyond the boundaries of music. Velma, an activist who has attempted to end her life under the pressures of organizing, tries to heal at the Academy of Seven Arts, an integrative community center much like those left in the wake of civil-rights-era cultural activism. During the conclusion of the ritual, the sky opens up and a storm floods the characters' and the reader's minds with a multivocal overflow of thoughts. As Velma begins to cross over into healing, she hears two songs playing at once: Ida Cox's "Wild Women Don't Have the Blues," which is described as "strains of some sassy twenties singer crackling low and indistinct," and Charlie Parker's "Now's the Time," which she hears as "an alto sax loud and insistent taking over the air, jarring her out of her fear of splintering, blaring through her head."[50] Velma begins to dance to the rhythmic cacophony of two songs playing at once, and one of the healers says to the other, "Dancing is her way to learn now. Let her go."[51] The climax of the book is doubly ekphrastic; Bambara writes music we cannot hear and dancing we cannot see, except through the "jazz fiction" of Bambara's prose, what Sasha Feinstein and David Rife define as "the near-magical capacity of the music to impact human behavior in all of its impressive variety."[52] Feinstein and Rife channel James Baldwin's observation on the liberating potential of jazz writing: "When I realized that music rather than American literature was really my language, I was no longer afraid. And then I could write."[53] Baldwin creates an undisciplinary genre of jazz as a language whose grammar could cross modalities from music to daily living. Bambara describes this when Velma comes into jazz consciousness: "And she'd have to travel the streets in six-eighth time cause Dizzy [Gillespie] said righteous experience could not be rendered in three-quarter time."[54]

Bambara wrote *The Salt Eaters* in a stream of jazz consciousness, which she describes through Parker's tune as "something muscular and daring, something borrowed first from books and imaginings then later from Palma's giggly narratives in the dark sharing a pillow, borrowed till she earned it for herself on that first piano in the church and learned to listen to linears and verticals at the same time, new time, rhythm bam."[55] Across books, storytelling, music, listening, and dancing, Bambara describes a *something* that encompasses a modality of borrowing and earning, of holding opposing ideas—the linears and verticals—together as a mode of understanding the world or, for example, writing a novel. Bambara offers us a chance to understand a new critical perspective on improvisation through the aesthetics of obligation, which I argue makes visible the imprint of jazz consciousness applied to activism, but it together seemingly opposing understandings of how improvisation works beyond music. On one hand, improvisation is a liberatory practice that "teaches us to make 'a way' out of 'no way' by cultivating the capacity to discern hidden elements of possibility, hope, and promises in even the most discouraging circumstances."[56] On the other, scholars, such as Vijay Iyer (also a jazz pianist and composer), Dan DiPiero, Gillian Siddall, and Ellen Waterman, focus on the uneven manner in which artistic improvisation translates to a better life. There are limitations to the synonymous relationship between freedom and improvisation, which DiPiero argues is "actually incoherent," yet I see both ideas operating at once in cultural activism: the possibility of liberation and the dedicated practice of working within and against constraint.[57] To hold these linears and verticals at the same time requires us to remember jazz as a dialogue with economic necessity and the creative response to waiting for a better future. It is informed by the conditions from which it emerged: through economic struggle and negotiation, radical repurposing, and collaboration with others as a means of survival. As Amiri Baraka writes of the jazz musician in *Blues People*, "At some point, always, he could not participate in the dominant tenor of the white man's culture. It was at this juncture that he had to make use of other resources, whether African, subcultural, or hermetic. And it was this boundary, this no man's land, that provided the logic and beauty of his music."[58]

Charlie Parker's studio recording "KoKo" offers a legendary example of how resourcefulness generates creativity.[59] Parker had originally wanted to record a jazz adaptation of Ray Noble's "Cherokee" but was stopped by the producer, who refused to pay royalties on Noble's song. Parker played the song again without the melody, just the harmonic changes, and created a song that propelled jazz to new heights. What started out as an economic decision evolved into an artistic tool that subverted legal limitations with an avant-garde sound, bebop. To an untrained ear, "Cherokee" disappears and "KoKo" becomes a new, independent composition, a *contrafact*. Created as a dialogue between the musicians and the constraints of the music industry, the contrafact is a method of repurposing that enables musicians to avoid paying royalties by writing new melodies over the harmonic structure of old standards that were often originally written by white musicians. The jazz contrafact emerged from necessity, but no one would deny "KoKo" as a work of art.

Just as Parker's pivot revolutionized a new musical method, cultural activists created works that were too innovative to be described as theatrical adaptations. I apply *contrafact* to cultural activism as a way of centering the everyday process of creating work against economic and legal constraint. Like many avant-garde artists, cultural activists such as the Free Southern Theater had little money to work with. Their archive swings back and forth between utopian writings of freedom dreams and the heartbreaking ledgers of an arts organization. The math on the back of brochures and pamphlets was always in the red, and the tone in their letters to donors was always a little desperate. But by adapting modernist theater from Europe, for example, they could have avoided paying royalties.[60] As the scripts they used were swallowed up in the atmosphere of the performance, elements of the plays remained. Their contrafacts of European theater became a new thing that stretches our understanding of what a theatrical adaptation can be. Okiji describes the analytic potential of jazz as a "playful tension involved in retelling a communal work in his or her own voice and within his or her own communicative capabilities," which creates a "negotiation of the desire to share in the tradition and the imperative to remain distinct."[61] The Free Southern Theater contrafacted European theater from Samuel Beckett and Brecht into performance pieces where the atmosphere and audience transformed theater into something distinct.

For an audience who had no knowledge of traditional theater, the bodies of the actors moving, the tones of their voices, the color of their skin all shaped the meaning of the performances more than any message written into the script. In the same historical moment as the Free Southern Theater, El Teatro Campesino began as improvised, picket-line performances that, like the Free Southern Theater, incorporated the environment of rurality and protest aesthetics into art.[62] Dolores Huerta recalls that cars and trucks would have to drive across thousands of acres, preaching the message of the union to strikebreakers.[63] Unlike traditional picket lines outside a factory, agricultural labor required a mobile picket line loud enough to be heard. In recorded footage of the March to Sacramento, El Teatro Campesino performed in a chaotic atmosphere. During the short, improvised skits, one can barely hear what people are saying—and yet the audience responds with cheers.

The contrafact spirals out beyond the Free Southern Theater and becomes a conduit for understanding the radical adaptations of everything in the process of social change: El Teatro Campesino contrafacted the Spanish morality play, originally used to convert indigenous peoples (chapter 2); activist theater contrafacted education (chapter 3); and craft-makers and farmers contrafacted cooperative economics (chapters 4 and 5). The contrafact resonates with adrienne maree brown's definition of adaptation as "the process of changing while staying in touch with our deeper purpose and longing," and it considers that when there is no model for the world longed for, nor funding for the vision, something new emerges from improvised subterfuge.[64]

Locating Activist Theater in Performance Studies

One event proved to the world the possibility of creativity in the civil rights movement, when activists tapped into the political potential of performance to plan the 1963 Mississippi Freedom Vote. The mock-election was a large-scale work of performance art and one of the most creative protests of the civil rights movement. It was organized by the Council of Federated Organizations, a supergroup of civil rights organizations, which nominated a Black candidate for governor, Aaron Henry, and a white activist for lieutenant governor, the Rev. Ed King. There was a real campaign and real ballots for an unofficial and unrecognized election. The point was to upend the misconception that Black folks in Mississippi were uninterested in voting and to show how the voting registration process was, indeed, racist. People turned out in droves: 83,000 votes cast as opposed to the 12,000 registered Black Mississippians.[65] The Mississippi Freedom Vote brought people into the Movement who previously had little to no investment in conventional politics or social activism and formed the Mississippi Freedom Democratic Party (MFDP) as an alternative to the Democratic Party. This performance was a massive organizing effort and it helped set the stage for Freedom Summer and much of the voter registration campaigns of the civil rights movement. Even though the election was a pastiche of the gubernatorial race, the enthusiasm for the candidates was not ironic or false. As Richard Dyer describes, pastiche "always both holds us inexorably within cultural perception of the real and also, and thereby, enables us to make a sense of the real."[66] The Freedom Vote and the MFDP acted as a process of holding the wider public in the reality of voter suppression and revealed the performativity of elections and the democratic process. Pushing pastiche to the next level, the Mississippi Freedom Vote proved that it was not the election that was fake, but rather the concept of democracy—there was nothing "real" to make sense of, except that the political process does not serve marginalized people.

During the process of creating the Freedom Vote election, participants gained a sense of autonomy in the democratic process and deepened their distrust of mainstream politics. In 1964, when the official Democratic Party at the national convention in Atlantic City decided to recognize the MFDP with a compromise of two seats, Fannie Lou Hamer responded, "We didn't come all this way for no two seats since all of us is tired."[67] If a seat (or two) at the table was the initial impulse for the Mississippi Freedom Vote, Hamer's sudden rejection of the offer of two seats changed the script. Hamer and the MFDP delegation claimed true representation, but also articulated a desire for political autonomy. The outcome of a campaign designed to generate more politically committed Black voters transformed into further disillusionment with the political process. What can we make from this refusal to compromise, which could also be understood as a failure? The answer is a change in what we consider success and failure in social movements, embracing improvisation as political strategy. We can accept that a study of critical connections and intimacy often offers unquantifiable results.

Performance studies examines the impact of relationality in the world and can bridge the work of theater with moments like Hamer's refusal and the mock election. Even though they did not emerge in urban art scenes, the Free

Southern Theater and El Teatro Campesino were integral to this moment of experimental theater and performance art. The techniques and methods developed by majority Black and Brown people—both activists and local people—during the civil rights movement created contemporary performance studies. In "The Unwieldy Otherwise: Rethinking the Roots of Performance Studies in and through the Black Freedom Struggle," Leon Hilton and Mariahdessa Ekere Tallie publish their syllabus "about how Black, Southern theatre and performance traditions—as well as embodied and transmitted genealogies of community engagement and activism—informed the intellectual, social, and political commitments that have suffused performance studies from its origins as an academic discipline."[68] They begin with the Free Southern Theater and expand outward to trace how their aesthetics have shaped performance studies methodologies. There is an obvious connection between one of the main founders of the field, Richard Schechner, and his involvement with the Free Southern Theater in its early days. However, Hilton and Tallie reach deeper than this connection to look at a community of shared ideas that builds toward how we witness and analyze performance.

The contrafact seeks to restore a deep history of resourcefulness for Black and Brown performance. Therefore, the performance of cultural activism aligns with what Soyica Diggs Colbert, Douglas A. Jones Jr., and Shane Vogel refer to as "behaved restoration" in their reversal of Richard Schechner's classic definition of performance as "restored behavior."[69] Behaved restoration has the power to "disrupt exploitative systems by making material repair or amends, however fleeting, to the exploited; that is, they can challenge the historic negotiation of populations and offer cultural workers in the present a useful past."[70] Performances, whether they be *Waiting for Godot* or the Freedom Vote election, opened channels of repair through connectivity, reflecting—rather than introducing—the collective organizational capabilities already present in the community.[71] Part of this restoration calls for a dismantling of the repetitive social scripts that determined how people should be or act, and especially how they should work. Looking at African American histories of performance, Daphne Brooks considers Brecht's techniques in terms of what she calls "Afro-alienation acts," which "render racial and gender categories 'strange' and thus 'disturb' cultural perceptions of identity formation."[72] With civil-rights-era activist theater, we can see actors "critically defamiliarizing their own bodies by way of performance in order to yield alternative racial and gender epistemologies."[73] Defamiliarization and Afro-alienation acts invest in the transformative power of performance, and within the archive of cultural activism, local people like Hamer shaped what that transformation could be. Their interpretations and participations shifted the outcome of performance from propaganda, or even a teaching tool, to one that exposes local ways of knowing. Through improvised happenings, activists learned what felt meaningful to their audience members and were humbled when they got it wrong.

Even though cultural workers tried to implement ideas from activist theater into their shows, the live performances were too noisy and too unpredictable to enact any set plan for their audiences. Activism reveals itself as a much more erratic and improvised form of collaboration; the intentions, the outcomes, the legacy come after the fact. We are called on to imagine performance as a *witnessing* of noise, where the spontaneous rise of the collective voice drowns out the script and opens space for new interpretations. Even though this reduces performance to spectacle, that does not foreclose the possibility for profound impact. For example, after a Free Southern Theater production of Amiri Baraka's *Slave Ship* in West Point, Mississippi, the audience threatened to revolt, and the actors had to bar them inside the theater out of fear that they would enact violence against local whites. In another example, the grape boycott in California inspired everyday people across the country to "act" out in their local supermarkets that stocked Schenley grapes: filling up their carts then dramatically walking away in protest without paying.[74] The public became part of the performances and what they improvised gives us a glimpse of how they felt at a crucial historic moment.

Activist theater of the civil rights movement happened in environments that were rural and makeshift, with audiences who, for the most part, had never seen a play. They shaped the process of making theater by amplifying their own voices in response to the action on stage. Keeping this in mind, performances did not act as theatrical representations of the civil rights movement but rather offered provocative frameworks for improvised meaning-making to happen in the community. Although the sounds of activist theater made nothing we might register as music, raucous sounds transformed an audience into a community. The constant commotion of activist theater redefines performance through improvised jazz, which, to use Heble's words, describes a "resistance to capture and fixity, its noisiness and clamorousness part of a refusal to give in to the kind of culture of acquiescence or nonparticipation which resigns itself to the way things are because (or so we are too often told) no other future is possible."[75] Anyone who has worked in organizing knows the difficulty of participatory democracy and consensus-based action. Reaching audible consensus can be both a pressure valve and a pleasure salve in the thorny process of making a new community.

The first chapter on the Free Southern Theater articulates how jazz methodology and the contrafact crosses to the visual space of the stage. In their production of Samuel Beckett's *Waiting for Godot*, dialogue between the interracial cast upended how audiences expected people to act toward each other. Beyond the stage, the environments in which they performed carried the potential for exponential meaning-making. Their audiences shattered the conventions of theater by disrupting performances and becoming involved with the play and more intimate with the cultural workers with which they interacted. Because audiences interpreted *Godot* differently than the Free Southern Theater originally intended, the activist-performers also became more intimate with what audiences felt and wanted from the Movement. I then turn to Gilbert Moses's production of Amiri Baraka's *Slave Ship: A Historical Pageant* in West Point, Mississippi where once again, audiences surprised the Free Southern Theater by disrupting the performance, this time threatening an insurrection against the white community. In tracing the different reactions of Moses's New York audience and the audience of West Point, Mississippi, I challenge the narrative of civil-rights-to-Black-Arts radicalism.

My second chapter turns to California and El Teatro Campesino's early *actos*, specifically ones performed on the farmworkers' March from Delano to Sacramento in 1966. I bridge my reading of visual jazz into their improvised acto *Governor Brown*, which played with language and tone in antiphony with audiences to make a mockery of antiunion efforts while at the same time making a case for inclusivity because even the white governor could join the union. Their ability to communicate through passionate sound, which I refer to as *participatory toning*, describes a technique that brings together call-and-responses found in activist, musical, and spiritual spaces. The March's use of Catholic symbols and rhetoric, for example the use of *peregrinación* (pilgrimage), embraced an alternative temporality to a settler colonialist framework of time. Rejecting the temporal limits on seasonal labor or conditions of citizenship, I explore how farmworkers and activists contrafacted theatrical conventions and religious ritual to create new expressions of faith in labor, as reflected in their acto *La quinta temporada*. Rather than argue that their use of religion was a subversive tool, I take seriously the union's methods of inclusivity and place their action in dialogue with Gloria Anzaldúa and Ana Louise Keating's *spiritual activism*. From this pairing emerges the means by which farmworkers redefined citizenship and labor in the United States through an indigenous-based temporality that could break the cycle of labor oppression.

My third chapter argues that civil-rights-era cultural activism and education activism developed a mutually symbiotic relationship. Not only were many cultural workers involved in both, but they brought the spirit of experimentalism into each, resulting in theater that transformed teaching. Plays such at the Free Southern Theater's production of *The Lesson*, a contrafact of Eugene Ionesco's absurdist play, exposed the roots of colonialism and white supremacy in American education. Other productions, such as the Free Southern Theater's *Does Man Help Man*, a contrafact of Brecht's *Baden-Baden Lesson on Consent*, and El Teatro Campesino's *Las dos caras del Patroncito*, transformed Brecht's concept of *Lehrstücke*, or learning-plays, into interactive moments for intimacy-making between performers and audience members. By bringing together bell hooks's pedagogical theory and her concept of dislocation with the Free Southern Theater's *The Rifles of Señora Carrar*, I mobilize the concept of the *presence of elsewhere* as a method for audiences to understand their own living conditions via another place and time. Throughout this chapter, I explore the complex role of cultural production within pedagogy, arguing how cultural activism resisted—and still resists—outcome-oriented approaches that demand proof of impact as a path toward legitimacy.

The fourth chapter brings together performance and economic reform in the craft cooperatives of Liberty House, a division of the Poor People's Corporation, which was an influential yet understudied program of the civil rights movement. As local people lost jobs for civil rights activity, activists turned to building cooperatives in the late 1960s and early 1970s, including craft cooperatives for quilts, fashion, dolls, and other items they could market to clientele in bigger cities. The cooperative project, I argue, was not solely concerned with economic improvement, but also as a revolution for how people labored in the U.S. (and global) South. I argue for a Black feminist approach to cooperative economic reform through the writings of Alice Walker, Toni Cade Bambara, and Anna Julia Cooper and read their work alongside fabrics in archives and photographs. From this textile-centered approach, I explore how intimacy between women working in cooperatives influenced the aesthetics of obligation in literary texts. In this incredible moment, not only did black sharecroppers and domestic workers absent themselves from the white-dominant economy of the South, they also used collective labor to build intimacy and forge a blueprint for community-based self-determination.

Part of the economic reform initiatives of the Movement included the creation of independent media through SNCC's photography and communications department, their publication company Flute Productions, the Free Southern Theater's television program *Nation Time*, and the independent media project, Southern Media, developed by Doris Derby. In this chapter, I examine how cultural workers experimented with technology, such as repurposing educational projectors, to make art/work within an intermedia format created between activists and local people in the Movement. The art objects discussed include filmstrips of cooperative labor in Mississippi and the farmworkers' strike in California, the poetry collection *Furrows*, which brought together Charlie Cobb's poetry with SNCC photography, and the unfinished projects of Southern Media. Using José Esteban Muñoz's definition of intermedia, I read these filmstrips, poetry, and television programming as conduits for intimacy between activists and local people that could traverse geographic space. The structure of intermedia art calls for readings that attend to the collaborative process, not only in the work's production but also in the formation of independent media collectives that could put the work out into the world.

My conclusion places the cultural activism of the civil rights movement in dialogue with contemporary organizations that focus on the relationship between cultural work and social change. There are many contemporary arts organizations in direct connection with the civil rights movement, but I step outside that lineage to consider three in particular: the Austin Project, an experimental theater collective in Texas; *The Panza Monologues*, a play created by Virginia Grise and Irma Mayorga and sourced from the San Antonio Chicana community; and Soul Fire Farm, a Black-owned collective farm grounded in social and environmental justice. As I trace the timelines of these various projects, there is never a decade since the civil rights movement devoid of organizations focused on the confluence of activism and art that works to, as participants of the Austin Project claim, "shift the way people experience art so that more deep engagement and transformation might occur."[76] The ways in which these groups engage with the tenets of cultural activism transcends the concept of artistic influence and calls for new frameworks—an ongoing dialogue across time, which I locate through the writing of Daphne Brooks, Fred Moten, and adrienne maree brown. A focus on this ongoing dialogue, I hope, can bring my framework of cultural activism beyond the limitations of this book.

The Revolution Will Be Improvised turns to intimacy as the driving force behind civil rights movement cultural work, where artistic collaboration emerged as a vital tool of activists seeking to build relationships with local communities. Just as activism and creativity were inseparable during the civil rights movement, so were many other factors that, from our twenty-first-century scholarly perspective, seem disparate: food production, avant-gardism, jazz, spirituality, labor, crafting, and pedagogy. The collective labor of collaborative art sought to reveal the experiences of everyday people in the process of social change; through their work, we become more intimate with their stories.

One

The Free Southern Theater and Visual Jazz Performance

That's what jazz is—it lays out a format for collective action.[1]
—Wynton Marsalis

In "The Greatest Love," an episode of the HBO series *Treme* that aired in 2012, two of the main characters, Toni Bernette and her daughter Sophie, attend an outdoor production of Samuel Beckett's *Waiting for Godot* in New Orleans at the London Avenue canal whose levee breached during Hurricane Katrina in 2005. As the characters in the play wait for something that never comes, the Treme character Toni Bernette begins to cry in response, a rare display of emotion from the hardened lawyer. The scene interweaves layers of fiction that resonate with real-life circumstances and experiences. Only through witnessing the Beckett play can Bernette feel the pain she shares with her many clients across New Orleans: disaster relief proved to be as elusive as Godot himself in the years after Katrina. In the fictional world of *Treme*, Bernette symbolizes the people fighting the legal battle against insurance companies and federal programs that failed to show up for the people of New Orleans. The weight of it all lands hard during the scene, when an audience member turns to Bernette and mumbles, "Motherfucker ain't coming. . . . The man, he ain't coming."[2] On the surface, one could see this scene and Bernette's reaction as a deflation of much-needed hope. Beckett's play opens the possibility for feeling despair and expressing anger at the realization that no one is coming. The truth of abandonment comes to these characters through the vector of the stage, which testifies to the power of theater to alter an audience's perception of their own reality.

Treme's play within the play channels multiple historical moments in spiralic time, bringing together Beckett's *Godot*, civil rights activism, and New Orleans. The scene in the episode is based on Paul Chan's 2007 production that also took place in the Ninth Ward and featured *Treme* actor Wendell Pierce as Vladimir. For weeks leading up to the performance, mysterious signs appeared everywhere around the city with Beckett's elusive stage directions, "A country road. A tree. Evening." As *New York Times* writer Holland Carter observed, "After a while the signs came to feel like a shared secret. . . . They added up to a visual network, art as a connective tissue for a torn-apart town."[3] Pierce explains the inspiration behind Chan's *Godot* in an interview for the *Times-Picayune*, calling the performance "a memorial, a community coming together."[4] He does not once mention Beckett; rather, he references a 1964 production of *Godot* staged in rural Mississippi by the Free Southern Theater, an integrated activist theater group that performed in areas across the Deep South during the civil rights movement. Pierce emphasizes the importance of the Free Southern Theater for New Orleans and the U.S. South and claims the Free Southern Theater's legacy as an inspiration for the play to act as a social commentary.

The *Treme* episode emphasizes the connection to the Free Southern Theater by casting one of its founders, John O'Neal, as the person in the audience who tells Bernette that Godot "ain't coming." Building on the Free Southern Theater's mythology, Pierce reflects, "At one performance in the Mississippi delta for sharecropper farmers, legend has it that at intermission a man turned to the director and said, 'Godot? He ain't coming.'"[5] Since many of these parallels would be unrecognizable to the viewer who is unaware of the Free Southern Theater's legacy, this scene suggests a lineage that exists beyond traditional narratives of the civil rights movement. The Free Southern Theater is present on the southern landscape like Chan's ubiquitous signs; their legacy is that same shared secret, or connective tissue, to a network of activist theater in the United States. O'Neal's cameo in *Treme*—most recognizable to the Black theater community of New Orleans—preserves local knowledge about the Free Southern Theater, while the play itself also makes global and historical connections to activist movements via Beckett's text.

When the Free Southern Theater decided to perform *Waiting for Godot* in 1964, they did so as an experiment, intending to see how local communities of sharecroppers and impoverished residents of rural Mississippi would react to such a controversial play. Those involved in the production—John O'Neal, Gilbert Moses, Doris Derby, and James Cromwell—were activists with SNCC who had migrated to the South for the civil rights movement. However, they were also theater people with more training in the arts than methods of organizing. As with many cultural workers in the 1960s, art and politics were inseparable. Cultural production became their method of protest, and their process hinged on bringing cast and audience together in dialogue. The production company of Chan's *Godot*, Creative Time, continued this community-based format in their approach to the staging of the play. Chan worked with activists and local people for nine months to better understand the needs and issues of the community affected by Katrina. The four performances were all free to the public, and at each site they created a "shadow fund" to help rebuild the site of the performance, echoing the spirit of the Free Southern Theater's obligation to its communities.[6] Finally, when *Treme* offers, but does not explain, the presence of O'Neal or the Free Southern Theater, the show engages an aesthetics of obligation by building a scene from the network of southern Black cultural activism. The aesthetics of obligation reflects the relationships and networks both material and spiritual that bring a work of art into being. The white characters, Toni and Sophie, serve as a bridge to translate the impact of the play to an HBO audience, but anyone in the know understands the scene as a tribute.

It's a strange tribute if we consider the Free Southern Theater's troubled relationship to *Godot*. In the Free Southern Theater's recounting of their own history, *Godot* and the other plays written by white authors, such as Martin Duberman, Bertolt Brecht, and Eugene Ionesco, represent a confusing growth period for what would become a Black liberation theater. *Godot* often polarized the fledgling theater. During the 1964 tour, O'Neal reflects in a letter written from McComb, Mississippi, "We nearly lost the group yesterday in a tift [tiff] about whether or not we would play GODOT here," and O'Neal continues to reflect on how the play opened arguments as to whether the theater would be a "theater theater or a social theater."[7] The group often argued about the play's relevance to a poor, Black audience. by 1969, their chairman Tom Dent asserted, "To bring Broadway, off-Broadway, even radical white theater as it exists today in America, to the black community Is most irrelevant. . . . If you want to be 'cultured' you got to dig *Godot*. Well I say goodbye *Godot*, we'll stick with Otis [Redding]."[8] The narrative repeated by the Free Southern Theater and its critics was that the theater grew alongside the Movement, turning toward Black-authored plays associated with the Black Arts Movement, such as *Slave Ship* by Amiri Baraka (LeRoi Jones). The story repeated was that the choice to stage *Godot* was a mistake from which the group evolved.

Despite the repetition of this narrative, *Godot* continued to be the Free

Southern Theater's most famous production. In 1968, New Orleans playwright Sharon Stockard Martin wrote a one-act play, *Proper and Fine, Fannie Lou Hamer's Entourage*, as an adaptation of *Godot* featuring a Black couple waiting in a retail store for help that never comes. The Free Southern Theater produced *Proper and Fine* in 1970, alongside Gil Moses's production of *Slave Ship*, offering audiences two critiques of integrationist aspirations. Years later, in 1977, as part of the foundational efforts of the powerhouse southern arts organization Alternate ROOTS, the Free Southern Theater produced *Godot* with the Academy Theater of Atlanta for the Florida Studio Theater in Sarasota. The director of the Florida Studio Theater, Marty Ardren, wrote a memo to all Alternate ROOTS companies about the success of this performance, using the performance as "an example of one kind of project Alternate ROOTS companies can do to help each other and strengthen ROOTS."[9] Three decades later, Chan and Creative Time would step in and continue dialoguing with the play as a tool for political activism. Over time, *Godot* has become a part of the history of Black theater in the South and continues to be associated with the Free Southern Theater. The spiralic history of *Godot* in the South is a tribute to a set of circumstances and mythologies created from the original production and tour in 1964. If *Godot* was a mistake, it failed successfully and created new theatrical forms whose influence lasted into the twenty-first century.

In their documentary book about their origins, *The Free Southern Theater by the Free Southern Theater*, they claimed that they were searching for "new idiom, a new genre, a theatrical form and style as unique as blues, jazz, and gospel."[10] The music comparison became a refrain they repeated over time in proposals, memos, and journal entries, especially by Dent, who venerated Black music as the standard for artistic achievement. In his evaluation of the Free Southern Theater, he praises the (male) jazz musician, claiming, "No matter how inventive his technical development or how suffused in his own vision, he can relate back to something real in people who share his experience and situation."[11] Jazz could be artistic and innovative at the same time it connected with Black audiences. For Dent and others in the Free Southern Theater, the comparison to music paves the way to an obligatory aesthetic: that art must be in dialogue with community. He continues, "Art is not an ivory tower exercise but always, basically, an act of communication."[12] Dent spent the majority of his tenure with the Free Southern Theater searching for this method, which went beyond the binary of Black or white authorship. As much as he didn't want to do white radical theater, Dent hoped the Free Southern Theater could also put away LeRoi Jones (Amiri Baraka) scripts in exchange for something more radical, perhaps not even called theater. This explains their early reluctance to stage African American plays such as Lorraine Hansberry's *Raisin in the Sun* or even their dissatisfaction with Ossie Davis's *Purlie Victorious*, which they toured alongside *Godot*. As they reached for Black and white absurd, abstract theater, they grasped content that could engender different and unexpected interpretations from their audiences, to open dialogue between the activists and the local people for whom they performed.

So much of the early material the Free Southern Theater produced, including *Godot* and *Slave Ship*, engaged with jazz as a performance method: an improvisational interplay between the performance of the play and the atmosphere in which it takes place. If we take the Free Southern Theater's desire for a jazz aesthetic at face value, we find a parallel between the experimental innovations in jazz musicology and the visual, or dramatic, jazz of the Free Southern Theater's performances, which has similar aesthetic roots in improvisation and communal experimentation. In other words, beyond simply incorporating jazz music or references into their art, the Free Southern Theater used the process of creating jazz as a blueprint for theater. They engaged the power of performance: taking white material not written for their time and place and appropriating it for the Black experience, making dramatic contrafacts the way Charlie Parker manipulated Ray Noble's "Cherokee" into "KoKo" as an act of subversive and radical improvisation. They kept the framework of the play and let their audiences and atmospheres complete the performance. Audiences reacted to these plays in visceral and unexpected ways, driving the Free Southern Theater toward further experimentation. In *Godot*, they created a performance that became its own conversation: a Black, southern adaptation with a life of its own.

Even though they rejected their early experimentations of the mid-1960s, I return to *Godot* and their reinterpretation of Bertolt Brecht's methods and read their early work as improvised creative flourishing. Through *Godot* and *Slave Ship*, I argue that the dialogue between audience and performance shaped the aesthetics of cultural activism. In these plays, audiences surprised the theater group and exposed the South, especially its more rural areas, as a place where theater could become something new, pushing Dent to consider language other than "theater" or "play" since audiences tended to name the productions in other terms, such as "meeting." The Free Southern Theater struggled to find the language to describe the South and why they felt that theater belonged there, a place neglected during the burgeoning of the Black Arts Movement. Gilbert Moses's 1970 production of *Slave Ship* offers a scene to describe the uniqueness of how a Southern audience could change a play because it offers a case study of the same play with the same director in two locations: New York City and West Point, Mississippi. By following their early avant-garde arc from Beckett to Baraka, we can witness how the Free Southern Theater used their environment to create performances that could open dialogue with local communities and reveal the surrealist conditions of segregation in the Jim Crow South and in broader national and global frames.

Locating the Free Southern Theater in American Protest Art

Even though the Free Southern Theater had their share of ideological struggles, from a twenty-first-century perspective, they were consistent in their service to communities across the Deep South, especially New Orleans, where they relocated in 1964. From their origins until their final performance in 1980, they remained dedicated to the spirit of experimentation and innovation and centralizing art in the struggle for social change. The Free Southern Theater searched for art that would serve even their poorest constituents and "add a cultural and educational dimension to the present Southern freedom movement."[13] While their professed goal was to register voters, many civil rights activists sought alternative methods that would enable people to gather together, interact with activists, and integrate spaces under the guise of entertainment. The record of audience reactions from their auto-documentary book, *The Free Southern Theater by the Free Southern Theater*, and newspaper and journal accounts reveal how the plays provoked people, sometimes angering or confusing them, and sometimes inciting them toward action and involvement in the Movement.

In Mississippi and the Deep South, the Free Southern Theater staged theater in Freedom Schools, churches, auditoriums, and even outdoors. They only received one rejection of their location requests for the 1964 tour, and it came from local activists in Neshoba County, Mississippi, which responded, "The difficulties attendant upon the visit of an interracial group would be too great. Someday the county may be ready, but not just yet."[14] Neshoba County became infamous worldwide that same year when local police and Ku Klux Klan members murdered three civil rights workers, an event for which the Free Southern Theater had to suspend performances in order to attend their funeral. Not only Neshoba County, but the whole state, became associated with racial violence. After Medgar Evers was murdered in 1963, Roy Wilkins described the Mississippi landscape as one of "inhumanity, murder, brutality and racial hatred."[15] The Free Southern Theater needed not only a plan for theatrical productions. They also needed a plan for survival—even to the extent that their participation forms for actors and volunteers asked whether or not they would have access to bail money in case of an arrest.

What the Free Southern Theater could do in this atmosphere of emergency, according to Julius B. Fleming Jr., was "encourage black southerners to forge new and more radical relationships to Mississippi's plantation geographies" and rewrite the script on how people existed in that particular time and place.[16] Fleming continues:

> What links the Free Southern Theater to these more widely remembered and celebrated forms of protest (like the sit-in) is that they all mobilized embodied performance to forge new relationships to their material environments, to alter the ontology of southern space, and ultimately rewrite the scripts of race, time, and black embodiment that were etched into the grounds of Mississippi and into the geographies of the Jim Crow South.[17]

The incredible cultural impact and significance of the Free Southern Theater has been well established by scholars such as Fleming, James Smethurst, and Joe Street who all draw attention to how, despite the violent atmosphere, the Free Southern Theater was able to produce controversial material, such as plays that featured revolutionary heroes of Black history (Martin Duberman's *In White America*), scenes where Black and white people embraced (*Godot*), and that humorously critiqued the South's racist paradigm (Ossie Davis's *Purlie Victorious*).

The Free Southern Theater operated as a locally focused theater group that also imagined itself within an international avant-garde. As Doris Derby's journal from the Free Southern Theater's initial meetings demonstrates, they imagined a theater derived from the theories of Marxist playwright Bertolt Brecht, the *carpa* theater tradition of Mexico, the migratory theater in Puerto Rico, the Soviet Blue Blouse theater that used performance to "give the latest news from the front lines," and the Chinese people's theater. However, Derby combines this with a theater that "arises out of our daily tasks and relationships," including everything from the persecution of artists by the House Un-American Activities Committee to "the use of chemicals in food."[18] Rather than claim that the Free Southern Theater's productions are *derived* from Brecht's ideas, their performances were an experimental assemblage of intentionally diverse elements and methods to produce a theater experience that would make possible a multiplicity of interpretations.

In their anthology of 1960s activist theater, James M. Harding and Cindy Rosenthal argue that the Free Southern Theater "belong[s] to a distinctly American activist avant-garde, one that has direct ties to an African-American community long excluded from histories of American experimental performance."[19] Their scholarship focuses on how the Free Southern Theater shifted and bent the boundaries of protest and how plays enabled communities to gather in potentially explosive circumstances under the guise of entertainment.[20] The extraordinary circumstances of the violence in the Deep South frame how scholars read the Free Southern Theater's aesthetics. As Fleming notes, "Their stages were often improvisational. Their set designs were skimpy as their budgets. . . . But even in the face of these remarkable circumstances, the Free Southern Theater transformed theatrical performance into a powerful genre of civil rights activism."[21] This narrative of resilience is echoed through Smethurst's observations that "there was always a certain feeling of improvisation and contingency in Free Southern Theater performances, especially as theater interacted with rural or small-town Black audiences on tours in the countryside."[22] Even though the landscape and atmosphere dictated the conditions for improvisational performances, the Free Southern Theater's relationship to improvisation intentionally put theater in dialogue with jazz and synced collaborative art with participatory democracy.

Their aesthetic innovations resonate with obligation by centering intimacy-making. Denise Nicholas describes their desire for intimate interactions as theater "presented in a way that they [the audience] emotionally and spiritually can tie, can tie into, which they did over and over again."[23] The Free Southern Theater used improvisational techniques to create emotional and spiritual tie-ins with their audiences, drawing them toward an earned intimacy made possible through theater. Producing unexpected plays, such as *Godot* and Eugene Ionesco's *The Lesson*, resulted in equally unexpected reactions from their audiences, who openly participated and disrupted performances. Dent described the atmosphere of the theater, claiming, "performers [are] confronted with people, especially children, who wander in and out at will, under the best of conditions. And who feel free, *as they should*, to talk and react vigorously to what happens on stage."[24] The raucous atmosphere of activist performances calls for a unique reading of theater, what performance studies scholar Diana Taylor calls *relajo*, to describe the uproarious melee, the "spontaneous disruption [that] shatters the given configuration of the group or community," bringing analytic focus away from the changes happening to the play to what's changing within the audience.[25]

Their attention to audience was a by-product of a gap between the college-educated middle-class activists and local people, who had their own ways of knowing and being in the world. Postshow discussions aided the Free Southern Theater in understanding their audiences, but even these were fraught with thorny moments that revealed a hierarchy that haunted activists. As Free Southern Theater member Denise Nicholas remembers, "So we, we talked, we had this incredible discussion with people who barely had a sixth-grade education . . . it flew in the face of everything, of every assumption that people have about people not having a formal education."[26] In his study of the Black Arts Movement in the South, Smethurst brings in Nicholas's recollection to prove that the Free Southern Theater's "generically mixed repertoire" could have an impact on its "frequently puzzled" core audiences of local people who had most likely never seen a play.[27] However, Nicholas also speaks from a position that reveals the expanse of privilege between mostly college-educated SNCC activists and the local people they wanted to engage with, who ostensibly were the same constituents they were trying to mobilize to vote.

In a letter written from tour, O'Neal both defends the use of *Waiting for Godot* while also addressing the issue with hierarchy. He admits they chose the play as "a kind of experiment" but, for that reason, they left the play in an "aesthetic limbo."[28] He then calls out activists for "a sense of self-aggrandizement which must necessarily be coupled with a same denigration of others."[29] Through his language, he searches for a way to do theater that leaves ego behind while remaining committed to producing a play that could offer meaning to the community and break down the "us" and "them" barriers he describes as such:

> The "WE" that I refer to here is the 'we who are *in the Movement*' the them I refer to are 'those who are *not in the Movement*'—including local Negroes. All of us—including the Free Southern Theater Company—have slipped into this bag whether we intended to or not. (digression: This, I maintain, is at the base of the problem about staff-community relationships that plagued the Waveland discussion.) By presenting *Godot* in a way we have challenged this kind of fallacious thinking—challenged it in ourselves as well as in others.[30]

Because no one can definitively know the meaning of *Godot*, the play offers an open conversation revealing to the Free Southern Theater how little they understood their audiences. O'Neal makes a case for using absurdist plays because they disrupt expectations and can open new channels of communication. After a long analysis of *Godot* and audience capacity ("they get the point"), O'Neal concludes: "The plays that are really relevant to the situation and to the particular point of view of this audience have not been written yet. It's that simple. We have to write them."[31] Their experimentations with adapting other theater pushed the Free Southern Theater toward art that could serve and reflect the community they created within. Almost immediately after moving to New Orleans, they began forming creative community workshops to generate new material.

In 1969, when the Free Southern Theater had its largest available funding, they also formed a series of workshops in poetry, drama, and dance, a literary magazine and newspaper, and a performance company for seniors. Their vision was always bigger than their pockets, which thinned out their capacity, and generated a funding problem that sits at the heart of radical arts institutions: accepting money from federal and private foundations. The Free Southern Theater began with sponsorship from artists such as Harry Belafonte, Paul Newman, and Bob Dylan, but quickly relied on grants from the Rockefeller Foundation, Ottinger Foundation, and the National Endowment for the Arts. The impression left by over a decade of archival evidence reveals that even though the touring company was central to the Free Southern Theater's funding stream, they poured their hearts into establishing a thriving, independent Black artistic community supported by the Black middle class. They foregrounded the community workshop so that artistic exploration and play would become an integral part of social movement activism. Inspired by places like Highlander and Karamu House Theater in Cleveland, the Free Southern Theater wanted to establish a blueprint for other theaters; and they did, because theaters such as Dashiki Project Theater in New Orleans, Carpetbag Theater in Knoxville, Sudan Arts in Houston, Roadside Theater in Appalachia, M Ensemble in Miami, and AlternateROOTS all emulated their method of community engagement. Creative workshops and cultural activism are one and the same, even though scholarship usually focuses on the final products of these exchanges. By tracing the early work of the Free Southern Theater within a jazz aesthetic, we catch glimpses of a theater discovering the aesthetics of obligation through the process of becoming intimate with their audiences.

Visual Jazz and the Aesthetics of Improvisation

In their search for a "new idiom" for creating art, cultural activists during the civil rights era imagined the possibilities held within jazz beyond playing instruments. Novelist John A. Williams, in his civil-rights-era book *The Man Who Cried I Am*, described the longing to approximate jazz in writing: "He wanted to do with the novel what Charlie Parker was doing with music—tearing it up and remaking it; basing it on nasty, nasty blues and overlaying it with the deep overriding tragedy not of Dostoevsky, but an American who knew of consequences to come."[32] The desire to stretch jazz beyond music into other art forms is at the heart of the civil rights avant-garde. For social movements, jazz and other Black musical traditions offered the possibility of deep transformation. As Robin D. G. Kelley describes, "[Music] created a world of pleasure, not just to escape the everyday brutalities of capitalism, patriarchy, and white supremacy, but to build community, establish fellowship, play and laugh, and plant seeds for a different way of living, a different way of hearing."[33]

Even though music appearss the least as an art object analyzed in this book, my approach concurs with Robert G. O'Meally, Brent Hayes Edwards, and Farah Jasmine Griffin that "jazz is not only a music to define, it is a *culture*," and that the effort to define this culture contains its own discourse that extends the musical process into poetics and politics.[34] Recognizing the power of music, I look at the forms of jazz creation and improvisation as a sonic blueprint for reading cultural activism methods, including radical adaptations of standards, which I discuss below, and the relationality of improvisation. By building creative spontaneity into civil rights and labor organizing, participants embodied the process of "tearing it up and remaking it," bringing jazz and the avant-garde to politics.[35] To put it simply, jazz improvisation depends on nonverbal communication; visual cues work together with sonorous ones to guide musicians in and out of solos, where individual interpretations serve the larger collective vision of the song. In relating performance to jazz, we can witness participatory democracy put into practice and what Vijay Iyer calls "traces of embodiment": the relationship between the body moving and the sounds produced from it.[36]

Through jazz, we are challenged to release our commitment to a specific outcome. As Fred Moten argues in *In the Break*, jazz is the "rematerialization of bourgeois space-time" through its form.[37] Moten emphasizes the *doing* of jazz: "Such production—such radically ensemblic, radically improvisational objection—is the unfinished, continually re-en-gendered, actively re-en-gendering project of the black (and blue and sentimental) avant-garde."[38] To be unfinished is central to Black expressions of jazz and improvisation and provides a direct challenge to completion or the seeking of an end goal or final product. Evoking this shift to the unfinished,

Daphne Brooks picks up Moten's conversation and extends "unreal time" into protests against police brutality:

> If, as Fred Moten (2011) has argued, "blackness is enthusiastic social vision performed in unreal time," these "disturbing" collective bodies translate and transition [Oscar] Grant's and [Trayvon] Martin's martyred "blackness" into the realm of nonstandard, civil disobedient time. . . . we are being hailed, beckoned to finish the performance, "to carry out the suggestions of the performer(s)," to think of the body as an open "channel for sonic resonance."[39]

Brooks argues that to be unfinished continues the dialogue with a future generation. The "sonic resonance" between the performers and their audiences was an investment, not in consensus but in continuation, and sought to define generational activism as a process that evolves with, rather than defines itself against, previous generations.

I see the Free Southern Theater not as artists who loved jazz music but as jazz performers themselves, using their bodies as instruments to rewrite theatrical standards, what I refer to here as visual jazz. Visual jazz describes the process by which dramatists radically altered the content or intent of a play by improvising off of the script with their bodies located in specific environments that encode them as racialized. The relationship between the Free Southern Theater and their audiences reformatted the plays to a call-and-response between art (the Free Southern Theater's production) and political message (what the audience perceived). The audience perception of the performance did not always align with what the Free Southern Theater wanted to convey. *Godot*, specifically because it was not written in or for the context of U.S. race relations, gave the Free Southern Theater hope that their performances could change perspectives of racial identity and then perhaps the social order. They sought to move audiences beyond a racially determined worldview by presenting a play *not* written about race relations with an integrated cast. However, audiences perceived an allegory for their own oppression as they waited endlessly for social change, which resulted in them shouting "We're not waiting" during one of their performances. Of course audiences saw race in the content of the play when racism determined every aspect of their public lives. The improvisation on Beckett's original text happened between the actors' choices and the vocalized response of their audiences. The play's tenacious criticism that "nothing ever happens" must be revaluated in front of an audience for whom nothing ever happening is a daily—and absurd—reality. Suddenly, *Godot* becomes an example of realism rather than absurdism.

Jazz and theater artists took white-authored material and radically altered its structure, intent, and context for a new audience. In this way, Black artists and musicians could balance inequities of artistic exchange, such as how white artists regularly took elements from the African diaspora and capitalized on it. The Free Southern Theater walked into theater's own realm of cultural borrowing. European dramatists, like Jean Genet in *Les Negres* (The Blacks), established an avant-garde tradition by appropriating performance techniques from other cultures. In addition, Brecht imported vaudeville and American jazz music into his dramaturgy, and theater director Max Reinhardt was inspired by his experience with the vaudeville-style production of *Shuffle Along* (1921), starring Josephine Baker, just to name a few examples.[40]

The process of visual jazz pushes theater beyond adaptation in the same manner in which Charlie Parker—and many other jazz musicians—did not merely adapt but transformed pieces of European music, such as Igor Stravinsky's classical ballet *The Rite of Spring*. The relationship between jazz musicians and Stravinsky mirrors the theatrical conversation the Free Southern Theater was having with European dramatists. Jazz musicians found something in the "folk-inspired forms and melodies . . . [the] extreme experiments Stravinsky devised in meter, rhythmic syncopation and dissonance."[41] Stravinsky's avant-garde provided a language for musicians to translate as their own, a parallel to how Beckett and Brecht created their own avant-garde through playwriting.

There was something in the raw matter of Beckett's original play that *worked* for artists to improvise on and transform. In jazz composition, a contrafact is a method of borrowing that enabled musicians to avoid paying royalties by writing new melodies over the harmonic structure of old standards that were often originally written by white musicians. At the time, the Free Southern Theater was paying royalties for Duberman's *In White America* and Ossie Davis's *Purlie Victorious*, which cost the Free Southern Theater at least $280 in 1965—a large amount for a financially struggling theater group. As far as their records show, the Free Southern Theater did not pay royalties for *Godot* or any other material from European playwrights, thus their decision to contrafact new, independent performances from free material was also an economic one. While it is a less romantic story, economic necessity provided the impetus for many of the Free Southern Theater's artistic innovations, including their poetry performance shows and their in-house community writing workshops that would develop a new generation of dramatists willing

The Free Southern Theater and Visual Jazz Performance · 39

to donate their writing to the Free Southern Theater. Money—and the need for subversion in a violent atmosphere—put the Free Southern Theater in a position to rework scripts and create something independent.

However, beyond the cost factor, artists were in dialogue with other artists pushing boundaries. To return to the Stravinsky example, jazz musician Darryl Brenzel notes, "Stravinsky was also pushing things a lot harmonically and I think jazz musicians in general have an appreciation for this. We tend to want to take a tune that people know and see how far we can take the harmony and still retain the tune."[42] I view the Free Southern Theater's productions as a contrafact rather than an adaptation in order to emphasize the performance's independence, what Harding describes as "apostate adaptations [that] owe no allegiance to the integrity of their European origins and have become experimental precisely because of that experimentation."[43] The Free Southern Theater made *Waiting for Godot* a Black play through the bodies of their actors and the environment of the Movement. A question Brooks asks is relevant here to understanding how the Free Southern Theater inhabited Beckett's play, "What does it mean to 'occupy' a song? To invade it? To play with and inside of its compositional and lyrical form with so much volatility that one jolts the listener, the spectator into a thrilling, moving, disruptive relationship with past, present and future, with old songs and new?"[44] As I move through the play, we can witness how the Free Southern Theater—even unintentionally—played with its composition.

Vladimir and Estragon's interracial relationship, as represented in the Free Southern Theater performance by Black actor Gil Moses and the white actor Murray Levy, respectively, carries the taboo of Black and white people waiting together in a society that had segregated waiting areas. This upends the core of the play by transforming what is supposed to represent the mundane—sitting together waiting—into a transgressive act of protest just by being present on stage together. During moments in *Godot*, scenes created a visual dissonance, such as the affection between a Black Vladimir and a white Estragon. According to Beckett's script, they hug and hold each other; they do not want to leave the other person to wait alone. One can imagine how uncanny this image must have looked within the segregated South and how those moments challenged the preconceived notions of how Black and white people should be acting together. *Godot* was meant to open audiences to an interpretation of their everyday racial milieu as absurd.

Within the first few minutes of the play, Vladimir establishes the dialogue of dependency that resonates between the couple throughout the play and comments to Estragon, "When I think of it . . . all these years . . . but for me . . . where would you be . . . ?"[45] When Estragon contemplates their separation, Vladimir responds, "you wouldn't go far," comically critiquing the white dependency on Black people in the U.S. South.[46] For the audience—who understood the performance to be a kind of protest simply because the event was organized by SNCC—the conversation adopts an ulterior meaning. The critique is especially evident in the way that the relationship between Vladimir and Estragon does not progress toward their common goal:

> ESTRAGON: Wait! (*He moves away from Vladimir*). I wonder if we wouldn't have been better off alone, each one for himself. (*He crosses the stage and sits down on the mound.*) We weren't made for the same road.
> VLADIMIR: (*without anger*) It's not certain.[47]

The characters' dialogue abstractly represents the debate between integration and separatist approaches to U.S. race relations—and it does so with a degree of humor. As James Cromwell noted, the Mississippi audience "looked at Beckett's play—right in the face—and they laughed right at the characters."[48] The irreverence of their laughter in the midst of the violence of the civil rights movement momentarily destabilized the oppressive social structure. Estragon argues for a separatist position within an integrated play, and Vladimir's indecisive response mirrors the skepticism inherent within the Free Southern Theater and other civil rights groups, which doubted integration was a viable option in the South. Vladimir's response would resonate with those in the crowd uncertain of integration's promises.

When the white actor playing Pozzo (James Cromwell) entered the stage in act I with a rope tied around the neck of the Black actor playing Lucky (John O'Neal) on his way to sell him in the market, the meaning was not ambiguous within the context of the South's history of slavery; the appearance of their bodies alone communicated a subtextual meaning *before* the actors even delivered Beckett's lines. As the play continues, the allegorical dialogue becomes so convincing that one would think Beckett did have U.S. racism in mind when writing the play. When Vladimir approaches Pozzo and Lucky he exclaims, "To treat a man . . . (gesture toward Lucky) . . . like that . . . I think that . . . no . . . a human being . . . no . . . it's a scandal!"[49] The clown-like naïveté of Vladimir's character gave a fresh reaction to this familiar image of oppression. During the production in McComb, Mississippi, an audience member interrupted the performance and stood up on the stage to shout, "slave . . . whupped him . . . no!"[50] O'Neal had argued that the man

Figure 2. The Free Southern Theater's *Waiting for Godot*, 1964. Free Southern Theater Records, Amistad Research Center, New Orleans.

on stage could not articulate his ideas and thus O'Neal overlooked how the man rejected the scene before him through his direct "no." The man's reaction protests against *any* existential debate over meaning; for him, the only reading applicable is an affective response informed by the context of his life. This moment suggests not only audience recognition of the scene's implications but also a need for vocalized response to the representation before them. An entry in Penny Hartzell's journal shows the effect of theater in this atmosphere: "The difference between their make-believe (TV and the movies) and real life becomes blurred during the plays. That's why, possibly, they usually don't listen to Pozzo. He is the white master and one need go no further than that; what could he possibly say to interest them?"[51] The Free Southern Theater did not expect such a politically charged result; rather, they explicitly stated that they wanted to help audiences "find the vocabulary"[52] for critical discussion, and to have their audiences debate the meaning of *Godot*.

Beckett's script contained the elements of universal oppression that resonated with southern audiences, especially the relationship between Blacks and whites strained by oppression and dependency. Lucky refuses to put down the bags he carries for Pozzo because, as Pozzo claims, "He wants to impress me, so I'll keep him."[53] When pressed to answer whether Pozzo desires to get rid of him, he again claims that "you can't drive such creatures away," thereby suggesting the psychological dependency on the master within the slave's mind.[54] Conversely, Pozzo's identity is dependent on Lucky: "But for him all my thoughts, feelings, would have been of common things."[55] There is also a suggestion of an abusive reciprocity in Lucky when Pozzo has a mental lapse, admitting that "He used to be so kind . . . so helpful and entertaining . . . my good angel . . . and now . . . he's killing me."[56] Comedy offers a moment of transgression as Pozzo and Lucky's absurd relationship becomes blurred with the everyday absurdity of racism and dependency.

The Free Southern Theater's stripped-down theater had the benefit of presenting this thin line between theater and reality. Director James Cromwell later reflected on how audience interpretations affected his relationship to the play: "The minister of the Baptist church in the black neighborhood in New Orleans said something to me that I had never heard really described as succinctly. He said the master is as tied to the slave as the slave is tied to the master—the reciprocity of that relationship. That was the beginning of my understanding of the play."[57] As much as the audience may have seen a dramatization of a traumatic history, they also saw this past within their own current context. In the second act of *Godot*, Pozzo's blindness renders him completely dependent on Lucky who remains tied to him despite the change in their power relationship. One audience member interpreted this scenario as allegorical to the conditions of 1960s Mississippi: "Maybe in this race relations business we should take the rope off our necks after the master goes blind."[58] With ease, the audience member creates a temporal shift from an image of a slave master to another master—the white southerners who were afraid of losing power during the legal enforcement of integration. Rather than trying to reconcile racial difference, the member's response argued for the more radical stance of separation and resistance beneath the seemingly innocent context of a play.

The audience member's reaction raises the question: What is the transgressive potential of entertainment? Beckett muses on this within *Godot* itself and, while critics have debated the play's engagement with minstrelsy, an integrated cast only thinly veils an obvious commentary on Black entertainment. When Pozzo forces Lucky to entertain the others with a dance, it broadcasts the familiar image of the minstrel: "Shall we have him dance, or sing, or recite, or think, or—?"[59] Lucky is forced to perform as Pozzo threatens him with a whip. Lucky's (O'Neal's) bad dancing transforms Beckett's vaudevillesque scene into an antiperformance of minstrelsy and a political commentary on the restricted position of the Black entertainer:

POZZO: He used to dance the farandole, the fling, the brawl, the jig, the fandango, and even the hornpipe. He capered. For joy. Now that's the best he can do. Do you know what he calls it?

ESTRAGON: The Scapegoat's Agony.

VLADIMIR: The Hard Stool.

POZZO: The Net. He thinks he's entangled in a net.[60]

The disappointment in Lucky's performance reverses the expectations accompanying the minstrelsy stereotype and pulls a commentary on minstrelsy to the surface of the original text. Beyond the humor, the Free Southern Theater's performance in a Mississippi context critiqued the behind-the-scenes reality of the exploitation of Black performance through a comparison to the exploitation of slavery. Lucky's performance makes a political statement instead of lighthearted entertainment, which also describes the Free Southern Theater's performance as a whole.

In the play's most controversial scene, the moment where Pozzo commands Lucky to "think," the Free Southern Theater production furthers the radical subnarrative of the play. Lucky responds in a tirade of disconnected words and untied fragmented significations, which critics of *Godot* have analyzed for its hidden intertextual meaning, or its mockery of Joycean prose. However, this criticism would add nothing to an audience previously unfamiliar with the larger literary context. Rather, the scene resonated with the audience's *environmental* context. The image of Lucky's voice agitating against Pozzo and Lucky's resistance is choreographed in Beckett's specific stage directions—"Lucky pulls on the rope, staggers, and shouts his text"— suggesting a specific message relevant to those in the audience without a political voice.[61] The words are meaningless and unintelligible, suggesting Lucky's inability to access authentic self-expression. Lucky refuses to stop shouting when the other characters attempt to physically restrain him, suggesting that even though the words he says are nonsensical, the *act* of speech is still a protest. Beckett separates language from action in Lucky's tirade, creating an independent narrative communicated solely by the bodies on stage. With the integrated cast, the audience sees actors restraining and holding down a Black man struggling to break free, an unmistakable connotation to the overall struggle in this temporal and geographic context. Just as Lucky's words in Beckett's monologue lack coherent meaning, O'Neal intensified their insignificance by expressing resistance through his body on stage.

Even further, when Lucky's body goes limp and he refuses to stand or return to work, the physical actions of O'Neal connote the same physical gestures of nonviolent forms of protest endorsed by SNCC—a canonical image of the civil rights movement. However, Lucky's passive resistance fails as Pozzo forces Lucky to hold his bags and silently return to his enslaved position. The scene transforms from a physically comic moment of resistance into a political commentary on the limitations of nonviolent protest. Yet again, absurdity is appropriate within the larger context of this performance: the Free Southern Theater's own contradictory dependency on the nonviolent SNCC and the militant Deacons for Defense for armed protection, not to mention the absurdity of risking violence in order to attend a play. This moment in *Godot* perhaps captured the sentiments of futility experienced by those trying to fight for equality through the Movement.

The production of *Godot* and its perception forged a new play from Beckett's script without letting go of the "tune" of *Godot*: the frustrations of waiting, the extent of human abuse and power, the thin line between intimacy and hatred. The actors' and audience's reactions imbued the play with a Black perspective in the same way jazz musicians used their technique and embodiment to contrafact songs: using economic constraint to create something subversive and original. The Free Southern Theater went beyond contrafacting Beckett's play; they also changed activism by altering the process of organization. Rather than mobilize for voting registration, these performances encouraged community gathering for entertainment, with spontaneous moments in which audience members expressed their political commitment to social change. For many—the shy, apprehensive, or uncommitted—attending a performance offered a safer way to gather than other protests. Theater changed the possibilities of what a political action can be, even as it retains the emphasis on gathering and mobilizing as a collective.

Theater pierced through the seriousness of protest and gave people the chance to laugh at the absurdity of racism. In 1969, the same year as their production of Gil Moses's *Slave Ship*, the Free Southern Theater produced a play heavily influenced by *Waiting for Godot, Proper and Fine, Fannie Lou Hamer's Entourage*, which Sharon Stockard Martin completed in 1968. While *Slave Ship* presents a world haunted by the violence and death from the Middle Passage, *Proper and Fine* is filled with humor and wit. The play centers on a couple, Afrique and Sam, waiting in a retail store and failing to get the white clerk's attention. After a long time waiting and being ignored, they finally begin to leave with the clothing, only to be accused of shoplifting by the clerk who had ignored their request for service. Stockard Martin's play revives *Godot*'s spirit of waiting for an absurd reason, but with a scenario more familiar to their audience: the experience of being denied service. The

The Free Southern Theater and Visual Jazz Performance · 45

dialogue references Beckett's play, such as the comedic back-and-forth misunderstandings and confusion over meaning of very basic things, such as the famous civil rights ballad "We Shall Overcome":

AFRIQUE: You said you wanted to hear a song to sing.
SAM: There are others.

Pause.

How about "We Shall Overcome"?
AFRIQUE: We shall overcome what?
SAM: He'll know that one.
AFRIQUE: Who will?
SAM: The man over there.
AFRIQUE: So what?
SAM: Maybe that'll make him want to come over here and wait on us.
AFRIQUE: While we're waiting on him.[62]

This scene draws directly from Estragon and Vladimir trying to amuse themselves to pass the time, and Pozzo's command of Lucky to entertain the characters. After they sing a few bars of "We Shall Overcome," the song works to get the attention of the people on stage, who clap for them, but the clerk still does not serve them. Stockard Martin also knew the audience would clap and has Sam claim, "Everyone else in the store is applauding us too."[63] The song works for attention, but not action. Like with the original *Godot*, the Free Southern Theater critiques the tactics of the civil rights movement. Singing songs doesn't get them equal attention, clapping is not service. And when the audience claps, they are implicated as well; supporting the arts is not enough either.

In the humor of this play lies a dark message about the failure of integration. The play not only makes reference to the absurdity of waiting for someone who will never come to help them, but Stockard Martin builds in references overtly drawn from the action in Beckett's play, such as foot pain and shoes being too tight. In a review of another Stockard Martin play in the Free Southern Theater newsletter, they describe how she "borrowed from the devices 'the theater of the absurd.'"[64] Anyone who had seen the Free Southern Theater's original version of *Godot* from their 1964 tour, which Stockard Martin may have, would recognize how she riffs and quotes the original in homage. The reference to Fannie Lou Hamer could represent her presence in the audience during the 1964 show in Ruleville, Mississippi, where she encouraged audience members to shout, "We're not waiting!" Even if Stockard Martin had not attended that particular show, Hamer's interruption was repeated in newspaper accounts and in journals as a popular Free Southern Theater story. *Proper and Fine* describes Hamer's uneven combination of commitment to nonviolence and militant beliefs for radical change. Stockard Martin makes clear in her play that Black people are still waiting for equality in retail stores, and critiques middle-class aspirations as the path toward social change.

Slave Ship and the Black Arts Avant-Garde

Almost all the Free Southern Theater's plays from this time period critique integration and respectability politics, but none more than their production of Amiri Baraka's *Slave Ship*, directed by Gilbert Moses. Moses directed the play at the Chelsea Theater in New York City in 1969 to much acclaim. The Free Southern Theater then produced a version of Moses's *Slave Ship* for southern audiences in 1970. *Slave Ship* is an experiential performance piece that depends on sound and setting to approximate the atmosphere of the Middle Passage. Baraka's script thus contains more stage directions than lines and it blends Yoruba rhythms with a soundtrack composed by Moses and incorporates the jazz music of Archie Shepp.

Slave Ship did not deviate from the style of performance the Free Southern Theater had already established, even though Baraka had never participated in one of their productions. Gilbert Moses brought the aesthetics and methods he'd learned from participating in the Free Southern Theater when he directed Baraka's play. Moses's *Slave Ship* is a conduit between the stylistics developed down south and the urban Black Arts Movement. At the Chelsea rehearsals, Moses depended on the actors' ability to communicate the heightened emotional state that would affect the audience: "Rehearsal rituals attempted to bring the performers together as a cohesive ensemble, the actors worked to develop a greater awareness of the social context of the performance and of the objectives of arousing the political consciousness and militant sentiments of their black audiences."[65] Moses placed his directorial emphasis on the environmental experience—what he termed *emotional space*—and despite Harry Elam Jr.'s claim that Moses "appropriated this technique" under the tutelage of Paul Sills, Peter Brook, and Richard Schechner, I would argue that Moses's technique derives from the Free Southern Theater's style of community engagement and their aesthetics of

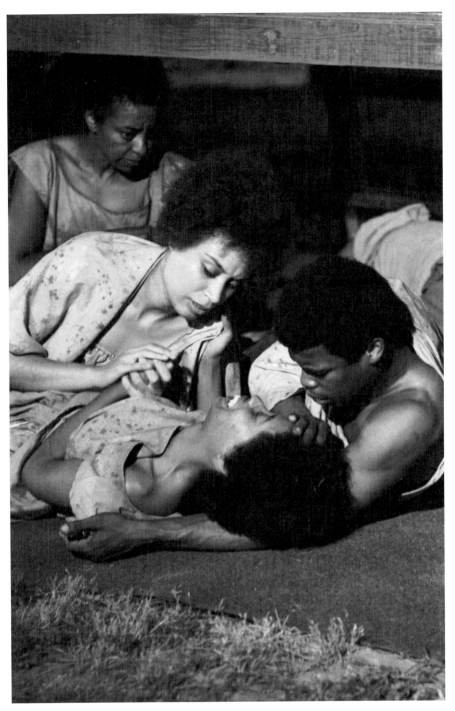

Figure 3. The Free Southern Theater's *Slave Ship*, 1970. Photograph taken by Doris Derby. The Doris A. Derby Papers, Stuart A. Rose Special Collections at Emory University, Atlanta.

obligation.[66] Moses encouraged actors to be politically active, in a sense re-creating a SNCC atmosphere in New York. Instead of training activists to be actors, the production in New York required him to train actors to be activists. Moses combined the Mississippi experience with Baraka's national-ist agenda and Archie Shepp's jazz sounds to re-create historical scenes that moved audiences to the brink of their capacity. As one reviewer commented, "There was no way for us [the spectators] to step outside of Gil Moses's pro-duction of Imamu Baraka's *Slave Ship*."[67] Moses was able to successfully re-create the experience of the Free Southern Theater, where theater combined with the entirety of the Movement, making it impossible for a spectator not to be a participant in political action. For this, Moses won an Obie Award and much critical acclaim in New York's theater world.

The play's movement between New York City and Mississippi reveals a cultural exchange; however, it also highlights the difference between the-ater in the Village and theater in the rural areas of Mississippi. *Slave Ship* transforms from a theatrical play to a place-based piece of performance art. Taking a cue from Smethurst's claim that the South worked with differ-ent temporalities than other locations during the Black Arts Movement, I read the North-South migration of *Slave Ship* as an opening to let go of the narrative of civil-rights-to-Black-Arts evolution. Instead, the specifici-ties of audience and location determine the play's style. There is nothing inherent in the South that gives it a different temporality; rather, the play changes based on the reality of the organizational structures formed in the afterlife of the plantation. As a mobile, public theater, the Free Southern Theater could not work with the conventions of a traditional theater—they pared the play's set down to a single raised platform. Tom Dent remembers the wooden platform as being an effective and economical set: "It symbol-ized both the slaveship (masters above, slaves prone underneath), the auction block in the new world, and the speakers platform from which the slaves are implored to rise up against their masters."[68] In Doris Derby's photographs of the Free Southern Theater's version, she captures the experience of the play: the actors playing enslaved peoples writhe and scream, presenting a claustro-phobic image of bodies crawling out from underneath the platform. When Black actors played white characters, they wore a white cloth mask wrapped around most of their face and head, which evokes images of Ku Klux Klan hoods. Screaming is the most prevalent dialogue in the play with a momen-tary cessation when one of the enslaved women kills herself and her child using their chains. A photograph of the woman holding the child shows an expression of fear and desperation. The outdoor theater could not use lighting in the manner that Baraka's stage directions called for; however, not having a stage meant that as actors writhed in the dirt under the platform, most of the audience wouldn't be able to see, only hear what they were saying. The use of the platform visualizes what version of history becomes visible (the world of white characters and their interactions with Black people) and the world below, the world of the Middle Passage and the planning of rebellions. The most poignant stage effect of the play, according to Derby's photographs, comes straight from the ground the characters are splayed on, which folds time against the site of ancestral trauma.

As the vignettes move chronologically through time, the slave ship is ever present. The play blends the conditions of slavery into the civil rights movement, calling attention to the afterlife of the plantation and how dynamics emerge over time. For example, the actor who plays the enslaved person who betrays Nat Turner's rebellion then plays "the same tom as before" but in a modern business suit, a "pseudo intellectual" preacher symbolic of the Southern Christian Leadership Conference and Martin Luther King Jr.[69] As the wooden platform transforms, the play visualizes an evolution of slave ship into the plantation, and then into ways these systems replicate even in the civil rights movement. As the preacher talks to an invisible white government official, he claims, "We will be non-violent . . . to the last . . . because we understand the dignity of the prudy mcbonk and the greasy ghost."[70] Like Lucky's speech in *Waiting for Godot*, the words slip between coherence and the dissolution of coherence into sound. The preacher's speech is supposed to be absurd and meaningless. As he speaks, the stage directions read:

> Then, one of the black men, out of the darkness, comes and sits before the tom, a wrapped up bloody corpse of the dead burned body, as if they just taken the body from a blown up church, places corpse in front of preacher. Preacher stops. Looks up at "person" he's tomming before, then, with his foot, tries to push baby's body behind him grinning, and jeffing, all the time, showing teeth, and being "dignified."[71]

The scene critiques the respectability politics of groups like the Southern Christian Leadership Conference, composed of suit-wearing preachers who negotiated with white-dominant mainstream politics to push forward legal reform. The way the preacher hides the corpse signals to the audience (both the white character on stage and the audience witnessing the play) that the suffering of Black folks at the hands of white supremacy will be concealed or downplayed by this version of a civil rights leader. The critique is specific to

Martin Luther King Jr.'s response to the 16th Street Baptist Church bombing in Birmingham that killed four children. Even though King expressed outrage in letters to President John F. Kennedy, his role in Birmingham was meant to calm the public and convince them to maintain nonviolence and not revolt. Baraka's play, on the other hand, wants to do the opposite: expose nonviolence as ineffective. Because the actor who played Uncle Tom is required to also play the assimilationist preacher, Baraka draws a direct line between those that thwarted Turner's rebellion and the contemporary Southern Christian leadership Conference. Eventually the actors "kill" the preacher and his head is thrown out into the audience—an incredibly controversial action considering how close historically this performance was to Martin Luther King Jr.'s assassination.

The play struck a chord with Black southern audiences and their responses exceeded the expectations of the Free Southern Theater. At the *Slave Ship* performance in West Point, Mississippi "the entire audience rose to its feet and joined with the actors waving fists and chanting, 'We're gonna rise up!'"[72] In Greenville, Mississippi, the audience tried to revolt during the performance and had to be persuaded to return back to their homes peacefully. As Kalamu Ya Salaam (Val Ferdinand) claims, the audiences of Mississippi and Louisiana understood the message of *Slave Ship*, despite a general lack of attention to its artistic merit, the kind of acclaim the production received in New York City. Salaam remembers how the Free Southern Theater performed a production along the shore of Lake Pontchartrain in New Orleans after Southern University would not allow the performance in their auditorium.[73] The outdoor atmosphere would have exposed the smells and environment Baraka desired in his stage directions, which would have been impossible in a traditional theater.

The Free Southern Theater's performance of *Slave Ship* contained all these elements of repetition over time; however, underneath the wooden platform, characters engaged in moments of care and strategy. Here, outside of the world of white interaction, we witness what Soyica Diggs Colbert, Douglas A. Jones Jr., and Shane Vogel call "restorative performance," a framework to the side of repetition, which extends performance studies into new configurations between past, present, and future. Taking inspiration from discussion of afterlives in Black and postcolonial studies, they place "attention on the things that matter most to care" and argue that "rather than see the past as a series of breaks or ruptures that return again in the present, the notion of afterlife traces continuities that may be obscured by the logic of progress, revolution, rupture, or reform."[74] Above the wooden platform, we see the past continuously emerging in breaks and ruptures; below reveals a set of interactions (captured by Derby's photographs) that display intimacies of care and touch that operate outside of what is historically recordable. As one central character shows pain in her body language, the others touch and hold her in her suffering. Their movements are a choreography somewhere between love and restraint—a restraint necessary as they try to keep the woman alive. Outside of the above-platform narrative, the story below and its restorative performance reveal processes that center intimacy between Black people and "the conditions of social life."[75] The kinds of strategy that result in the play's revolutionary conclusion emerge from gestures of communal care.

In their discussion of performance beyond repetition, Diggs Colbert, Jones, and Vogel read Baraka's writing on theater and production of *Slave Ship*, albeit only the script itself, not the Free Southern Theater performance. They claim that *Slave Ship* "best manifests the aesthetic and philosophical principles he outlines" in "The Revolutionary Theater" and describe the relationship between the play and atmosphere: "The play's ritualistic energies emerge from its atmospherics, which Baraka seeks to achieve through dance, harrowing wails and euphoric utterances, music (especially drumming) and spectacle."[76] From these atmospherics, the play "exceeds itself as the repetition of form or representation."[77] In other words, the play's immersive experience of the Middle Passage is both referential in content and singular in its power. Baraka wanted a theater that could inspire "actual explosions and actual brutality," which it came closer to in Mississippi than in New York, despite the fact that the Mississippi version would not have the budget or possibilities for the kind of spectacle a physical location in New York City could provide, even an off-off Broadway one.[78] This does not have to do with any romanticized notion of regional difference, but rather as a result of the ongoing dialogue the Free Southern Theater was having with audiences and the resonances of performance locations that were also places of protest. The production asks us to understand the particularity of place, drawing our attention to the relationship between theater and audience in that moment.

Conclusion: The Impact on Performance and Theater

The potential of the Free Southern Theater's performances to challenge the social order did not go unnoticed by Richard Schechner, one of the original board members and advocates of the Free Southern Theater and later a key founder of performance studies. The environmental factors involved in creating the Free Southern Theater's *Godot* are echoed in Schechner's definition of performance as "the whole constellation of events . . . that take place in/ among both performers and audience," evolving into his "broad-spectrum approach" that extends a performance into a myriad of social processes: "formal ritual ceremonies, public gatherings, and various means of exchanging information, goods, and customs."[79] The broad spectrum that frames the Free Southern Theater's performances was a product of its environment that intermingled activist networks and unlikely locations with theater. Schechner's theories germinated from his experiences with the Free Southern Theater in Mississippi and New Orleans before they later evolved into the discipline that influenced performance studies, which is why the Free Southern Theater easily fits into a performance studies paradigm. What Schechner could not imagine, taken up later by Diggs Colbert, Jones, and Vogel, are ways in which performances could be exponentially singular in their engagement with repetition—"to the nth power"—and do the work of restoration with a focus on reparation and radically different futures.[80] Through its innovative use of environment, the Free Southern Theater anticipated what would become a central tenet of performance theory: that performance can alter social identity through people interacting with their surroundings and each other.

As easily as one could say that audience involvement stems from Brechtian aesthetic theory, one could also point toward the setting of the local church, community center, or any other area that allowed people to participate openly. Or that Antonin Artaud's, Beckett's, and Brecht's derisive attitude toward formal language was suited to a community without access to formal literacy and education. Performance aesthetics draw from a variety of cultures without necessarily fusing them together, what Erika Fischer-Lichte calls "interweaving cultures"—a concept she intentionally chooses instead of hybridity.[81] Tracing the history of modern theater though this process, Fischer-Lichte emphasizes how "the interweaving of cultures in performance has neither led to the westernization of non-Western performances nor to the homogenization of performances globally."[82] In other words, one culture can borrow from another without necessarily compromising its own set of aesthetics, thus rejecting the hierarchical idea of influence. When applied to the Free Southern Theater, the relationship between avant-garde techniques and local materials interweave together without being alloyed.

Despite the Free Southern Theater's marginal status in the Black Arts Movement, they share many connections to avant-garde theater and Black drama theory, which at times favored avant-gardists in the same breath in which they rejected Western or white drama as a whole. Exemplary of this paradox is Amiri Baraka's manifesto on Black Arts drama, "The Revolutionary Theater," that rejects the dominant white literary tradition and calls for the "conquest of the white eye" by channeling the French dramatist Artaud's *The Conquest of Mexico*—the primary example of the aesthetic theory titled "Theater of Cruelty" (1938) from which Baraka draws in his essay.[83] Baraka, Ed Bullins, and Larry Neal each noted the value of avant-garde theater as a revolutionary form yet found it necessary for a Black aesthetic to come from the Black community.[84] As Mike Sell notes, "Lacking real estate, an ideologically unified model of community, and a sure foothold in the African American community, the most advanced segments of the Black Arts Movement chose the transient, situational, performative forms of avant-garde and theater to forward their goals."[85] Even within the same text or interview, they would reject the Western forms they identified as revolutionary: "The Revolutionary Theater, even if it is Western, must be anti-Western."[86] The Black aesthetic's complicated relationship to avant-garde theater practices is difficult to comprehend much less discuss. However, when thinking of it through Fischer-Lichte's "interweaving cultures" paradigm, and the concept of visual jazz, their process emerges as an artistic exchange that radically alters the history of theater as it relates to the daily life of the Black community.

In the years after *Slave Ship*, the Free Southern Theater continued to perform works by nationally renowned Black dramatists, including those they had previously rejected in the earlier years of experimentation, such as Lorraine Hansberry and Langston Hughes. However, this decade has been viewed by critics (and even by its own members) as a period of decline, leading to the theater's final performance in 1980. As the Free Southern Theater inspired a variety of satellite groups, different core members funneled their energies and finances into other community programs. The Free Southern Theater's cultural work moved into the urban New Orleans environment, developing arts programs such as BLKARTSOUTH, as a community-based arts collective in New Orleans. Even though this deviated from the Free Southern Theater's identity as a theater and its association with the Movement, BLKARTSOUTH continued the methodology that the Free Southern Theater established. As Smethurst argues in reference to the performance/activism network of BLKARTSOUTH, "the circuits for certain sorts of grassroots political organizing and for grassroots, community-oriented arts performances were often the same."[87] They are just one example of myriad groups established from the Free Southern Theater's network, whose impact on the South, especially New Orleans, positions itself as a living legacy, as it did with the *Treme* episode.

The Free Southern Theater still has an impact, not only through its legacy and memory but also through replications of its method. In addition to inspiring other groups, the method and *process* of the Free Southern Theater has continued as an integral part of cultural history—a living record of the Movement's impact on artistic production. From the perspective of southern performance and culture, 1960s-era activism did not die; and different organizations carry their performance aesthetic, which is still relevant for contemporary issues and artistic expression. As the *Treme* episode suggests, political, ideological, and cultural exchanges of civil-rights-era activism constitute a wide network, one that offers a glimpse into the exchanges between activists and the people whose lives were affected by the civil rights movement. The following chapter continues this through line to California, where El Teatro Campesino's performances on the March to Sacramento improvised scenes and interpretations of the farmworkers' strike. The cultural work of their improvised actos envisioned new ways of being through labor reform and contrafacted spirituality to reimagine concepts of citizenship and belonging. On the picket lines and in the midst of their most arduous campaign, performance experimented with new modes of public communication that solidified into a tradition within Chicanx culture.

Two

Creative Labor

*Spiritual Activism, El Teatro Campesino, and
the Farmworkers' March*

In California in 1966, farmworkers marched from Delano to Sacramento to raise visibility for the Delano grape strike and boycott, a massive labor campaign against the exploitation of migrant and seasonal workers. The strike was organized by a coalition of activists: Larry Itliong and the Agricultural Workers Organizing Committee and Cesar Chavez and Dolores Huerta with the National Farm Workers Association. They marched to the state capital both to drum up support for the strike and to demand recognition by Governor Edmund "Pat" Brown. The boycott and strike placed pressure on the growers to fold to their demands for better working conditions and recognition of the union, making the Delano strike one of the most successful campaigns in U.S. labor history. Their end goal—to have the governor recognize the union on the steps of the Capitol on Easter Sunday in Sacramento—reached toward an improbable height. However, in process, the March to Sacramento created solidarity and a sense of farmworker consciousness through its many stops along the way to the capital. It began with about seventy strikers but swelled to thousands of supporters who walked 370 miles in twenty-five days. Even when one of the major growers, Schenley, folded near the conclusion of the March, the farmworkers continued onward, honoring their commitment to arriving in Sacramento on Easter Sunday.

They called the March *la peregrinación*, or pilgrimage, and conducted their protest during the Lenten season, the most sacred time of the Catholic calendar. They embraced a multiethnic and interfaith community and held Protestant and Jewish services along the March, but the Catholic symbolism dominated the atmosphere as marchers carried a banner with the Virgen de Guadalupe above the letters NFWA (National Farm Workers Association) as they passed rural towns and agricultural fields. They weaved through the San Joaquin Valley, stopping at churches in small towns. Their point was not speed or efficiency (though they covered many miles each day) but building community through pilgrimage, using the religious language of intentional and spiritual movement across geography. Even though Lent is usually associated with somber reflection, the community connected through expressions of joy and creativity. The farmworkers' theater, El Teatro Campesino, performed *actos* or short improvised skits each evening, and musicians played the popular folk song "De Colores" on guitars, while strikers and their families, priests, nuns, and civil rights activists sang along. The value of El Teatro Campesino extended beyond a tool of communication or propaganda for the union; it expressed theatrical forms of political resistance dating back to and before Spanish colonization. The creativity farmworkers brought to the March and its improvised performances contended with difficult issues, presented impossible scenarios, and challenged audiences to imagine new ways of relating to each other.

The farmworkers' strike and the Black freedom struggle in the South emerged from disparate events and are distinct movements. Oliver Rosales's research on Black and Brown coalition activism in Bakerfield, California during the civil rights movement emphasizes how organizers of protests "were influenced by events going on in the South" and formed similar tactics to face a common enemy, such as the White Citizens Councils that existed in California as well.[1] An editorial from the National Farm Workers Association newspaper *El Malcriado* claims that the renters' strike in support of the farmworkers sought "the same courage which has been shown in Alabama and Mississippi," just one of many moments of comparison made in both *El Malcriado* and SNCC's newspaper *The Movement*.[2] The connections happening in California were part of SNCC's continuous widening outward beyond the South. SNCC's involvement in both arenas was part of the organization's shift to labor concerns, spearheaded by SNCC field secretary Mike Miller and the development of the San Francisco Friends of SNCC chapter in Northern California. As Lauren Araiza argues, "In reflection of the West's demographics, the fight for civil rights took on a decidedly multiracial form by demanding social justice on behalf of Latinos."[3] *The Movement*, SNCC's official newsletter, which predominately covered activity in the South, began to turn toward the farmworkers' struggle in California, making an effort to unify these movements as a way to emphasize the larger-scale changes that movements in the 1960s were hoping to fulfill.

Placing these movements together runs the risk of conflating the two or taking a comparative approach, which Brian Benhken warns against in his book *The Struggle in Black and Brown*. He notes that historical narratives of either cooperation or conflict between the two movements "unfortunately flatten a varied and exciting history."[4] Through a focus on artistic experimentation, my approach appreciates the commonalities between these movements as indicative of the necessary moves of cultural activism and their emphasis on creative communication—both here in my discussion of theater and in chapter 5 when I turn to media experimentation. In terms of performance, the emergence of El Teatro Campesino and the Free Southern Theater coevolved independently and spontaneously of one another, even though they have often appeared side by side in histories of American activist theater groups. Their emergence reveals a lot about the conditions in which they formed: audiences that needed free and open communication, a feeling of participation and involvement, and the ability to make theater in challenging geographies. The similarities between El Teatro Campesino and the Free Southern Theater did *not* emerge from the SNCC network, nor was it magic; rather, it evidences a tactical strategy arising from the conditions of social movements trying to transform predominately agricultural areas.

The simultaneous emergence of El Teatro Campesino and the Free Southern Theater evidence the demand for art forms that could respond to contingent, ever-changing material conflicts. When conditions are plagued with violent oppression and a lack of resources, people get creative. The two theaters were both shaped by their audiences, communities, and participants, they both relied on an improvisational dialogue with the site in which they performed, and they were both mobile theaters. Most importantly, they were both sites for intimacy-making between activists and local people, creating ties between people that were reflected in their creative process and in the performances themselves. The spate of experimental theaters during and immediately after the civil rights movement testifies to a need to call into being new forms of relationality alongside political movements reshaping politics and economics. The success of a theater like El Teatro Campesino gives credit to farmworkers and the traditions they kept over generations as they transformed the future of Latinx and American performance art. As El Teatro Campesino created and interpreted meanings within their performances, they engaged with a process of belonging that transformed the concept of a union into something that could meet the unique demands of migrant workers, noncitizens, secondary citizens, and nonindustrial, agricultural labor—a massive reformation that called for creativity and cooperation. Like the other examples that form the archive for this book, the March calls on us to witness how people created the conditions for intimacy as a form of political and artistic praxis.

Through extensive interviews with participants in El Teatro Campesino, historian Yolanda Broyles-González emphasizes the oral tradition of Chicanx, Mexican, and indigenous theater practice that resulted in the actos of El Teatro Campesino. Drawing on the comedy of Mexican icon Cantinflas and the native "buffoonery" theater Spanish colonizers reported witnessing, El Teatro Campesino developed a theater for the underdog that communicated through humor.[5] The strongest influence was Mexican *carpa* theater, or tent shows, which one observer from the 1930s called "the highly cultivated art of improvisation."[6] In their own words, "actos are not written. They are created collectively" and represent a "social vision," which Broyles-González interprets to mean, "Even the classic actos—which have been adopted for performance by Chicano theatre groups throughout the United States and in Latin America—were never rehearsed by El Teatro Campesino using a script."[7] Actors using gestures and language-play emphasized the interaction between words spoken and what audiences perceived and heard in the noise of the March and on the picket lines. The limited archive of these performances on film and in photographs gives us a better sense of the performances, in a way that the script cannot. "It was for the most part based on human body movement and expression and not on language," Broyles-González argues. "Words only refined the substantial meaning carried by physical action. It was, indeed, a visual art."[8]

El Teatro Campesino's process embodies participatory democracy, the political backbone of SNCC and other civil rights organizations, based on principles of dismantling hierarchies and being inclusive to all voices. Sometimes inclusivity translated to sheer noise: performers and audience members shouted, cheered, and improvised dialogue. I refer to this process of inclusive noise-making as *participatory toning*, in which sound, rather than the exchange of ideas alone, brings people into nonhierarchical political action. The collective sound-making happens in the framework of the performance, and through improvisation transforms both performance and audience. In what Gillian Siddall and Ellen Waterman describe as "sounding the body," we can see the possibilities opening through participatory toning:[9]

In embodied improvisations, subjectivities are formed and re-formed in the profound and unpredictable dissolution and recombination of identities, whereby misfires can lead to cohesion. There is no clear sense of individual agency here; indeed, there is a sense of loss, or at least the fluidity of identity, but also of the capacity for individuals and communities to change based on their willingness to engage with others, embrace the intimate chaos, and recognize that meaning and sensuality cannot exist separately.[10]

As an ancient sound practice of embodied healing, toning honors the potential for what Gloria Anzaldúa and Ana Louise Keating identify as transformational healing to repeat itself through spiralic time. As music therapist Shelley Snow and her coauthors note, "Toning encompasses a variety of vocally based interventions that utilize sounds rather than words." Rather than melody or rhythm, "sounds are generally freely improvised with specific therapeutic intentions."[11] Through the collective and improvisational noise during El Teatro Campesino's actos, toning could become a collective action meant to incite rather than relax, but was no less therapeutic for workers forced to be passive in their labor and quiet about their rights. By extending participatory democracy into performance and sound, participatory toning brings a mind-body approach to the study of political action.

Together, the actos' optical and audio registers within the acto create a fluid and multilayered "message" that resonates beyond entertainment or didacticism. Chavez warned Valdez that because El Plan de Delano, was written down, it could be perceived as too didactic or miss the point of the March. "Cesar was particularly insistent, however, that the emphasis be put on actions *not on the words*," Valdez remembers. "Thus: the first article of the Plan is that 'este sera un movimiento de hechos y no de pronunciamientos [this will be a movement of actions and not of manifestos]."[12] Chavez's concern was warranted since many of their actions could not be easily recorded, while El Plan de Delano has been reprinted many times over. Chavez's request calls for a reading of the March that focuses on action and movement over words and script. Extending this to the actos, I read liveness and improvisation beyond words transcribed from recorded performances in the archive. By listening to oral histories of activists and participants, watching the visual archive of the performances, and reading descriptions in reviews and other writings about the performances, I engage in an imaginative re-creation of El Teatro Campesino's performances alongside the narrative content. Embracing critical fabulation as a methodology, I excavate not meaning but imagined experience to argue for El Teatro Campesino's ability to move with fluidity around the concepts of identity and temporality. Within El Teatro Campesino's use of *rasquachismo*, a term popularized by Tomás Ybarra-Frausto and means making something out of nothing, they converse with medieval morality plays through the mobility of outdoor performances, the personification of abstractions in *La quinta temporada*, and the *carpa* tradition of irreverent humor, stock characters, and audience participation. El Teatro Campesino took elements of theater derived from the religious colonization of indigenous people and reshaped it into a tool for labor organizing.

El Teatro Campesino went beyond the conventions of agit-prop theater and toward an *aesthetics of obligation*, where the meaning of the acto emerges from the relationships formed in its making instead of a predetermined political ideology. Obligation, the ties that bind people to one another, does not form automatically as soon as one gets his or her union card and in many cases El Teatro Campesino knew that transforming a disparate group of people into a family would cause conflicts. Through humor, the discomforts of social transformation emerge aesthetically through conflicting or paradoxical scenes. These conflicts expose ways in which we can be bound to the very person oppressing us or that we feel discomfort with the person—or organization—in which we are participating.

Humor also became an exercise in relief from the stress of the strike. The raucous, sometimes bawdy evening performances staged by El Teatro Campesino on the route to Sacramento provided a counterpoint to the March's reverential tone as a penitential pilgrimage. The March was a high-profile symbol of the farmworkers' plight and thus curated an image that emphasized civil rights tactics of nonviolent protest and unity. Much of this unity was reflected in the sacred symbolism of Catholicism, which made the irreverent performances even funnier. The actos brought forward tensions and differences that, on the surface, seems to contradict this display of ethnic and religious solidarity, and yet the spiritually reverent and theatrically raucous worked well together. As Broyles-González argues, "Although heavily criticized by Marxist critics at the time, the miraculous also served to question and challenge the established order. In its own way the miraculous could mock, pull a trick, or defy business-as-usual and overturn the seemingly immutable social order."[13] Broyles-González observes El Teatro Campesino's indigenous spirituality in their post-1970 Theater of the Sphere, in which the theater, now separate from the movements, focused on incorporating Mayan and Aztec spiritual practices and worldviews into their performance practice.

However, I look earlier than their intentional shift and trace elements of these practices as they emerged spontaneously during the March and in the artistic expression of the actos. The first part of this chapter analyzes how spirituality complements the labor movement by experimenting with what relationships and identity might look like in a new economic order. The combination of spiritual and material expressions of protest become legible as a network of care within the union.

The second part of this chapter looks to the actos performed along the March. El Teatro Campesino's characters were created based on the political realities of the farmworkers, including personifications of corporations—actors donned signs that said "DiGiorgio Fruit Corporation" and "Bank of America"—and even abstract concepts like "Hunger." However, it was the daily lived experiences of the workers that provided the spark for the improvisatory actos. In the first acto discussed in this chapter, *Governor Brown*, the performers staged their version of Governor Brown's attempt to get strikers to return to the fields by making an appeal to them over the radio in Spanish. The farmworker playing Governor Brown begins in an Anglo-accented "bad" Spanish, but as his Spanish-speaking gets better, he begins to rally for the union cause and must be dragged off stage by other performers. The second acto, *La quinta temporada*, adapts the medieval morality play genre by personifying the seasons and describing their hardship for seasonal and migrant laborers. The fifth season referenced in the title represents unionization, arguing for a future temporality free from the yearly cycle of capitalist exploitation. In these actos, activists and farmworkers took up issues important to "La Causa" and through improvisation opened diverse meanings and invited audiences to be agents in the act of meaning-making.

By approaching the strike and El Teatro Campesino from a community-based perspective, I challenge the narrative that centers solidarity around Mexican and Chicano identity. In El Plan de Delano, the written record of the strike erases people marginalized within their own social movement, including women and Filipinx people who were integral to it. The "sons of the Mexican Revolution" are male inheritors of a patriarchal version of history, even though Dolores Huerta was one of the initial organizers.[14] The Mexican icon of la Virgen de Guadalupe as "the patroness of the Mexican people" created popular memory of the strike as a Mexican American campaign, which erased the leadership efforts of Filipino activist Larry Itliong and all Filipinx people who contributed to the March.[15] El Plan de Delano has become representative of the March, while Filipinos, Puerto Ricans, Black folks, and women have been relegated to footnotes until more recent interventions both scholarly, such as *The Dolores Huerta Reader*, and artistic, such as *Larry the Musical*, that tell a more diverse story of farmworkers.

La Peregrinacíon and Indigenous Temporality

The farmworkers formed a different kind of evangelism through combining religious practice with labor organization and the media coverage made public their faith-based approach to work, one that emphasized *believing* in the union in a deep and spiritual way. As Chavez remembers, "Every day we had Mass, held a meeting, sang spirituals, and got them to sign [union] authorization cards."[16] This union evangelism was folded into the "workplace religion" of the farmworkers, and unionism became a part of religious practice, carrying influence from the civil rights movement in the South.[17] The transformation of protest into faith-based action reflects what Ana Louise Keating and Gloria Anzaldúa call *spiritual activism*. Spiritual activism interconnects religion and labor, changing both in the process. "The important point is our inter-relatedness—not the particular labels used to explain or describe it," they write, and argues that spiritual activism eschews ideological labels and focuses on connectivity between ideas, the "underlying commonality [that] takes a variety of forms."[18] The spirit of spiritual activism resonates with the March's engagement with liberation; however, they did in fact name their belief system as Catholicism. Understanding how the farmworkers worked with and through Catholicism as a modality for labor reform opens a pathway for understanding the March's overwhelming combination of religion, radical politics, performance, and cultural expression through mutual obligation.

Beyond its potential for inclusivity and community-building, Catholicism offered a historical and cultural trajectory alternative to the confines of the United States and its legal systems. To be clear, I do not argue that the Catholic Church offered a path for liberation from the United States government; both colonized the San Joaquin Valley at different times. However, for workers to identify with the Catholic Church as a worldwide institution to which they belonged diminished the feeling of powerlessness associated with their lack of access to full citizenship and reminded each other—and the public—that a sense of belonging is contextual. The commonality between religious beliefs and workers' rights allowed an official space for agricultural work in the labor movement, and in turn creates a space for Brown bodies in the corpus of the United States, regardless of language, papers, education, and poverty. This reading does not analyze Catholic theology, nor does it make the argument for a moral community or even a sense of belonging through shared religious practice. Rather, the way Catholicism emerges here begins with the longer history of encounter between indigenous beliefs and the Catholic Church, which is a story of violent subjugation, resistance, subversion, and radical adaptation.

The alternative temporality of both the Catholic Church and indigenous survivances shaped a vision of what a union could be, especially because in the United States unions faced barriers incorporating agricultural workers in the wake of the 1935 National Labor Relations Act, which excluded agricultural labor. By survivances, I mean the elements of Catholicism that emerge from a blending between missionary and indigenous cultures, what Broyles-González calls "the subversive nature of the syncretism between Catholic and native philosophy and cultural practice."[19] Indigenous temporalities echo in Catholic rituals and worked within this labor movement by removing marchers from capitalist or "settler time," to use the term popularized by scholar Mark Rifkin.[20] The malleability of religious symbols and doctrine comprises a transformational method needed to encompass such a diverse campaign. This fluid design emerges from indigenous knowledge practices as well as survival tactics. These elements are difficult to locate and call on us to imagine their fugitive place within the dominant religion.

The March's emphasis on self-reflection and penance transformed a labor movement from being reactive to introspective. The March focused on forgiveness and "penance for all the failings of Farm Workers as free and sovereign men," calling on workers to reflect on their own transgressions and the desperate conditions that caused them.[21] The goal was to generate empathy toward the strikebreaker because the strike's success depended upon the farmworkers welcoming former scabs into the union, which would mean overcoming feelings of betrayal. Aside from this, spiritual self-reflection exposed a system that keeps labor mobile, desperate, ignorant, and deprived of rights, rather than emphasizing the ethical failings of other individuals. For example, rather than condemn Governor Brown in their acto, farmworkers welcome Brown into their union. As they anticipated the factionalism that plagues social movements, the strike encouraged forgiveness as a tool to continue moving forward. Religion is not solely a tactic for circumventing a legal barrier but rather a way of transforming how organizations and politics happen. The commonality between religious beliefs and workers' rights, espoused within a framework of spiritual activism, extends to the malleability of concepts such as "union" and "church." As malleability spirals outward, it can then imagine a world where agricultural workers form labor unions and a country where they could belong regardless of language, papers, education, and economic status.

However, to lean into Catholicism with La Virgen de Guadalupe and actions such as contrition was a risky move on the part of activists. Not only could it potentially isolate participants from different religious and cultural backgrounds, it also aligned the movement with foreignness at a moment in labor history when unions were actively trying to be compatible with mainstream American values based on whiteness. Parallel to this, in the 1960s, Catholics were establishing themselves as compatible with Americanness.[22] As many non-Black and non-Brown Catholics leaned into the mainstream as a path to whiteness, the farmworkers pulled in the other direction by creating a religious labor practice laden with "foreign" imagery. Even though they invited other religious groups to express themselves through worship services during the March, all other religious and nonreligious people followed Chavez's aesthetic, spiritual, *and political* commitment to Catholic social teaching: a pro-labor, human rights-based doctrine of liberation.

La Virgen de Guadalupe was about more than Catholicism. As Elaine A. Peña argues, the presence of La Virgen manifests the power of making space sacred, which happens "only when devotees' embodied performances—their voices raised in ecstasy, their praying and dancing bodies in motion, the labor and care they offer—inscribe their histories, beliefs and aspirations on the environment."[23] The combination of Catholicism and unionism influenced how a union could function as a spiritual place, and the union began to serve a larger purpose beyond better working conditions. Both religious and political doctrine garnered a flexibility that could make it site-and-community specific. Religious studies scholars refer to this as "lived religion," which emphasizes how religion manifests in the everyday lives of believers. Sharon Erickson Nepstad's approach focuses on how this plays out in "engagement with various social, economic, and political issues."[24] Lived religion, for Nepstad, means the creative application of Catholic social teachings to social movements via small daily acts that can influence the larger platforms and goals of activism. Even though Nepstad distinguishes lived religion from popular/folk religion, which "denotes the scope of practices beyond officially sanctioned religion," it is impossible to separate them here, where people from different communities were brought together to create an assembled lived religion specifically for the union.[25] Communities brought together by work, as Kristy Nabhan-Warren argues, practice a "politics of inclusivity" that acts as a collaboration between a wide community of various religions, denominations, and nonbelievers in order to keep workers safe in the face of violence. Reading Nabhan-Warren's contemporary analysis of Catholic inclusivity back into the moment of the March, the religious aspect of labor mobilization must be inclusive to others, including strikebreakers, as a way of demanding that a country become inclusive of them. Even when Schenley and other growers went to the bargaining table and recognized the union, the marchers refused to stop because a deeper kind of recognition was at stake.

Beyond recognizing the centrality of social justice activism to Catholicism and the religiosity of union organization, I want to understand popular religion through a framework that recognizes indigenous thought and practice. In Dylan Miner's *Creating Aztlan*, indigeneity is at the heart of Xicanidad and the discursive homeland of Aztlán. Miner argues for "engaging precolonial indigeneities alongside colonial, modern, and contemporary Xicano responses to colonization,"[26] and excavates this relationship from codices to lowriding culture. Following Miner and Leanne Howe's invitation to transcend the "Western history of social science" through tribalography, I am attentive to the stories told through improvised performance along the March and how, as Howe claims, they "pull all the elements together of the storyteller's tribe, meaning the people, the land, and multiple characters and all their manifestations and revelations."[27] I read the March itself as a performance of indigenous temporality and movement as it survives and is held within Catholic traditions.

Miner's description of the codices as "postcontact texts [that] were an amalgam of both Indigenous and European form and function" transforms the codex from archival object to theoretical vector.[28] Even though the original codices were destroyed by colonizers, the ones created and performed during the colonial period were, as Miner argues, "embedded with an Indigenous time-space."[29] Therefore, the colonial-period codices, which were folded like an accordion, enfolded Spanish Catholic imagery and indigenous modes of experiencing and enacting time. The codices were meant to be interpreted and performed, but when the performances that accompanied the codices disappeared during the colonial period, as Miner argues, so did a set of knowledges that could make the codices understood by others. As a contemporary codex, the March unfolds to expose how Catholic belief systems and labor mobilization touch up against indigenous storytelling, and the concepts of Lent and peregrinación stand in place for expressions of indigenous time unable to be understood by a Western audience.

The evening performances along the March recover a method of storytelling about migration, movement, and transformations of identity. The first performance each evening of the March was a reading of El Plan de Delano, which was modeled after the Zapatista's Plan de Ayala, that interwove the story of the strike, Catholic social teaching doctrine, and civil rights movement discourse. The performance of El Plan de Delano channeled tribalography by enacting a method of communication centuries old. The actos of El Teatro Campesino did the same by expanding on the sketch of an idea so that the heart of the performance was improvisation. Expanding the accordian and reading the March through the conduit of the codex opens spiralic time, a mode of indigenous temporality described as the "privileging of pattern over exceptionality."[30] In Gina Caison's discussion of spiralic time, she witnesses these patterns across deep time to reframe anticolonial revolution as a pattern rather than any specific, exceptional historic event. Caison's meditation on the root of the word *revolution* leads her to conclude that "at its core, then, discussions of revolutions are discussions of spirals," and I place the labor revolution in California within spiralic time and indigenous temporality—a pattern in the unexceptional and continuous revolution against settler time.[31] By calling it a pilgrimage during Lent, the March changed not only space but time. The marchers reached beyond a capitalist version of agricultural time, which the strikers disrupted every day through their absence from work. On a spiritual level, farmworkers engaged with a countertemporality that upended settler notions of monocrop agriculture and migrant labor.

The correlation they built between mobility and peregrinación reclaimed *migrant labor*, as farmworkers took control over how and where they moved. As Juan Herrera argues in his study of Chicanx activism in the Bay Area, "movements *produce* space" and "produce landscapes shaped out of the reconfiguration of social relations and the meeting of multiple historical trajectories."[32] The March accelerated the production of place-making with their pilgrimage through the San Joaquin Valley as the marchers met with and stayed among farmworker communities along the route. In this way they created a sensibility that José Esteban Muñoz describes as the idea of a Brown commons, which is "not about the production of the individual but instead about a movement, a flow, and an impulse to move beyond the singular subjectivity and the individualized subjectivities."[33] Keeping on the move physically represents the fluidity Muñoz describes within Brownness, a way to embrace a feeling without claiming the rigid boundaries of an identity category. In their early actos, El Teatro Campesino destabilizes the categorization of bodies, but this critique of identity made for uncomfortable scenes in a labor campaign that used ethnic and racial identity as an organizing tool. El Teatro embraces this paradox by creating atmospheres of transformation through narrative, audience participation, and religiosity that blends elements of tra-

Governor Brown and the Possibilities of Improvisation

ditional spirituality—both Catholic and indigenous—with a faith in labor.

El Teatro Campesino takes a framework used by missionaries—drama and spectacle—and transforms it into a union campaign to liberate workers. In their new version of the morality play, they do not erase, but rather express, indigenous practices of interpretation through performance and by stepping outside of settler time. The performers make parallel contrafacts of Catholic methods of conversion and epic theater's use of personification to expose systemic oppression and advocate for a Marxist-based politics. In the former, they keep elements of the genre but transform the didacticism of the morality play into a playful possibility for a unionized future. In the latter, they transform the expository qualities of Marxist theater, such as Brechtian personification, with a spiritual message: social change calls for a ritual yet to be imagined. In both cases, the references to other theatrical traditions challenge those genres to make space for more imaginative possibilities for audiences, placing creativity at the heart of social movement activism. The sparseness of their performances serves to mock the professional theater and its desiderata of good acting and impressive set design. Without those things, the actos hold a warped mirror up to the inherent theatricality of politics, or perhaps by eschewing the trappings of the professional theater, they swallow up the entire terrain of the struggle into their theater, from the fields along the route of the march to the statehouse in Sacramento. As I argued in my previous chapter on the Free Southern Theatre's production of *Waiting for Godot*, what seems absurd to mainstream audiences better reflects the reality of farmworkers who were told, for example, that they could not have toilets because they would not know how to use them, or that the growers were going to provide them with an alternative "union" they could join in lieu of their own.

The performances repeat a pattern dating back to colonization, but the improvisation on, or riffing off of, that pattern dialogues with the contemporary moment of the labor movement. The actos provide a framework for performance that could be—and has been—replicated by other theater groups and activists, whose art emerges from the aesthetics of *cultura norteña sin fronteras*, or a Southwest culture without borders. El Teatro Campesino appropriates medieval drama through *carpa*, an improvised, carnivalesque form of entertainment associated with the underclasses. *Contrafact*—a term used within jazz musicology to name the radical adaptation of songs—

describes this method of transformation, which makes something new while keeping the structure of an original piece for both creative and practical purposes. El Teatro Campesino upends the form of medieval traveling theater, whose purpose was religious education and moral conformity, and whose origins could be found in the evangelical zeal of Franciscan missionaries dating back to the sixteenth-century colonization of what is now called Mexico. Through *rasquachismo*, the personification of missionary theater transforms in a way Diana Taylor describes through her definition of *rasquache* as something "citational, recycled, and transposed into a context that brings about the reversal from high to low, from reverent to irreverent."[34] Any reverence the strikers may have had for a government controlled by commerce could be eviscerated with humor.

And yet, when it comes to Catholicism, *rasquachismo* falls short, considering the March's commitment to belief and reverence for its iconography. To encompass the seriousness of their faith, *rasquache* expands to be a broad, slippery, and inclusive term, and I read the contrafact through the *rasquache* aesthetic, combining jazz approaches that riff, digress, and transform ideas to make sense in the live moment in which they happen. By making a contrafact from Catholicism, they elevated a protest into a ritual, making spaces of labor sacred, and in doing so, reminding the world of migration in the human experience—not only through the ancient/contemporary practice of pilgrimage but also the ancient/contemporary practice of indigenous mobility.

In *Governor Brown*, the contrafact opens space in the smaller scale of the improvised acto, to expose and transform the "special case" of U.S. agricultural labor and the racialization of the power dynamics within agribusiness. Farmworkers performed *Governor Brown* at different locations along the March, as well as at the historic Azteca Theater in Fresno to a large crowd of over a thousand strikers and supporters. In the acto, Augustin Lira, a farmworker, actor, and musician, plays Governor Brown and takes the stage, mimicking Brown's broken Spanish. As Lira's improvised speech continues, his Spanish becomes more fluent; his message also turns from being a mimic of Brown's to becoming more politically aligned with the strikers: "lo que acabo decir . . . todas las mentiras, yo creo movimiento, queiro la peregrinacíon, quiero la huelga, que viva la marcha!" [whatever I just said . . . it was all lies, I believe in the movement, I want the pilgrimage, I want the strike, long live the March].[35] Within minutes, he joins the side of the strikers, refuting his original statements and passionately calling for the strike and the march. As the audience joins in with shouts of "Viva!," they drown out Lira's voice. Other actors dressed as antilabor politicians and capitalists forcibly remove

Figure 4. El Teatro Campesino's *Governor Brown*, 1966. El Teatro Campesino archive at the University of California, Santa Barbara.

Lira from the podium as the crowd continues to cheer.

Even with amplification, Lira's speech, which he shouted, is difficult to understand. Of most importance in *Governor Brown* is not necessarily the dialogue, nor which language Lira speaks to the multilingual audience, but rather the musicality of his protest and the universally understood "Viva!" echoed back by the enthusiastic crowd. Through his tone, Lira's zeal for the cause would be legible to those sitting in the back that could not hear the action and those that did not speak Spanish. The improvisation of sound, and the intimacy fomented in the act of creating the acto, spills out into the audience as they match Lira's tone, a communion of noise.

The participatory toning between the shouts on stage and the audience happens through their mutual crescendo. As the audiences enact liberation through sound, they not only create a sense of unity and belonging but also manifest an absurd fantasy on stage—that if he could speak Spanish, the real Governor Brown would join the union. As the actions of participatory toning and performance suggest, to form a union means more than signing a card or even understanding the issues—it is a transformative and full-bodied experience.

Through the call-and-response of participatory toning happening in these performances, we can listen to "critical connections" forming between people.[36] It is to this aspect of organizing that contemporary activist-artist-scholar adrienne maree brown gives her attention, asking via Grace Lee Boggs, "what our movements would look like if we focused on critical connections instead of critical mass." Intimacy is necessary for social change and deserves our attention as both political strategy and artistic expression. Interactions and collective sound-making helped to form critical relationships through intimacy-making, a strategy that moves focus away from the critical mass protests and outcome-based model of social movement success and toward moments that reflect the network of care happening in the movement. By reorienting the audience's attitude toward a fictionalized Governor Brown, the audience of farmworkers could feel empowered to transform others and bring them into the union—even the governor.

Governor Brown develops a new vision of the spreading of ideas and transforms what had been vilified by Red Scare advocates (that labor activism was akin to communism) and xenophobic politicians (that workers coming across the borders from Mexico, the Caribbean, and the Pacific were infecting the U.S. both literally and metaphorically). Lira played on the idea of infection as the character Governor Brown's Spanish-speaking overtakes him and converts him to the union, making movement across ideological borders possible. There is a reverse embodiment that occurs in the scene. Instead of Lira temporarily *becoming* Governor Brown by acting, the character of Brown alters when being inhabited by the body of a Chicano farmworker. In the imaginative space of the play, it is Lira who holds the power of transformation, and the crowd is invited to participate in the process with their emotional reaction. The performers make the argument that Governor Brown can become a revolutionary, even if it is just in the imaginative space of the play.

By imagining Governor Brown as a Chicano revolutionary, they challenge ethnic-and-religious dominance by focusing on the fluidity of ethnic, racial, and political identities, a method appearing across many of the other improvised early actos. Characters transform; sometimes they awaken to join the Union; other times they change for the worse, such as in *Las dos caras del patroncito*, discussed in the following chapter. With later plays, such as *Los vendidos* (The Sellouts), El Teatro Campesino would mock cultural stereotypes while *at the same time* make a case for strategic essentialism. For the strike, which leaned into the Catholic iconography of their Mexican and Mexican American community, Chicanx identity forms as something flexible, and performances engaged with the limits of this model. They promoted the message of unity through diversity while at the same time openly recognizing the limits of solidarity along racial or ideological lines. The actos provided strikers a necessary critique of strategic essentialism and offered an outlet to process and discuss the many conflicts that make up coalition activism.

A process-oriented approach to the March brings to the surface the histories of patriarchal attitudes and paternalism that plagued members, especially women, who often bore the brunt of material and creative labor, and opens a path to recognize these limitations while appreciating how elements of religious and political ideologies emerge within collective action. Despite these limitations, through the interconnectedness of spiritual activism, farmworkers and actors told stories of transformation through their bodies and how they contrafacted the world around them through their Brownness. If we follow Chavez's advice to read actions instead of words, the March emerges as a Brown commons, where the Brownness of those participating is "conferred by the ways in which one's spatial coordinates are contested, and the ways in which one's right to residency is challenged by those who make false claims to nativity."[37] In *La quinta temporada*, El Teatro Campesino reaches across time to unearth those false claims and engage with indigenous presence in the union effort, imagining a future outside of settler conceptions of time.

La quinta temporada: Making Catholicism Work for Labor

In *La quinta temporada*, indigenous temporality combines with union futurity through lived religious practice. The seasonal cycle in *La quinta* suggests just that: modes of being in the world hide within dominant discourses of time. To recall, according to Sharon Nepstad, lived religion operates outside the official religious structure and embeds into what we might consider secular aspects of living—in this case, union mobilization. These spaces become sacred through the embodied practices of believers, but actually this goes both ways: the presence of workers worshipping reminds us that religion has always been intertwined with labor. In the play, a farmworker is subject to the cycles of seasons and labor exploitation until a fifth season appears to create a livable existence: the fifth season is the farmworkers' union personified. *La quinta* takes a spiritual approach to envisioning a new political future in the idea of a new sense of time existing beyond capitalism's linear temporality but also beyond the temporality of the natural world. Religious aesthetics help make visible a secular possibility on the horizon of the strike: a union that changes not the order of nature itself, but the order of power among workers, growers, and the state that has been made to seem natural and unchangeable. Catholicism's alternative seasonal calendar (Lent) opened the door to dis-

Figure 5. El Teatro Campesino's *La quinta temporada*, 1968. El Teatro Campesino archive at the University of California, Santa Barbara.

course about alternative timescapes, but *La quinta*'s fifth season of unionism breaks through as an example of indigenous futurity grounded in spiritual activism.

In the spiralic time of indigenous resistance in the place now called California, the coming together of the union enters into the pattern of revolution against exploitative labor. In other words, the unfolding process that *La quinta* asks audiences to engage in goes into the past of indigenous resistance and temporalities while gesturing toward a future where indigeneity thrives. As Leanne Howe argues, tribalography emerges through storytelling, and, as Miner continues, emergence is the ethnogenesis that could "materialize Xicano peoplehood or sovereignty."[38] In the case of the union, the process of ethnogenesis within which the March and the actos engaged discovers workers' consciousness at the heart of the revolutionary pattern.

The fifth season represents a major shift in economic and social relations, the freedom dream with the power to change the conditions of the natural world. All the characters within the agricultural labor system were made into stock characters and personifications, often wearing signs around their necks indicating their role. In *La quinta*, the personifications of the seasons and of Hunger expose the relationships between the politics of labor and agriculture's collaboration with the natural world represented by the weather. Summer appears, dripping with fruit and money. As the farmworker takes the money and places it in his back pocket, Don Coyote, the labor contractor, lifts it out and gives it to the grower/*patron* character. The scene creates a physical humor that is also depressing—the farmworker cannot keep a dollar in this exploitative system. The cycle of economic exploitation becomes as cyclical as the seasons and begins to look just as natural.

By visualizing these relationships, El Teatro Campesino creates nuance within stock characters and, most importantly, a visionary break within this cycle. Reading personification as reductive contributes to a tenacious reading of the early actos as unsophisticated. Jorge Huerta argues that because of the conditions surrounding the actos, "There was neither room nor need for psychological realism . . . as in the medieval morality plays, the villains and heroes were always clearly defined," a reading in which Lira's interpretation of *Governor Brown* doesn't fit.[39] Although critics have noted ways that *La quinta* provided consciousness-raising to its audiences and "provoked laughter in the audience to arouse their social awareness,"[40] audiences of farmworkers didn't need the consciousness-raising of agit-prop theater for social awareness; after all, they were strikers who lived this as a daily reality.

Personification does not simplify but rather builds intimacy between humans, nature, and systems of power. By reducing these to stock characters and then defying the conventions of drama to have those stock characters change, El Teatro Campesino repeated the message that anything can be dynamic: including people and their access to power. It is empowering to imagine a white politician such as Governor Brown as changeable; and even more so in imagining that there could be another season on the horizon. When power is in the hands of the growers, seemingly apolitical personifications, such as Winter and Hunger, are used against the farmworker. The deployment of these environmental and biological elements against the farmworker allows the acto to perform how power works concretely, insinuating itself into the very rhythms of the seasons and the bodily needs of the worker. In order to decouple seasonal rhythms from agribusiness and denaturalize this economic relationship, the fifth season envisions an end to the strife between workers' bodies and changes in the weather by reducing capital's ability to use each one as disciplinary tools. By creating another season, the acto suggests a supernatural experience; however, by making that season the season of the farmworkers' union, the acto makes real a utopian future, arguing that what you believe in is, in fact, already here.

In this way, performance serves as a model for confronting the paradox of individual identity faced by minority groups within social movements as they negotiate the need to form flexible solidarities in response to the divide-and-conquer strategies of capital. *La quinta* further complicates reductive notions of solidarity through the character Don Coyote, the labor contractor or middleman, who exploits the workers for the rancher. Yet he is also a target of abuse and oppression by the boss because of his shared ethnic identity with the workers. As such, he is "*one of the most hated figures in the entire structure of agri-business*,"[41] and his character exemplifies how El Teatro Campesino challenged a broader system beneath the surface of their more overt critique of the grower. Don Coyote steals from the farmworker and exploits him in the name of the boss, yet in the face of Winter (a character conceptualizing the hardships of the offseason), the contractor shares the same fear of poverty and suffering as the farmworker. Don Coyote turns to the character Campesino, exclaiming, "Lío es lío, yo soy tu tío, grillo."[42] The messy entanglement suggested by the phrase "I am your uncle" not only refers to the exploitation of the farmworkers but also the familial relationship the workers have to the contractor. The oppressed worker in the acto is related to the oppressor. Once again, El Teatro Campesino does not condemn an individual's actions but rather points toward systemic injustice.

La quinta moves between scales—the interpersonal relationships and the larger systemic issues—through the modality of intimacy-making, which I define as the process of building trust and community with others in social movements. Intimacy is difficult in a system meant to keep the workforce separate but necessary to the inter- and intraethnic coalition required for a labor campaign. In her article on Anzaldúa's work, Keating synthesizes a definition of transformative healing that resonates with the difficult work of intimacy: "Self-healing and social transformation are mutually supported and interdependent: inner healing facilitates direct engagement with other people and the external world, thus leading to social transformation; social transformation inspires, enhances, and increases inner healing."[43] *La quinta*, on the surface, is a play about an exploitative system exploding into a brighter future, but as constituents engage in the performance or the act of participatory toning in the live performance, they are opened to healing from the traumas of the system that is at once current and ancient. The fifth season transforms the reluctant intimacy between labor contractor and farmworker—the bond of family or ethnicity—into solidarity through unionism.

Conclusion: Changing the Nature of Labor

By looking at how the actos contrafacted theatrical genres, we witness their contribution to transforming performance and cultural activism. El Teatro Campesino's performances facilitated solidarity that could simultaneously reach across ethnicities, nationalities, and languages while also containing space in which to critique coalition—an outlet for the exhausting work of making unity happen. However, beyond the aesthetic contributions, El Teatro Campesino's performance methodology both reflected and shaped the politics of the Movement. Their callback to ancient practices referenced a time before the industrial era and the style of union organization that emerged from a specific kind of labor. Unionism itself also needed a creative reimagining in order for the campaign to work. As a workforce of Brown agricultural laborers with uneven access to citizenship, traditional organizing techniques would fall short of serving their constituents. The creativity called on by *La quinta* (and the other actos) to imagine new relationalities and a new world order was needed to reimagine unionism from workers' rights to human rights. Farmworkers needed a union that included a scope wider than the workday or workplace, a union that extended pathways to citizenship, full-family care, and a sense of interfaith community wellness.

In the wide scope of labor organizing in the United States, a long-standing labor movement has continued to make gains for workers' rights, while legislation, such as the 1947 Taft-Hartley Act, has made unionization efforts increasingly difficult—and almost impossible for agricultural workers. Legislation has had uneven approaches to labor rights, and labor scholars such as Rick Fantasia and Kim Voss view creativity as the strategic solution "to build unions as organizational vehicles of social solidarity."[44] The community-oriented structure of the farmworkers' strike offered a model for contemporary worker centers, defined as organizations that operate outside the National Labor Relations Act that provide organization and aid to workers. Worker centers prepare workers to resist oppression in the workplace as well as in other aspects of society with no direct connection to labor, such as citizenship and ethnicity. The worker center may be a late twentieth-century invention, but the method of collective labor organizing outside of official channels has deep roots in a country colonized for profit and dependent upon exploited labor. The March and the farmworkers' strike open labor beyond its legal history and even beyond the limited perspective that focuses solely on the workplace. Cesar Chavez place the wider scope of what a union could do at the heart of the campaign:

> And these problems are the problems that deal with citizenship and language and racial prejudice so that when we deal with those problems then we have to add to our program . . . for example our MLK [Martin Luther King Jr.] farm worker fund where we deal with social services away from the employer-ee relationship. For instance, getting a social security card . . . we have to then tend to those needs and then that makes us like a movement cause we're doing more than just the traditional collective bargaining work that unions do.[45]

However, Chavez goes on to say that "other unions did the same thing we're doing in those days when it was necessary for them to do."[46] Chavez points out that even though agricultural labor seems exceptional because of the legal barriers and obstacles to citizenship, in fact, all unions once faced those same obstructions. He shapes a vision of labor that excludes the white supremacist paradigms that have dominated both pro- and antilabor actions in the United States. Intentionally brushing that aside, Chavez and other leaders impacted U.S. labor by getting creative with history and mobilization so that farmworkers could make real a world where Brown agricultural workers could determine their own futures. From this perspective, the goal and achievement of the U.S. labor movement has been to negotiate a livable life for workers and their families.

The creative approach to labor organizing "took on a life of its own" and became a framework for improvised activist performances across the country, according to Dolores Huerta, who tells the compelling story of the United Farm Workers in her oral history. People who were not trained actors took elements of El Teatro Campesino's performances into the public sphere and made a spectacle out of protest. In New York City, students from Stonybrook University in Long Island picketed outside of grocery stores in support of the grape boycott, waving United Farm Workers flags. When the store owner criticized the flags, the students exchanged them for American flags at a local dime store and continued their picketing. The improvised flag exchange is in the spirit of El Teatro Campesino's performance, an easy and inexpensive way of making a bold statement with multidirectional interpretations. The American flags reveal the performativity of ideological symbols, simultaneously mocking the Stars and Stripes while emphasizing the Americanness of boycotts and protests. It did not matter what banner they waved, the protesters stated in their gesture, what matters is taking up space.

Additionally, at supermarkets across the country, both activists and ordinary people participated in performance-protests by enacting "park-ins" and "shop-ins," disrupting places that sold grapes to raise awareness. In one supermarket in Stanford, California, activists attempted to fill the parking lot of the local Safeway with cars so consumers couldn't park. When that didn't work, they improvised a tire change that blocked the entrance and took forty-five minutes to clear. Then they "shopped" but left the carts filled with goods in the aisles. It was difficult for store owners to have an adequate response to their actions precisely because of the protestors' flexibility. It was even difficult for customers to know that this was about a grape boycott. Anything that could be a protest could also be an everyday scenario and vice versa. By purchasing American flags and changing car tires, they created action outside the expected boundaries of protest.

By placing the messages "join the Union" and "boycott grapes" secondary to the action of taking up space, making noise, and moving unconventionally in the public sphere, protestors across the country left open space for multiple interpretations and expressions of political and cultural commitment, much like El Teatro Campesino did through their actos. Within cultural activism, as we saw in the previous chapter, cultural workers surrender the end goal, and a certain amount of power, to their audiences. The inclusivity of improvisation welcomed a broader national and international audience to participate in the Movement from a distant location. Elements of the actos were a precursor to El Teatro Campesino's version of the Pastorela, or Shepherds' Play, which they started performing when they moved to San Juan Bautista after separating from the strike. There, in the former Spanish colonial outpost, they would perform within *pastorelas*, which they transformed through Theater of the Sphere, a method derived from Maya and Aztec spirituality to bring participants closer to indigenous worldviews through study and movement practice. In this way, performance as a method of communication is always proximate to teaching others. In my next chapter, I continue my discussion of El Teatro Campesino's performances, as well as the Free Southern Theater's, and argue for how performance methodology both reflected and shaped civil-rights-era education reform by inviting audiences and local people into the process of learning.

Three

A New Lesson for Activism

Art Education and Performance

———

In 1967 the Free Southern Theater produced a version of Eugene Ionesco's absurdist play *The Lesson* at Tuskegee Institute in Alabama as part of a tour of historically black colleges and universities across the South.[1] They cast Murray Levy as the aggressive, violent professor and Jacyln Early as the ill-fated pupil. Levy was white and Early was Black, keeping in line with the Free Southern Theater's tradition of integrating the cast of their performances. The casting of Levy and Early transformed Ionesco's script into a commentary on racism and sexism in education. In Ionesco's script, whenever the pupil challenges the professor during the lesson, she is silenced, belittled, and made afraid to interrupt or speak her mind. However, the lessons the professor imposes make no sense; for example, he gives meaningless definitions to words and demands the student memorize them. The nonsensical lesson escalates as the student gets more confused and frustrated. The professor continues to rage against the student and finally murders her. Her body is removed as another student takes her place.

In the discussion after the Free Southern Theater's performance, the dean of Tuskegee critiqued their adaptation of Ionesco's script, asking, "Are you not doing violence to the spirit of Ionesco's play by minor alterations in the script to give it a racial application?"[2] However, the Tuskegee students privately commented to the Free Southern Theater that "the Dean resembled Ionesco's professor," insinuating that the education they were receiving at Tuskegee aligned with Ionesco's dramatization of epistemic violence—despite the fact that their dean was Black and Murray Levy was white.[3] Far from creating a sense of uplift, the Free Southern Theater's version of *The Lesson* exposed and further opened fissures within a space that represented

Figure 6. The Free Southern Theater's production of *The Lesson*, 1967. Free Southern Theater Records, Amistad Research Center, New Orleans.

Black progress in higher education. Through the dialogue that emerged between the Free Southern Theater and the Tuskegee students, the performance takes on a new meaning: that there can be no progress through a system of education that colludes with colonialist and white supremacist attitudes toward learning.

In the tradition of agitprop political theater, the Free Southern Theater's performance of *The Lesson* doesn't fit the imperative to build solidarity and commitment to the ideologies of the political organization. If the civil rights movement built itself on a platform of integration, this play makes the opposite argument: that white supremacist education is illegible to the Black community and therefore should be resisted. In one short act, the dream of equal access to educational spaces contorts into an absurdist nightmare. The performance also critiques nonviolence as an approach to social change: in the play the student resists the professor's lessons nonviolently and gets killed in her efforts to comply with him and reason with his logic. Audiences could read a subversive conclusion to the play: that integration will only result in violence, a message that hit close to home for those trying to integrate schools. The

Tuskegee students witnessed Jacklyn Early's character struggling to survive a system created to harm her, and the students' response to the play shows the danger of how racism and collusion with white supremacy could permeate even a historically black institution.

The Lesson represents how civil-rights-era cultural activism questioned, interrogated, or critiqued the platforms of the Movement through the process of collaborative art-making. The Free Southern Theater valued performance for its ability to produce unexpected dialogue through interactions with local people. Their documentary book, *The Free Southern Theater by the Free Southern Theater*, does not record the minor alterations they made to Ionesco's script; instead, it focuses on how the students and dean reacted. In this way, outcome is important, but not an outcome based in the play's financial success or even the conventional aesthetics of theatrical productions; rather, their aesthetics focus on the obligation they held to the communities in which they performed. I refer to this process as the *aesthetics of obligation* via Toni Cade Bambara's definition of cultural work, which places art-making as always rooted in community engagement. From the aesthetics of obligation, new meanings within pedagogy emerged that centered relationships over learning content and having transformative experiences over achieving benchmarks. The plays discussed here—the Free Southern Theater's *The Lesson, Does Man Help Man,* and *The Rifles of Señora Carrar,* and El Teatro Campesino's *Las dos caras del patroncito*—did not represent a singular ideology of the social movements they operated within. Instead of being didactic, these performances leaned into the absurd and experimental. Their audiences were not self-selecting theater enthusiasts; rather, they were comprised of local people: sharecroppers, farmworkers, domestic workers, families, and whoever happened to be nearby. As audiences interjected, annotated, and participated in the moment, their experiences shaped what activist performance could be.

The performances of the Free Southern Theater and El Teatro Campesino revised education by moving away from the concept of the lesson, with all its didactic and moral implications, to new modalities. Art education scholar Rúben A. Gaztambide-Fernández identifies the possibility of new approaches to creative methods that are "not simply positive or negative, diminishing or exalting, but that are complex, open to interpretation, and always irremediably particular."[4] In other words, it's a version of learning focused on the specific needs of the moment and therefore cannot know the answers to the questions ahead of the lesson. Reading plays as modes of liberatory education traces their complexities and particularities through patterns of interaction with audiences. The Free Southern Theater's commitment to dialogue reveals the relationship between civil rights movement activism and new modes of teaching and learning. In this chapter, I trace their avant-garde method of cultural production as emerging from the education reforms sparked within the civil rights movement.

Defining Art Activism as Education

Education and social movement activism share the same pressure to prove "a definable, observable, measurable output," which, as Gaztambide-Fernández argues, creative practice inherently resists.[5] Having to prove that there will be a specific outcome limits the creative process that seeks to make something new and unknown happen. Educators and activists, then and now, struggled with the relentless need to prove their impact in order to receive funding; the stakes were high in programs such as the Child Development Group of Mississippi (which later became Head Start) to prove that federal and donor investments would close the gap of social inequality. Even the Free Southern Theater had to make a case for some kind of provable impact on their funding applications. However, through plays such as *The Lesson*, activists playfully responded to this pressure by leaning into the absurd and getting away with overtly controversial subject matter. Even though these plays were not direct products of the education philosophy discussed in this section, they express the need to search for new methods of communication and modes of expression. Understanding the pedagogical activism of the Movement teaches us how performance taught others.

Even though education activism is a less widely celebrated aspect of the civil rights movement, its organizations had an incredible impact on how education operates in the United States today. In his study of the Freedom Schools, Jon N. Hale notes "how central education was to the local grassroots civil rights movement," and states that they were initially conceived as a path to increase access to civic engagement through basic knowledge such as literacy, but later developed into a wider initiative of consciousness-raising meant to empower people for social change.[6] Beyond correcting a system meant to "maintain the social, political, and economic status quo that always worked in favor of white segregationist land and business owners," *The Lesson* and the other plays in this chapter exemplify how education activism during the civil rights movement sought to rewrite the script of how learning happens by addressing social inequality and epistemic violence.[7]

However, this well-intentioned initiative came up against obstacles of

A New Lesson for Activism · 83

prejudice and paternalism even within activist circles. One of the education reformers of the civil rights movement, Maria Varela, made note of internal prejudices in her analysis of the Selma Literacy Project. There were class disparities between what she calls "Outside people" (defined as SNCC activists who are middle class, educated, and many of whom were from the North) and "Inside people" (local people with alternative modes of literacy and knowledge).[8] Varela suggests the issue is less about race, because four-fifths of the staff was Black, and more about the difficulty of the Outside people overcoming class prejudice and the "barriers of communication" between the two groups.[9] As Varela works through the realities of these barriers, she suggests that traditional educational materials and methods are part of the problem:

> The materials which exist are inadequate and insult the dignity and style of life of the black-belt Negro community. In addition to this, the existing materials and theories about teaching adults attempt to impose a formal and alien style of learning which takes little or no cognizance of the adult's own style of learning. As a result, new theories must be built around value assumptions and goals contained in this paper.[10]

Varela seeks to disrupt the barriers of communication through the materials with which the Outside people and the Inside people engage each other. On their own accord, the students at Tuskegee reflected on the outsider/insider tensions at their own institution, between the dean's vision of education and what students knew to be true about their own experiences.

Much like the work of Paulo Freire's *Pedagogy of the Oppressed* (1968), Varela argues that education had to eschew transferring content knowledge from teacher to student and be reformatted as a method of liberation. Varela stresses the need for creative solutions that could break the Outsider/Insider pattern and build relationships based on mutual respect and dignity. Arguably the most celebrated educational reformer of the twentieth century, Paolo Freire writes about dignity in *Pedagogy of Freedom*: "Reflecting on the duty I have as a teacher to respect the dignity, autonomy, and identity of the student, all of which are in the *process of becoming*, I ought to think also about how I can develop an educational practice in which that respect, which I know I owe to the student, can come to fruition."[11] Without direct reference to Freire, activists found a *process for becoming* through art so that "both the teacher and the students know that open, curious questioning, whether in speaking or listening, is *what grounds them mutually*."[12] Varela's call for "new theories" lay the groundwork for experimentations with self-reflexive learning environments that could transform both instructor and learner. She grounds her perspective on her participation in a 1963 summer program in Atlanta, which she says "forever changed my view of education and the role of self-esteem and pride in learning."[13] The National Student Association and SNCC had developed an educational program composed of SNCC workers and young, mostly Black teenagers from the South who had engaged in local activism. The program included African and African American history, and as Varela recalls, "Students had never encountered this history and it changed their engagement in the summer course material."[14] In undoing and remaking her own knowledge, Varela could then begin to imagine education for others.

Resonating with the internal tensions SNCC workers confronted, bell hooks observes how racism in education can be so deeply entrenched as to negatively affect interactions between Black people. In *Teaching Community*, hooks expands on racism in education as a wider sociological issue:

> As long as educators are unwilling to acknowledge the overt and covert forms of psychological terrorism that are always in place when unenlightened white people (as well as unenlightened people of color who have internalized white-supremacist thinking) encounter people of color, especially people of color who do not conform to white stereotypes, there can be no useful understanding of the role shame and shaming plays as a force preventing marginalized students from performing with excellence.[15]

As hooks argues, all activists, whether engaged in learning or not, have to question their own prejudices and confront them. By seeking out controversial themes, activist theater could spark hard conversations and self-reflection, for both the audience and the performers.

Education philosophers such as hooks, Varela, and Freire consistently blur the lines between places of learning and society. It's no surprise that one of the great education philosophers, John Dewey, also related the experience of engaging and creating art as rooted in community, rather than sequestered away in museums "in isolation from the conditions of their origin."[16] When speaking of art objects, Dewey claimed that the "task is to restore continuity between the refined and intensified forms of experience that are works of art and the everyday events, doings, and sufferings that are universally recognized to constitute experience."[17] In other words, to restore art's place within social life as a functional part of it. As activists witnessed the need for new modes of communication, they created art reflective of the community and the particular moment that generated it—an active art that is impossible to separate from its formation.

In their experiments with theater, performers in the Free Southern Theater and El Teatro Campesino continuously questioned their own collusions and limitations as they created work and collaborated with their communities. They engaged with hooks's admonition that "teachers must be actively committed to a process of self-actualization that promotes their own well-being if they are to teach in a manner that empowers students," placing the focus, as Varela does, on educators as much as students.[18] Within the large-scale project of civil-rights-era education reform, performance claimed a right to complexity that disrupts the relationship between activist theater and propaganda. Plays such as *The Lesson* did not promote or encourage political commitment to a single cause; instead, they developed content from which activists could learn more about their audiences and themselves.

Because there is no strict boundary between pedagogical and artistic experimentation within cultural activism, elements of education run throughout this entire book. Here, I focus on this mutually symbiotic relationship and argue that it is impossible to separate innovations in pedagogy from experiments in performance and art. After all, many of those trying to reform education were artists. As cultural activists integrated new and experimental pedagogical practices into their artistic production, they made performance a method for learning through participatory democracy, a process of relationality that sought to dismantle hierarchies within social movement activism developed by Ella Baker and practiced by SNCC. Leaning into participatory democracy meant shifting the outcome from conventional aesthetics to that of the transformative experience. In doing so, activists rejected didactic material and even any singular message. As experimental learning mixed with avant-garde performance techniques, the open exchange of knowledges meant plays would act in unexpected ways. The students in the audience at Tuskegee opened up about their education to the Free Southern Theater and shared how they understood the limitations of their institution via the play. This moment of intimate exchange may have been the extent of the play's outcome, but as adrienne maree brown argues, interpersonal interactions act as a fractal that connects to the whole.

Small moments of intimacy have power within them to incite social change. Varela understood the Selma Literacy Project as not simply a means of spreading literacy but as a place where critical connections could form. Here, adrienne maree brown's emphasis on relationality in social movements meets Freire's attention to the self-in-community, as he states that "being in the world" is a "'presence' that is relational to the world and to others . . . that can intervene, can transform, can speak of what it does, but that can also take stock of, compare, evaluate, give value to, decide, break with, and dream."[19] Both Freire and brown focus on how relationality can lead to a sense of agency and participation in social change. Applying brown's concept of emergent strategy shifts focus from larger organizational goals to the intimate moments fomented in the performance space. I see brown's theory of the fractal at work in activists' attention to local, particular interactions, which in this context means the intimate moments taking place on stage and with audiences. The question is no longer, *what did audiences learn from the play?*, but rather *how did people relate to each other as they experienced the performance and what did performers learn from the audience?*

In relation to the last question, cultural production creates a container for difficult conversations by dislocating audiences through both abstraction and the *presence of elsewhere*, plays set outside the U.S. and the specificities of its racism, colonialism, and politics. I argue that *elsewhere* offered both a wider scope of solidarity and an opportunity to contemplate values in alternate realities. Dislocation can move beyond the colonizing project that hooks identifies as "set classroom time."[20] According to hooks, dislocation from the "structured classroom" offers "the perfect context for free-flowing thought that lets us move beyond the restricted confines of a familiar social order."[21] Activists would have to improvise as the learning process happened, a tactic Freire embraces to "create the possibilities for the production or construction of knowledge."[22] The existing structures only reinforced the power dynamics already inherent between college-educated activists and those with nontraditional forms of education and literacy. Cultural workers and educational activists found themselves dislocated as they established educational and artistic programs beyond institutional walls and in community centers, churches, and agricultural fields, faced with the challenge to improvise as they went along.

Las dos caras del Patroncito and the Limits of Racial Solidarity

El Teatro Campesino's acto *Las dos caras del Patroncito* (The Two Faces of the Boss) addresses the theme of white collusion and "teaches" by modeling the complex relationality between farmworkers and the growers, or *patrones*. The use of the diminutive in the word *patroncito* suggests how this relationship is an intimate one, and like their other actos, such as *Los vendidos* and *Governor*

Figure 7. El Teatro Campesino's production of *Las dos caras del Patroncito*. El Teatro Campesino archive at the University of California, Santa Barbara.

Brown, exposes the instability of identity. In my discussion of *Las dos caras*, I consult the script published in Luis Valdez's *Early Works* and through photographs from the El Teatro Campesino archive. Knowing these were improvised, the final printed product recorded by Valdez years later would have been a version that resonated best with farmworkers and strikers. In *Las dos caras*, the character of Patroncito, a land-owning farmer, berates the character of the young farmworker, continuously calling him "boy," micromanaging his actions, and even patronizing him with hollow gestures of friendship. Both the Patroncito and the Campesino would have been played by farmworkers, so for the sake of differentiation, the Patroncito wears a pig mask—an easily removable signifier. The body of the farmworker beneath the Patroncito's mask destabilizes the oppressor's identity as the audience perceives him as a role to be performed—not only with masks but also other signifiers of his power. The stage directions for the Patroncito's entrance—"driving an imaginary limousine, making the roaring sound of the motor"—imbue his performance with a hyperartificiality, which codes the dialogue he then speaks to be interpreted as performed lies.[23] Valdez claimed the acto was written as a response to the "phoney 'scary' front of the ranchers."[24] El Teatro Campesino used humor to mitigate fear of the ranchers: the pig mask and imaginary limousine provide campy props to represent symbols of power. Moreover, when the Patroncito demands that the Campesino speak English, the migrant-worker audience would have been aware that the person behind the mask has the ability to understand Spanish, thus amplifying that English is here a performative language of power—transforming language itself to become a prop or costume. Without the funds for elaborate staging, the makeshift costumes and cheap props barely mask the performer in his role. Having a farmworker playing the part of a rancher would expose how the real rancher's power relies on a group of symbols that can be removed like a mask.

Therefore, when Patroncito grows weary of the pressures of being a capitalist boss, he simply takes off his mask and hands it to the farmworker. He desires what he views as the carefree life of the farmworker: "Sometimes I sit up in my office and think to myself: I wish I was a Mexican," he muses, before continuing on a paternalist rant about how the farmworker receives free food and housing at the labor camp.[25] Then, at the behest of Patroncito, the two characters proceed to change their clothes and props that mark their positions of power(lessness). The Patroncito gives the farmworker his cigar and whip while taking the farmworker's hat and shears. The previously oppressed worker begins to turn on his former boss, subjecting him to the same oppressive language and abusive working conditions. By the conclusion, the Patroncito exclaims, "You know, that damn Cesar Chávez is right," and cries, "Where's those damn union organizers!"[26] The grower can easily become an oppressed farmworker simply by wearing the sign that reads "CAMPESINO." Costumes change easily, and so do the characters' social roles, as El Teatro Campesino humorously destabilizes their power as fixed entities.

The acto is in dialogue with various elements of epic theater and commedia dell'arte, such as stock characters and masks. Through these methods and themes, El Teatro Campesino drew on traditions in theater to enact what seems absurd: that one could change the hierarchy of power with the ease of exchanging a mask. Valdez locates these methods in Bertolt Brecht's *Lehrstücke*, defined as "teaching plays" and identifies himself as "an educator."[27] In the spirit of Lehrstücke, the participants (all the people involved in creating and shaping the acto) created "lessons" by offering scenarios that would incite dialogue between people in the audience, or the farmworker-actors. However, the Lehrstücke method matters as a political platform and an aesthetic style in the farmworkers' movement only because it was brought into dialogue with local communities.[28] Valdez may have promoted the idea that the early actos advocated for the union through audience instruction, but his perspective suggests that farmworkers needed to be taught that they *should* join a union and falls into a patronizing view of what it means to teach through theater. As I discussed in the previous chapter, Yolanda Broyles-González's counterhistory of El Teatro Campesino reveals how the actos relied much more on the improvisation of the performing farmworkers than any script or directive. Since those participating in the acto wouldn't need to be convinced to join the union, farmworkers creating *Las dos caras* had other intentions in crafting this funny and poignant story about power exchange. The acto promotes the idea that all it would take to compromise one's own political beliefs would be a few props or, to extrapolate further, a shift in power. This argument is counterintuitive to propaganda and even risks making tenuous the concept of a stable union.

The conversations happening around the acto remain unrecorded and unknown except for the sounds of audience reactions in later recordings, but we can speculate from the acto that those involved in the farmworkers' movement were awake to the complexity of labor relationships and wanted to remain vigilantly self-reflexive in their relationship to power. The acto intentionally fails to keep characters fixed within the axis of good and evil, reflecting the real-life scenarios where a scab must join the strike and be incorporated into the union. *Las dos caras* makes a risk worth taking that destabilizes the relationship between race and labor, which has historically divided workers in U.S. labor movements. The celebration of a racial identity in a labor movement—specifically a Mexican American/Chicanx identity—often plays into the white supremacist institutional and social forces that have created a racialized approach to labor. El Teatro Campesino offered their audiences a lesson in navigating strategic essentialism without falling prey to fixed notions of identity. The strategic essentialism of the farmworkers' movement called for an identity-based aesthetic, even though the body of farmworkers and activists was composed of multiethnic, multicultural, multigenerational people. The farmworkers could not depend on an idea of racial solidarity to drive their labor movement, yet they had to make an appeal through a sense of shared identity—whether that be ethnic, religious, or working class—in order to persuade strikebreakers to walk off the fields and join the union.

The identity paradox emerges from the complexities and hypocrisies of immigration law and the "imported colonialism" of the Bracero Program and its situation within the longer history of capitalism's exploitation of migrant labor.[29] During the tenure of the Bracero Program, Brown agricultural workers became what Mae Ngai has called an "impossible subject," a "social reality and legal impossibility," or a subject whose access to rights is compromised by their disassociation from U.S. citizenship.[30] "The actual and imagined association of Mexicans with illegal immigration was part of an emergent Mexican 'race problem,' which also witnessed the application of Jim Crow segregation laws," as Ngai argues, and "the legal racialization of [Mexican and Asian] ethnic groups' national origin cast them as permanently foreign and unassimilable to the nation."[31] The complex process of racialization impacted the prejudice with which white and enfranchised Americans viewed Brown bodies as always already illegal. The agricultural labor in California complicated this divide because Puerto Ricans, African Americans, and white farmworkers suffered a different but interconnected loss of rights even as they maintained their citizenship. Each time growers emphasized racial difference to justify inhumane treatment, they implicated all poor people forced to work in substandard conditions: they were specific in their racism and general in their cruelty.

Las dos caras del Patroncito offers a response through an absurd scene where farmworkers could meditate on, and laugh about, the relationship between identity and labor roles. The play argues for the audience to disconnect racial identity and political commitment, warning a working-class audience about the seduction of upward mobility and positions of power. In its rejection of any simple message of union solidarity, the play mirrors the diverse identities and perspectives that comprised the farmworkers' movement. The audience can then extend the scene to the larger social processes to which the characters correlate. The result is that the acto can question the method by which society assigns the individual body restrictive roles, such as "Chicano/a" or "farmworker." Beyond this, the acto opens up possibilities for the audience to conceive a future where individuals are no longer defined by limited labor and ethnic roles. A new lesson (or warning) emerges from *Las dos caras* beyond the instrumental imperative to "join the Union," as scholar Jorge Huerta claimed when he argued for the actos' simplicity. The early work contains more nuance; in reality, many of these actos meditate on the formation of identity and interactions between varying degrees of power in both agriculture and activism.

The play's complexity calls on us to reevaluate how Valdez discusses Brecht and Lehrstücke as inspirations for theater that could teach lessons. For Brecht, the epic theater is both "a highly skilled theatre with complex contents and far-reaching social objectives" and also as simple as an everyday street corner car accident.[32] Erwin Piscator and Brecht sought to make audiences aware of the performativity of theater through a similar use of obvious props, stock characters, and slippage between actor and character, a technique evident in *Las dos caras*. The audience's awakened awareness would call on them to think critically of the politics of the piece, and thus of the political situation as a whole. In other words, it would call attention to the presence of real people and real conflicts exerting pressure on the imaginary world of the play.

Reading Lehrstücke through civil rights cultural work, learning shares affinity with Gaztambide-Fernández's call to action for education: "Rather than making a case that something called 'the arts' should be applied like a magic salve onto the lives of the youth, the argument should hinge on the understanding that the lives of all students are always-already imbued with creativity and symbolic work."[33] Lehrstücke was transformed by the interpretations of everyday people working for social change and these performances emphasized the defamiliarization that Brecht was so famous for. Approached cultural production as a reassessment of social conditions. In Brecht's "A Short Organum for the Theater," he writes:

> Such images certainly demand a way of acting which will leave the spectator's intellect free and highly mobile. He has again and again to make what one might call hypothetical adjustments to our structure, by mentally switching off the motive forces of our society or *by sub-*

Figure 8. The Free Southern Theater's production of *Does Man Help Man*, 1966. Free Southern Theater Records, Amistad Research Center, New Orleans.

stituting others for them: a process which leads real conduct to acquire an element of "un-naturalness," thus allowing the real motive forces to be shorn of their naturalness and become capable of manipulation.[34]

El Teatro Campesino substitutes masks for the larger historical and political process by which white people have access to land ownership in California and Brown people do not. By suggesting that the roles of oppressed and oppressor are interchangeable, audiences and performers alike are encouraged to consider whether social change is more complicated than just taking down the boss. Indeed, both the farmworker and the patron are players within the larger capitalist system, and the acto remains ambiguous about whether or not the farmworker is victorious or whether he continues to be imprisoned by the cycle of oppression. The farmworkers playing Patroncito would also add in their own experiences of how bosses act beyond what Valdez could write in the script, and *Las dos caras* would take on new specificities each time it was performed. It makes a mockery of all components of the capitalist system, never making clear who is the hero and who is the villain. Each time the acto was performed it created new worlds of thought exchanged between people, or even further, in the private minds of audience members as they asked themselves, *What would I do in a position of power?* These moments remain in the realm of speculation and outside of the realm of scholarly analysis, even though they are present in the spirit of the acto. They reveal how cultural production opens space to think through the dangers of fixed ideologies. The influence of Brecht then becomes less about a model for teaching and more evidential of the trust activists had in their spectator's "free and highly mobile" intellect.

The Free Southern Theater, the Brechtian Theater, and the Presence of Elsewhere

Trust does not always translate to understanding, however. As we see in the Free Southern Theater's production of *Does Man Help Man* and other early plays derived from European material, content foreign to the United States enabled activists and audiences to feel out disparate sets of knowledges. Originally titled *The Baden-Baden Lesson on Consent*, the Free Southern Theater's adaptation of *Does Man Help Man* took material written by Brecht, Elisabeth Hauptmann, and Slatan Dudow and contrafacted the play to resonate with the particular places and audiences in which they performed. The short play features a clown, Mr. Smith, who is slowly dismembered by two other clowns. The play offers audiences the chance to debate consent and bodily autonomy. In the context in which it was performed, *Does Man Help Man* ignited arguments and even physical altercations about its significance and meaning. I contextualize the Free Southern Theater's pedagogical plays within Lehrstücke and the way in which civil-rights-era Mississippi offered the kind of environment sought out by Brecht and other avant-garde theatre revolutionaries seeking to create transformative experiences about political commitment. For most audience members, this was their first experience with a play, and most activists entered into the unfamiliar space beyond the traditional theater for the first time. If local people felt unfamiliar with theatrical spaces and conventions, the performers had the reverse sentiment, understanding how theater worked but not how it worked in the unique and challenging locations in which they performed. Dislocation, as hooks defines it, acts as a pedagogical method that transforms teaching. For activist theater, dislocation acts as a theatrical tool that could place audience members within a space analogous to, but separate from, their quotidian living conditions.

If Brecht intended Lehrstücke to present audiences with abstract scenarios that would challenge their view of the world, the Free Southern Theater took this a step further by opening space for mutual transformation between performer and audience. In other words, the Free Southern Theater was being more experimental than intentional, as a means to learn about audiences via their reactions to the material. During the play, two clowns alleviate the complaints of the third clown, called "Mr. Smith," by dismembering him slowly. Each time Mr. Smith vocalizes a pain, for example his left foot, the other clowns remove the body part with a saw until all his limbs have been removed. When he complains about unpleasant thoughts in his head, they saw off the top of his head. The play concludes with the "Crowd" shouting, "No man helps another." From this abstract scene of violence, the audience at Bethel Lutheran Church in New Orleans produced politically relevant responses: "Mr. Smith was variably seen as a symbol of the whites, the blacks, capitalism, and Viet Nam."[35] With all of these differing perspectives, the Free Southern Theater interrogates the act of helping and of assistance and aid, which seems counterintuitive to the role of activism during the civil rights movement. No matter what Mr. Smith symbolizes, the play hinges on a gap in communication about asking and receiving help and this miscommunication results in abusive behavior. The theme of violence and empty consent would have resonated with a Black audience in the South as a cautionary tale about receiving aid: that sometimes the solution is more harmful than the problem. Even civil rights organizations could be accused of this kind of harm; after all, so many Black people tried to register to vote only to lose their job as quickly as Mr. Smith loses a limb.

When hooks describes the process of dislocation, she emphasizes defamiliarizing the "familiar social order."[36] As I discussed in my first chapter, the defamiliarization of the conditions of racism in the U.S. South formed a key component of cultural activism and the main philosophy of the Free Southern Theater. As they sought to manifest freedom dreams through theater, the Free Southern Theater created new scenarios of embodied movement that resonate with approaches to Black performance seeking to disrupt how people expect Black people to act. In Daphne Brooks's "Afro-alienation acts," Brooks alters Brecht's techniques as she observes how Black performers "render racial and gender categories 'strange' and thus 'disturb' cultural perceptions of identity formation."[37] The actors were "critically defamiliarizing their own bodies by way of performance in order to yield alternative racial and gender epistemologies."[38] Because the Free Southern Theater's performances are also dialogues with their audiences, the creation of new epistemologies was being improvised in real time. One of the benefits of contrafacting European theatrical influences such as Brecht was that ideas created in a different context had the potential to question and disrupt the status quo.

Figure 9. The Free Southern Theater's production of *The Rifles of Señora Carrar*, 1965. Free Southern Theater Records, Amistad Research Center, New Orleans.

The abstract characters in *Does Man Help Man* invited audiences to contrast their worldview of relationality through characters created outside the context of U.S. racism, not to avoid or circumvent the realities of racism, but to approach it from a different perspective. The words written by Brecht could change their understanding of how a racialized body "should" act, and their readings of the play challenge the idea of an abstract character—everything means something (even theater of the absurd!) in the Deep South states in which they performed. The dislocation of what is real and what is being performed was meant to enable an audience to rethink their relationship to their political situation and "play" with the concept of change. But what if the institution is the United States? Dislocation takes on a deeper meaning when applied to the context of U.S. racism. Cultural activists used the performance space to extend beyond the borders of the country as a method to break minds away from the institutionalized racism that embeds itself into every aspect of daily living. The *presence of elsewhere* employed in pedagogical performance created a temporal and geographic analogy as a method of consciousness-raising and used the immersiveness of theater to create fleeting moments of transnational solidarity with an imagined other that can also be a proxy for the self.

In 1965 the Free Southern Theater produced another Brecht play, *The Rifles of Señora Carrar*. The original was adapted from John Millington Synge's *Riders to the Sea* by Brecht and Margarete Steffin, and takes place *elsewhere* in a fishing village in rural Spain. The practice of inhabiting or imagining alternative spaces bears a relationship to a progressive learning experience: *elsewhere* teaches us something about where we are. In order to achieve this, the Free Southern Theater used a projector to project images of rural Spain in the background of the performance. They most likely gained access to the projector through education program funding and repurposed the projector for the play, further connecting pedagogy and performance. *Carrar* takes place during the Spanish Civil War, where a group of villagers are debating whether or not to take up arms against the fascist Falange. The main character, Teresa Carrar, tries to remain uninvolved throughout the play; she uses poverty as an excuse to remain external to the conflict happening all around her. The language of the play bridges the Spanish Civil War and the civil rights movement through the challenges of political commitment in poor regions struggling to survive. The line repeated in the play, "We're poor; poor people can't make war," aligns with sentiments from local people during the civil rights movement, such as Ezra Cunningham's "You can't eat freedom. And a ballot is not to be confused with a dollar bill," which Greta de Jong mobilizes to show how, "for many people, obtaining such basic necessities such as food and shelter was a more immediate concern than was voting."[39] Carrar also does not wish to see her sons sacrificed for ideological reasons for which she no emotional or personal investment.

Yet, in response, Carrar's brother and the other villagers repeat the mantra, "If you do not act, you act for the enemy."[40] They want her to unearth the family's rifles, locked up and hidden away beneath the floorboards. After her son dies senselessly as a civilian casualty of war, she finally commits to action and reveals the rifles, handing them to her sons as they leave for the front. In the photograph, actress Emalyn Hawkins stands in front of a projected image of a Spanish peasant woman. The images projected during the play invite audiences to imagine peasants *elsewhere*, yet for those watching the performance in rural areas, the pastoral image also acts as a conduit to the here and now. Both Hawkins and the projected image *are* Teresa Carrar, suggesting that there exist multiple Carrars faced with the choice of whether to become politically involved. Rather than asking the audience to forget the original script and become lost in the local context of the performance, the projections remind the audience that the play is simultaneously here and elsewhere, and that the words being said on stage apply to rural Mississippi as well as to Spain. Brecht and Steffin's play may have been written to encourage political involvement, but as this theme travels to Mississippi, the message becomes secondary to the intimacy-making across different locations and periods of time.

The production dramatized the debate over militancy from multiple perspectives, offering audiences a variety of interpretations on political commitment. However, at the play's conclusion, the Free Southern Theater staged a scene where Black men hold rifles triumphantly, a singular image of the radical world of the civil-rights-era South. Within this comparison, the dialogue exhibits ideological differences within the community as well as a heated debate over militancy and armed self-defense. As Maria Varela remembers:

> Armed self-defense was rampant in black households throughout the south. Civil rights workers were consistently defended by armed local black people in their houses. The Klan knew where to ride and where not to ride in the black belt south, as they anticipated gunfire in response to their terror. It's the northern media that decided to call armed self-defense as "radical militancy" which is evidence of their ignorance of black culture.[41]

Echoes of this reality made their way into the show's commentary. Free Southern Theater artistic director Robert Cordier commented in an after-show discussion, "you can't stand around and do nothing while people all around you are being shot, because you yourself will be shot."[42] Cordier makes use of the doubling of "you" to address both a general "you" and the specific people in the audience that evening. The play makes the same gesture as it oscillates between the universal of political commitment and its application to civil rights movement debates on nonviolence. Even though the Free Southern Theater projected images of rural Spain throughout the production, the final image would have been unmistakable as a symbol of Black militancy in the middle of a play calling for arms against the oppressor. To put this in historical context as well, this occurs in the year before Stokely Carmichael's watershed "Black Power" speech in Greenwood, Mississippi, which would give words to an image the Free Southern Theater created on stage a year earlier. Brecht's script called for arms against Franco, but the image on stage created a visual contrafact so that the structure of the play remained Brecht's, but the familiar images of violence on Black bodies and the radical vision of black militancy were too pertinent as images of the civil rights movement to be ignored.

This conclusion to the play brings out the emotionality of Brechtian drama and of activist cultural production in general. A production like *Carrar* highlights ways in which Brecht and his collaborators experimented with emotional registers, as Brecht explains: "We need a type of theatre which not only releases the feelings, insights and impulses possible within the particular historical field of human relations in which the action takes place, but employs and encourages those thoughts and feelings which help transform the field itself."[43] Cultural activists understood the role of dialectical engagement with feelings and how they would play out within an abstract concept such as political commitment. In what may seem counterintuitive to Brecht's "scientific approach," Free Southern Theater member Gail Mount recalls that "just as there was an alienation between the actors and their various roles, there was a separation between the play and the audience . . . a grateful separation that enhanced thought and emotions."[44] Mount brings together the alienation effect of Brecht's drama with the emotionality of the Free Southern Theater's productions. Plays like *Carrar* and *Does Man Help Man* create an interplay between emotional response and defamiliarization, placing feelings as central to critical thinking.

The *presence of elsewhere* seems at first to contradict Varela's call for materials relevant to the Black experience in the U.S. South. However, the Free Southern Theater reached for Brecht's *The Rifles of Señora Carrar* to approach the civil rights movement in ways that could resonate with their constituents' concerns with poverty and how at times being poor felt more prescient than political commitment. The imaginative work of the *presence of elsewhere* called on audiences to think through familiar situations and what they thought of as rebellion. Fluidity was relevant for the South and "Mississippi's closed system," which the Free Southern Theater saw as a "vacuum."[45] Mississippi, haunted by its description as the closed society, opened up into a dialogue between distant locations and hyperspecific locality. Dislocation thus serves a purpose toward intersectional thinking, as audiences could connect *and disconnect* racism to issues of poverty and political commitment.

Any effort to liberate Mississippi from its global reputation would have been a revolutionary maneuver, and thus the Free Southern Theater infused rural areas with images of elsewhere, collapsing global sites of resistance with modest performance spaces in the South. *Carrar* and the other "learning plays" of the civil rights movement introduced controversial topics such as self-defense that subverted, or at least challenged, the ideological framework of the Movement, placing critical thinking above political commitment. Geographic fluidity epitomized a greater sense of resistance to mainstream oppression in both politics and art because theater was not beholden to place. Even if the production quality and atmosphere made it difficult to understand the play's content, the act of gathering contributed further to the act of intimacy-making.

Conclusion: The Right to Complexity

Both the Free Southern Theater and El Teatro Campesino intertwined dislocation and defamiliarization to create a transformative experience for audiences and activists alike. Activist theater in the 1960s catapulted European avant-garde theater to new possibilities by dislocating performance away from the space of the theater and into the community, carving a path for education to do the same. The Free Southern Theater and El Teatro Campesino share a similar critical narrative challenged in this book: that their earlier, improvised work—the art produced closest to the protests—was less sophisticated than their later, more developed art. This detracts agency from those improvising on and shaping cultural activism and relegates the desire to teach to something simple, or less artistic, as if art meant for consciousness-raising (or for poor people) has less merit. To force these improvised experiences into a traditional understanding of didacticism or propaganda reinforces a false belief that art cannot be produced in the immediacy of a social movement without traditional resources or by workers without formal education in the arts. Instead, from a method-focused approach to social movement activism, art education was central to the civil rights movement and social justice is central to art education. We can understand education reform through performance since they are all expressions of the same method of fomenting intimacy, transforming *how we learn* and *how we teach* to *how we relate*.

Cultural activists asked the same questions as progressive educators: how to teach without being didactic, and how to enter into nonhierarchical dialogue in the process of social justice. Returning to Varela's call for relevant teaching materials, the first value of the Selma Literacy Program is "that man should participate in the basic decisions of his society in order to live a fully human life."[46] The statement opens a broad enough purview that could upend a multitude of systems. Everything, including education, should emerge from a process that enables a fully human life. The performances of El Teatro Campesino and the Free Southern Theater define "fully human life" as the right to complexity—of interpretations and emotional responses that may be in conflict with each other. The pedagogy of these plays opened space for people to maintain the right to be diverse in their perspectives as they worked together.

The call for a human-rights-based approach to liberation echoes across Freire, hooks, Varela, Cesar Chavez, and into Bettina Love's twenty-first century call for abolitionist teaching. Love argue that we should "build new schools . . . based on intersectional justice, antiracism, love, healing, and joy."[47] Love cites nineteenth-century activist Anna Julia Cooper's call for "recognition of one's inherent humanity" so that students may demand "undisputed dignity" from the world around them.[48] Thinking through Cooper's use of the term *inherent*, Love situates humanism within a universal frame, while activists and educators recognized how locally specific the expression of humanity could be. The role of creativity—which is important for education theorists and cultural activists alike—makes space to open dialogue about the meaning of being human between a universalism that eschews racial difference and a local specificity that must address how racism shapes people's daily lives.

As bell hooks argues in *Teaching Community*, we must confront collusion with white supremacy in order to effectively create a transformation, and therefore the difficult angles of social justice work cannot be avoided. As contemporary education continues to be threatened by hegemonic political forces that are currently dismantling the progressive movements of the civil rights era, it behooves us to look at the moment when activist educators tried to imagine a teaching life beyond racist and oppressive institutions. The great attempt in the latter half of the twentieth century to reform these institutions from within struggles to survive in the first half of the twenty-first century. Witnessing ways in which people—both activists and local people—redesigned systems of communication and transformation from the grassroots can offer us moments of inspiration and an understanding of failures and triumphs as teaching moments for educators today.

As creativity became an essential path to social change, activists and local people expanded their media, using anything and everything. Performance unraveled the basic conventions of drama into a set of techniques applied to cultural production beyond theater. The topic of the next chapter examines the craft-making cooperatives of Liberty House and the world-building of the Poor People's Corporation. Activists transferred the art of collaboration found within theater into the power of economic reform for poor people looking for a future beyond sharecropping, domestic labor, and unemployment. Tracing intimacy-making as both an artistic and pedagogical mode of praxis, I spiral out to the political-artistic implications of experiments with new modalities of labor. The imprint of intimacy emerges everywhere.

Four

The Fabric of Social Change

Liberty House and Craft-Making Cooperatives

————

Wasn't but a piece of room the school, with a shed tacked on in back for storage and sudden meetings. The furniture was bandaged but brightly painted. The chemistry equipment was old but worked well enough. The best thing was the posters. About the co-op, about Malcolm and Harriet, and Fannie Lou, about Guinea-Bissau and Vietnam. And posters done by the children, the pictures cut from magazines, the maps—all slapped up as though to hold the place together, to give an identity to the building so squat upon the land . . . [people] determined to get now and to be what they'd been taught was privilege impossible, what they now knew was their right, their destiny.

—Toni Cade Bambara[1]

Inspired by her own activist work in the South, Toni Cade Bambara's 1974 short story "The Organizer's Wife" depicts a cooperative in a rural Black community. The building is a symbol of the cooperative as a whole: the walls are held together by the art the people create. The paper itself is not strong, but it supports the structure with a sense of identity, albeit one that is not politically fixed. Rather, the posters on the co-op walls attest to a long, fluid tradition of activism, from the nineteenth-century abolitionist Harriet Tubman, to civil rights icons Fannie Lou Hamer and Malcolm X, to the anti-colonial movements symbolized by Guinea-Bissau and Vietnam. Moreover, the specifics of these figures are less important than what they symbolize—upheaval, reform, change—and how they bring people together. Bambara's approach to reading social movement activism makes space for the messiness of community-building and cultural work, which often comes together as a collection of overlapping issues and projects. What the cooperative can do, Bambara argues, is make community happen through a claim to "privilege impossible": a feeling of ownership that can transform squatting into right and destiny. This chapter explores the bold attempt made by activists and local people to establish a cooperative economy in the South and attests to the creativity incited by cooperative labor. This creativity spread into the photography and literature that emerged from the cultural work of cooperatives and which reveal an economics based in Black feminist approaches to autonomy. The everyday work of people reforming labor has both its own creative expressions and literary afterlives in the writings of Bambara and Alice Walker. This chapter traces the "crooked stitches" where the pragmatic meets the sublime and argues that the cooperative movement's commitment to others was an artistic strategy as much as it was a political one.[2]

Writing about the civil-rights-era cooperative movement, especially the craft cooperatives, comprised and managed mostly by women, calls for an approach that can bring together disparate pieces of evidence outside traditional conversations about activism and economics. Not only did Black sharecroppers and domestic workers absent themselves from the white-dominant economy of the South but they also used collective labor to build intimacy and forge a blueprint for community-based self-determination. My approach to the cooperative movement begins with textiles, fabric, photographs, and storytelling as a starting point for understanding Black feminist economic theory at work. In this chapter, I examine the fractal between cooperatives and collective creativity, and what enterprises owned and operated by majority Black women can tell us about Black autonomy during the civil rights movement.

The cooperative movement of the 1960s was a collaboration between many civil rights organizations and people who wanted to help farmers and unemployed people compete in an economy meant to keep them poor. The history of cooperative formation is a complex multistate initiative and has been covered by historians elsewhere as an integral part of the civil rights movement.[3] Formed in 1967 and continuing through today, the Federation of Southern Cooperatives organized the many cooperatives of the South, the most famous being the Freedom Quilting Bee of Gee's Bend, Alabama. One of the Federation's cooperatives, Liberty House, handled the marketing and distribution of over a dozen craft cooperatives under the auspices of the Poor People's Corporation, established by Jesse Morris in 1965. Liberty House had its central office and retail store in Jackson, Mississippi, which was managed by Doris Derby. The Poor People Corporation's purpose was to offer "financial and technical aid for poor black people in the state of Mississippi who want to go into business for themselves."[4] While the numbers differ, at its peak the Poor People's Corporation organized over 800 people—former domestic workers, sharecroppers, and unemployed people—into worker cooperatives. For artisan workers, they provided raw materials and training to create quilts, dolls, leather handbags, and candles, to name a few. They brought together farmers and craft workers with the hope that they could gain autonomy over the means of production of goods and establish minority-owned industry.

Liberty House opened a store in Greenwich Village in New York City, and then expanded to two more stores in the city, as well as additional locations in Detroit and near Harvard Square in Cambridge. The materials made in the South were sent to Liberty Houses where they sold "hand-crafted products from poor people from Mississippi, Louisiana, Florida, Georgia, Alabama, & Alaska as well as Africa, Mexico, Guatemala, Canada, & other parts of the world."[5] Images of Liberty House in the New York stores show walls and tables crowded with merchandise, and young activists such as Abbie Hoffman and Ellen Maslow preaching to customers about buying goods from and for people who wished to support self-determined labor. Their connection to indigenous communities living in the U.S. and in countries that we might identify as part of the Global South evidences an interconnectedness through economic models rather than race or region. As workers tried, through Liberty House, to sell their goods in urban centers, they created a limited liberatory economic process, which capitalized on marketing to consumers who wanted to aid poor people's "self-help" initiatives while devising a system through catalogue and mail order (and putting people like Abbie Hoffman at the front desk) to limit the encounter with those consumers through the cooperative model.

Liberty House also became a cultural center and integrated the selling of goods with creative workshops and literary experiences, including one benefit at the Harlem store featuring The Last Poets, listed as Nikki Giovanni, Jackie Earley, Sandra Lein Jones, and James Radcliff. Liberty House continued to function this way until 2015, when it finally closed its doors due to expensive rent in a changing city. Despite this longevity, Liberty House does not exemplify economic success. They claimed to buy the craft-makers' products regardless of whether they sold or not, and when they reneged on this promise due to lack of funds, production stopped.[6] The financial narrative of Liberty House is essential to understanding how it impacted people's lives. The evidence of complaint in the archive, detailed later in this chapter, reveal the complexity of its structure, and how it offered a safe enough environment for women to vocalize criticism and express discontent. The carework of intimacy-making—of tying one's well-being to the well-being of others—has as much capacity for fomenting love as it does for frustration and anger. The challenge for cultural workers was the ability to hold it all and keep organizations going.

In an interview about the co-ops, Derby claimed, "You know we're not making big salaries. So, the reason people stay with the program is more meaningful, spiritual as well as practical." The *aesthetics of obligation* connects art and politics with the ties that bind people to one another, and in the case of cooperative-based art, this aesthetic emerges from networks of intimacy based in spiritual nourishment that came not from organized religious practice but labor reform. Tracing the spiritual aspects of cooperative labor is difficult to do through the archive. Literary representations, while fictional, have acted as their own archive of women's work in the Movement, chronicling the daily struggles that often counteract the idealism of civil-rights-era imagery.[7] Alice Walker's fiction discussed in this chapter, her short story "Everyday Use" and novel *The Color Purple*, shows how narrative can open a Black feminist perspective on civil-rights-era politics and reflect the complex textures of intimacy-making.

Although this chapter moves away from theater, the performance cultures of the civil rights movement influenced the methodology of practice in the design of Liberty House and the Poor People's Corporation. James Smethurst connects civil rights movement/Black Arts theater to cooperatives, reading Liberty House "as an institution that connected grassroots African American people as artists in the African American tradition, much as the FST [Free Southern Theater]-BLKARTSOUTH would do in its performances."[8] One scholar, Anne Gessler, goes so far as to claim the Free Southern Theater was a cooperative.[9] A methodological thread between theater and cooperatives is Thomas DeFrantz's observation of movements that *"make Black bodies strange"* in their motions.[10] People opted out of white supremacist economies of sharecropping and domestic labor for white families and began making clothes and quilts in black-owned-and-operated cooperatives. They did so in defiance of expectations of what their hands *should* have been doing and what work was *supposed* to look like for poor folk in the South.

Collaboration and self-expression were still central to the cultural work of cooperatives, and the jazz contrafact informs how I read political and economic adaptations, especially when it comes to the word "self-help"—a contentious term often used by activists and journalists when describing the cooperative project. Beyond the fixedness of concepts used when discussing cooperatives, which range from uplift and self-help to Marxism and communism, activists and local people approached this terminology with fluidity, evocative of the walls of Bambara's co-op in "The Organizer's Wife." Walker's writing also reflects a search for new meanings and definitions in her monumental and controversial text *The Color Purple*, which mirrors the complexities of the cooperative movement. In Walker's novel, sewing and Black entrepreneurship make liberation possible, and the book does not easily distinguish between business and love. The controversy around both the cooperatives and Walker's novel opens the question: *What happens when necessity, rather than ideology, forms the foundation of creative action?*

The Poor People's Corporation, Liberty House, and the Messiness of Freedom

Among the various ideologies of the civil rights movement, cooperative ownership has been seriously overlooked, even though it was practiced widely and effectively throughout the 1960s. Much of this has to do with the political complexities of cooperatives not fitting in the various narratives of the Movement, such as integration with white mainstream society, including department stores, and the more revolutionary angle to dismantle capitalism. As the federal government moved toward legally protected integration through legislation, such as the Civil Rights Act of 1964, the cooperatives advocated for self-organization, what we might retroactively label separatism (they would not have called it that). The records of the Poor People's Corporation show that they wanted to be independent from any external funding, including those supporting many civil rights programs. Derby had participated in a variety of programs that depended on a hybrid of federal and private foundation funding, such as the Free Southern Theater and Mississippi Child Development Fund (which would become Head Start) and, in an interview about the Poor People's Corporation, emphasizes how the red tape of external funding prevents an organization from actualizing its mission.[11] The Poor People's Corporation wanted to create community-supported programs that would be free from outside influence.

Liberty House made real a vision of an alternative economy based on craft-making and anti-industrial production and consumption, and how economic transformation could foment a new social order. The author of one article for *Manas* describes this vision:

The Bleecker Street store, for example, is selling large quantities of

African-type jewelry made by the Harlem Workshop. Along with quilts from Mississippi it is displaying quilts made by a co-op in Selma. A Liberty House store which opened in a Negro community might allot some of the margin on the sale of goods from Mississippi to finance craft classes, having in view the establishment of production units in its own neighborhood. The store, of course, would be a convenient outlet for whatever was made. And in it black people could be trained in retailing, advertising, publicity, and even community organizing, with the store as a functioning base. This would not be abstract, like the training programs offered by some anti-poverty agencies, and would certainly be less expensive! According to the manager's judgment, the store could be opened on weekends or evenings for Freedom School classes, craft education, consumer education, and political education. Liberty House stores across the country could handle merchandise produced by the co-ops fostered by the other stores, and all the stores could be linked by a newsletter published at Liberty House headquarters, P.O. Box 3193, Jackson, Miss.[12]

At the Poor People's Corporation Training Center in Edwards, Mississippi, this vision was already a reality. Located in a former plantation house, Mt. Beulah, the center housed five workshops, classrooms "for teaching small business management, bookkeeping, and cooperative principles," and accommodations for over two hundred people.[13] The training center was seen as a radical improvement from the conditions in which many people were working and offered a utopian vision, or a freedom dream, of Black poor people occupying and repurposing a plantation to build community wealth.

The problem activists and local people faced was deceptively simple: people were losing jobs because of civil rights movement activity, and they voiced their most urgent concerns over poverty and exploitative labor. Through cooperatives, civil rights workers joined the long history of labor organizing, of the effort to move people of color and poor people away from an economy shaped by white supremacy and racism. Through craft-making and sewing, activists confronted the dual-headed beast of sharecropping and domestic labor for whites, an exploitative labor system that seemed airtight.[14] As David A. Davis explains, "Although sharecropping was primarily an economic arrangement, it significantly influenced the South's rigid system of social stratification, its one-party political system, and its culture," with the only chance of escape being migration out of the South.[15] Trying to change this system meant confronting what felt impossible.

As Jessica Gordon Nembhard notes about the history of Black cooperatives, "When there is a narrative, the history is told as one of failure," and even when there is success, it is "little understood, and even less documented."[16] Nembhard's writing on Fannie Lou Hamer's Freedom Farm exemplifies the strenuous circumstances cooperatives faced, everything from the difficulties of management with such few resources, to bad weather. "The question is not so much why Freedom Farm failed," Nembhard quotes Kay Mills as saying, "but how it managed to operate as long as it did."[17] Although Nembhard's rhetorical maneuver is small, her reframing shifts attention to other kinds of investments that are unquantifiable, but present in the history of Black economic reform. Tracing the spirit of cooperation is more difficult than following the money, and any narrative focused only on the ledger misses half the story. Even though Liberty House "did not achieve its economic goals," Smethurst argues (via Kalamu ya Salaam) that artistic enterprises in the South emerged within the region's history of successful "economic institution building" and a "tradition of communal self-reliance," which made "nationalist visions of separate Black economies and states and other polities plausible on the grassroots level."[18] Activists recognized the extent to which the conditions of success and failure were important, but focused on the reasons why folks were willing to take a pay cut and double their work for an experimental and risky enterprise. They hoped they could collapse the systems of sharecropping and domestic labor that perpetuated the conditions of the plantation.

In a radio interview about the foundation of the cooperatives, Derby explains, "This is a self-help program by black people for black people to create employment in Mississippi."[19] By downplaying the efforts of the cooperatives to form an independent economy and move Black people away from the white-dominant labor structure, I read this statement as reflective of how Derby kept safe the intentions of the program by performing compliant maneuvers with her rhetoric. An article from the *Wall Street Journal* better describes some of the tensions emerging from the cooperative initiative. An interviewed woman claims, "The whites don't like it a bit—for every woman who comes to work out here, that's one more gone from a white woman's kitchen."[20] In this racialized economic model, Black labor directly benefits white employers and the wage earned does not compensate for that work nor does it heal the severing between the worker and his or her own family and community.

Because cooperatives sought to disrupt the status quo, people such as

James O. Eastland, the racist, antilabor senator from Mississippi, called the cooperatives communist. An article in the Poor People's Corporation newsletter detailed Eastland's misunderstanding of the cooperative structure:

> As usual when such folks notice that poor people are trying to be independent, Eastland put up a cry of "communist." . . . People like him feel they have to attack groups like the PPC [Poor People's Corporation] when they are afraid that poor people will be successful at making jobs for themselves that they will not be afraid of losing when they go to the polls to vote Eastland out of his job.[21]

Their desire to build capital within the community prompted the Poor People's Corporation to advocate for economic restructuring within a Cold War atmosphere, even if this contradicted the anticapitalist sentiments of many SNCC workers. And so, despite the fact that the cooperative model relied on people buying their products, they were willing to walk a politically ambiguous line to get to a position of self-sufficiency.

The language describing the initiatives of the Poor People's Corporation could be tricky and sometimes described self-help as opposite to government support and as a way to keep Black people in the South. For example, in a 1969 interview with Derby for *Newsfront* she navigated through a set of leading questions by the interviewer that insinuated anxiety about Black migration to Northern cities, emphasizing that the Poor People's Corporation enabled more Mississippians to stay in the South to work.[22] A more explicit example of this rhetoric was articulated by Mrs. Leo (Sima) Felsen, a white woman from Long Island, New York, who was a dedicated advocate for the co-ops and even traveled down to Mississippi to train women to sew. In an interview where she promotes Liberty House's products, she made it clear that "I didn't only do this to help them. . . . I think it also helps us in the North. There's so little opportunity for Negroes in the South that too many come to the north to make money and that causes so many problems for our cities."[23] It's unclear whether these perspectives were part of a larger strategy that kept Black people safe from harassment and encouraged even racist whites to open their pocketbooks. In her interview, Derby makes the case that when local southern whites figured out that Black people were trying to be self-sufficient from government support, harassment of the co-ops stopped. The language she used was politically malleable: it could be used to make a case against government support and federal programs, but at the same time, it could make a case for Black autonomy: "At least we feel that we're independent and we don't have any strings attached to what we're doing and we're developing our own programs according to the needs of the people of Mississippi."[24]

However, this meant that activists had to reorient their leftist politics and suffer criticism from others who didn't feel like "self-help" was radical enough.[25] The reactions of activists show the scrutiny placed on their initiatives, as Ellen Maslow wrote in 1969:

> It would be a drastic mistake to dismiss this proposal [for cooperatives] as "ugly capitalism": the coop program is frankly evolutionary rather than revolutionary. That's the best we can do in today's America. Besides, how can it be called ugly that 200 former cotton field workers and maids in Mississippi are now independent craftsmen? Let's be realistic and try to get something concrete going.[26]

Maslow reacts to an unknown interlocutor who rejects their self-help platform and its base in raising Black capital. She places blame on "today's America," referencing the anticommunist and racist attitudes that make cooperatives seem like the only viable pathway to autonomy. Abbie Hoffman gave a more nuanced response to naysayers, naming the intention of cooperatives as an effort to "develop in practice some of the ideals of participatory democracy on an economic level."[27] As he argues, "The concept of worker-owned cooperatives fit not only idealistically but *realistically* given the nature of rural, Negro communities," so that, in other words, land ownership would result in voting and Black farmers could "overcome the psychological problems that the segregated system fostered."[28] Hoffman's point, albeit paternalistic in tone, reflects the desire of SNCC activists to have cooperative labor begin the reparative work they believed participatory democracy offered, and thus the cooperative is a stepping-stone to further liberation.

Somewhere in the ideological confusion of what exactly a cooperative was politically, Black and poor people were able to gather together and imagine a world beyond the white-owned economic structure of the Deep South. Hoffman's argument about psychological harm both resonates *and is in conflict* with bell hooks's writing on work in *Sisters of the Yam*, where she claims, "It is a tragic irony that many more black people suffer undue anxiety and stress as a result of racial integration . . . many black people work at jobs in integrated settings where the presences of racism may bring added tension to the work setting."[29] Hoffman points to segregation and hooks discusses the stress of integration, and together they limit possibility for a way out. In an effort to think beyond both, cultural workers and local people poured their creativity into forming something new through craft-making, even though cooperatives are not new in the history of Black labor. Black-owned cooperatives enabled activists and local people to collaborate toward labor reform that focused on fostering intimacy within one's own relationship to work and, simultaneously, within one's relationships with others.

Even though the Poor People's Corporation may seem like an outlier, it fits in with a long tradition of black economic autonomy, rooted in farming and land. This includes the Southern Tenants Farmer's Union and the Alabama Sharecropping Union of the 1920s and '30s, Garveyism, and Fannie Lou Hamer's Freedom Farm founded in 1969. "Revolution is based on land," Malcolm X claimed, despite being mostly an urban organizer. "Land is the basis of all independence. Land is the basis of freedom, justice, and equality."[30] This tradition extends further than post-Reconstruction freedom movements. As Monica M. White argues in *Freedom Farmers*, food cultivation as an act of resistance can be traced back to seeds carried in the hair of enslaved peoples across the Middle Passage and their garden plots on plantations that preserved food knowledge. White looks at how agriculture became "a space and place to practice freedom" and over time constituted what she calls "commons as praxis."[31] She begins with the everyday lives of black farmers to open theories of social space. White brings attention to Booker T. Washington, who, she argues, is too often the straw person to prop up post-Reconstruction discussion of W. E. B. Du Bois and the "talented tenth" echelon of black intellectualism. White argues, "Our historical memory has been profoundly affected by those narratives of the civil rights movement that, in emphasizing the 'talented tenth,' have failed to capture the roles of black working-class men and women and thus often have ignored the legacy of black farmers and those living close to the land."[32] So much of the history of Black agricultural reform has been mediated through an alliance between middle-class Black intellectuals and poor people, including Washington and Tuskegee Institute. This does not elide the ways poor people have organized and resisted over time, but draws our attention to how they have been represented. The cooperative movement was comprised of middle-class, college-educated activists working alongside farmers, employing Ella Baker's method of participatory democracy to discourage hierarchical power relations between them. This was an admitted challenge for people like Derby and Morris, whose Blackness did not elide the class difference between them and their constituents.

Baker's history with cooperatives reveals the extent to which cooperative philosophy impacted the civil rights movement. As a young organizer with the Young Negroes Cooperative League, Baker developed "a long-range view of the cooperative movement" as Barbara Ransby argues. "To them," Ransby continues, "the concepts of cooperation and collective action were the ideological pillars on which this larger movement was to be built." Baker's philosophical vision shaped how SNCC operated and mobilized, placing cooperatives as central to the Movement, rather than an offshoot or side project. Imagining a new economic order was vital to social movement activism.[33]

The long history of Black economics exists in tandem with Black philosophy. Black feminist philosopher Anna Julia Cooper discusses issues of labor in her 1899 publication, *A Voice from the South*, with a perspective so astute and futuristic that scholar Jo Davis-McElligatt describes her as a "black feminist augur."[34] Cooper advocates the kind of Black owned and operated economic uplift imagined by the Poor People's Corporation as a path to what she calls "social wealth," which attaches labor reform to the significance of intellectual and artistic life. To say Cooper was ahead of her time is an understatement. She calls for equal pay and wages for domestic workers, claiming, "if men will not or cannot help the conditions which force women into the struggle for bread, we have a right to claim at least that she shall have fair play and all the rights of wage-earners in general"[35] In the same publication, she makes the case for domestic labor compensation because it "reliev[es] the man of certain indoor cares and enabl[es] him to give thereby larger effort to his special trade of calling."[36] Cooper called for demands that would not be met in her lifetime and not even in the twenty-first century after multiple waves of feminism. Despite these radical claims, Cooper was a product of her time, and much of her reasoning—whether it be subversive or not—is grounded in heteronormative ideals of marriage. As far as the criticism Cooper faced in her own time, she was accused of being an accommodationist, according to Davis-McElligatt and Vivian May. Davis-McElligatt responds to these critiques, stating, "Cooper's analysis presciently examines how marginalized peoples challenge rigid phenomenological paradigms, and develops a critical spatially located interdisciplinary comparative feminist framework which she believed would alter perceptions of black women's agency and political future."[37] Cooper's writing helps to frame the cooperative movement's self-help and uplift as a feminist project flexible to the needs of its locales.

Cooper argued that the Black community needed a more flexible approach to the debate between agricultural-trade work and intellectual life. In her opinion, both could be in the same family, and it was the meeting of different intelligences—physical and intellectual—that would accumulate social wealth in the community. Social wealth is an abstract idea of community value that links the fate of the individual to the fate of the race. It is tied to accumulation of capital but also some other, hard-to-define essence, which is cultural but never deviates too far from labor: "Wealth must pave the way for learning. . . . Labor must be the solid foundation stone—the sine qua non of our material value," and skilled craftwork and trade must come from the community.[38] Because Cooper grounded her ideas in labor, she saw hope in the agricultural communities in the South, where "the colored man virtually holds the labor market."[39] Her argument that poverty manifests itself differently in rural areas would be shared by civil rights workers who faced unique struggles organizing in similar areas. Rural economies meant rethinking tactics of mobilization and economic liberation, especially because of the widespread attention to industrial labor in the history of unions and worker consciousness. By focusing on agricultural and black women's labor, Cooper decenters industrialism as the origin of labor-thinking and places it within a historical perspective that centers slavery and its aftermath. She argues that if Black people could obtain a fair share of the profit of the labor they had to expend for others, their wealth would close the 250-year gap of social wealth. Cooper demands reparations for what was lost, focusing on the effect of labor estrangement on the artistic and intellectual life of the worker:

> There are other hungerings in man besides the eternal all-subduing hungering of his despotic stomach. There is the hunger of the eye for beauty, the hunger of the ear for concords, the hungering of the mind for development and growth, of the soul for communion and love, for a higher, richer, fuller living—a more abundant life! And every man owes it to himself *to let nothing in him starve for lack of proper food.*[40]

In this passage, Cooper refuses to separate cultivation from culture so that she may argue for the importance of southern/rural agriculture as the base of power if the scales of labor and profit are balanced. To be clear, she did not advocate for a "go slow" method but rather a means of building a separatist, community-funded social wealth that would not depend on patronage or white capital.

Cooper calls for a process that I refer to as intimacy-making—a dialectal retort to Marxist concepts of alienation—to make work intimate with one's creative and spiritual life. She anticipates powerful repercussions resulting from intimacy-making for women, claiming, "We need women who are so sure of their own social footing that they need not fear leaning to lend a hand to a fallen or falling sister," noting how relational repair is necessary for labor reform.[41] To heal oneself and heal together is predicated on removing oneself from harmful encounters with racism at work. The conversation continues over a century later with Saidiya Hartman's *Wayward Lives, Beautiful Experiments: Intimate Histories of Social Upheaval*, which describes waywardness as "the avid longing for a world not ruled by master, man, or police . . . the practice of the social otherwise, the insurgent ground that enables new possibilities and new vocabularies; it is the lived experience of enclosure and segregation, assembling and huddling together . . . a *beautiful experiment* in how-to-live."[42] Cooper would have been scandalized by Hartman's queer subjects that defy a commitment to heteronormative family structures, one of Cooper's highest values, and yet they resonate across time in their desire for beautiful experiments of how to live better lives. Viewing the craft cooperatives within the framework of Black feminist beautiful experiments, we can see how cooperatives situate their own ideological framework, improvised from their resources. Black cooperatives deviated from the expectations of civil rights movement programming and even traditional labor mobilization. In doing so, they created a new path toward labor value and social wealth.

Archival Textiles and Performances of Everyday Use

This section steps away from Liberty House cooperatives to trace textiles within the cultural activism of the civil rights movement and how fabric art engaged an aesthetics of everyday use. By reading textiles as objects that hold narrative and communicate information, I intersect studies of performance, textiles, and Black and feminist cultures. Textiles often provide insight where the text-centered archive fails and contain the histories of women, colonized peoples, and people whose access to literacy and authorship has been compromised by white supremacy. The Freedom Quilting Bee from Gee's Bend, Alabama has received the most artistic and critical attention of any craft cooperative of the Movement, and scholarly writing about their quilts offers a perspective to how scholars and quilters have discussed Black women's cooperative craftwork. In her reading of Black women's quilts, Patricia Turner moves through debates on art and utilitarianism. Scholars, curators, and the public imbue Black quilts with lore about the underground railroad and narratives of West African influence and authenticity, and as Turner shows, there is as much evidence to prove as to disprove many of these assertions. An inconclusive inference Turner makes is that these communities are too diverse, both in Africa and in Black southern culture, to draw any singular blueprint for a Black quilt. Following Turner's observation that "quilts mirror

Figure 10. Head Start workshop, *gele* wrapping. Photograph by Maria Varela. From the Doris A. Derby Papers, Stuart A. Rose Special Collections at Emory University, Atlanta.

much about the quilters," the materials crafted by civil rights activists reveals how working with textiles created pathways to intimacy, even if many have only lasted as photographs.[43]

While there was no quilt to read in Doris Derby's archive, there is a faded tie-dyed cloth and a collection of photographs taken by Maria Varela, who captured Derby's workshops with women in Canton, Mississippi, as part of her organizational work with Head Start. In the photograph above, Derby and two women wrap fabric in the tradition of the Yoruba *gele*. In a manner that anticipates the Black Arts Movement's embrace of pan-African aesthetics, Derby integrated crafts and fabric materials from her visit to Nigeria into the cooperative movement. In her oral history, she describes her experience in Nigeria, which she visited in 1960 through an NAACP scholarship, and argues for the deep connections between African and African American culture: "When I did go to the South, I had things with me and I used to show African art in Head Start programs and churches. I took African dresses.... I wanted to share what I knew, what I learned about African culture, so that people know that there is not a void."[44] The photograph documents how cloth binding symbolizes the closing of this void.

The subject of the photograph is *not* the violent atmosphere of Mississippi, which Leigh Raiford argues has dominated the cultural memory of the civil rights movement.[45] Instead, Varela captures an image of joy between Derby and two local women as they play with fabric and engage in activities extraneous to the dominant white-supremacist labor system. Varela decenters Derby whose back is toward the camera and keeps the focus on the local women and gestures of intimacy, as one assists Derby in wrapping the *gele*. In the composition of the photograph, the eye follows arms that lead into the central woman's face, framing her and attending to her. The arms of the two attending women reach out in support. Even though the photograph is clear and sharp, it evokes movement: the movement of the arms as well as the fabric. They may be ostensibly learning the process for the first time, but their hands perform tasks that engage with embodied knowledge and together create a choreography that reaches toward an ancestral past. Wrapping cloth, as Beverly Gordon observes, materially and symbolically represents care: "Enfolding cloth can provide reassurance and protection" in both a metaphoric and material way.[46] The hair wrapping tradition, Gordon notes, derives from the process of creating "micro-environments" of protection from extreme elements.[47] Derby's workshop holds this dual purpose by expressing forms of diasporic touch to nurture the spirit and developing cooperatives that could create an economic micro-environment for Black workers as a barrier from the extreme labor conditions of the South.

The relationship between textiles and influences from Africa on Black southern culture is a contentious issue in quilt studies. Scholars of Black quilting have detailed possibilities of West African influence on fabrics and patterns, including what Eli Leon has termed "models in the mind," to trace how these patterns survived the Middle Passage into the twentieth-century South.[48] Yet it just as easily could have been Derby's showcase of Nigerian textiles and the ingenuity of women wanting to try new patterns that inspired "African" aesthetics and ended up on a quilt. Because intimacy between women, especially Black and poor women, has historically been left out of archival documentation, textile influences and lineages largely remain elusive, breaking apart traditional academic systems of knowledge that place a burden on the site of origin. Turner reads Alice Walker's short story "Everyday Use" as reflective of the "genealogical epiphany" that these quilts and "handmade objects were worth preserving."[49]

In "Everyday Use," a southern matriarch confronts her daughter, Dee, over the inheritance of the family quilts. Dee has moved away and changed her name to Wangero, expressing a Black nationalist Pan-Africanism. She has also recently altered her view of her southern heritage, coming to see it not as a source of embarrassment, but as cultural capital. Turner notes the timeliness of Walker's publication in the 1970s, when "real-life Wangeros who had avoided quilting lessons from their kin were starting to enroll in classes and buy books on the subject."[50] Wangero wants to take her sister Maggie's inheritance—the family quilts—with the excuse, "Maggie can't appreciate these quilts! . . . She'd probably be backward enough to put them to everyday use."[51] Wangero says that she would hang them, transforming heritage into art and making the bold claim that her mother and sister do not understand their own heritage. Walker's story explains the distortion of meaning and value in relation to textiles and concepts of heritage. For the mother, heritage exists in the embodied knowledge of quilting as a practice. When Wangero makes a case for preservation, the mother's counterargument is that Maggie can always make another quilt, since she learned from her relatives.

When looking to Derby's *gele* workshop, once could read this as an attempt to superficially impose Yoruba heritage on Mississippi women in the same way that Wangero tries to inflict an external cultural value of art that exists outside the family's own internal system of value in labor, memory, and use. Perhaps some of the women in Derby's workshop felt the same way about Derby's Yoruba artifacts; however, what Varela's photograph captures in the moment is mutual value in joy and collaboration. This suggests how wrapping *gele* played with embodied knowledge and performed a connection to an ancestral past without adhering to a specific political ideology. Derby forms her interpretation of West African fabrics based on what was available to her in Mississippi, and in doing so creates moments of intimacy between a Black woman from New York and the southern women she lived among. As the women and children in the series of photographs dye fabrics and figure out patterns of hair wrapping, they engage in labor with potential for spiritual nourishment. Derby claimed that she wanted to close the void between Africa and the U.S. South, yet the intimacy visible in Varela's photograph reveals that the void being closed was between herself and the local women she organized.

Walker's story represents the South as complex terrain for identity formation, which Riché Richardson explores both as a scholar and quilter. If Wangero represents a post–civil rights movement effort to reorient southernness as authentic connections to the past, Richardson sees this in contemporary "linkages to the Africana South" that enable Black people to "embody new notions of southern subjectivity that were inconceivable and illegible in the past."[52] Richardson traces new images of southernness through Beyoncé's "southern epistemology" at work in the music video for "Formation," noting the power of tapping into an extended assemblage of symbols that "visualizes landscapes historically linked to African American subjectivity through a history of slavery and the lingering repercussions of this history, which conditioned the South as a symbolic ancestral home in the African American imaginary."[53] The complexity and at times illegibility of the southern cooperative movement emerges in material traces of Derby's cultural work, which evidence the ways in which linkages to the Africana South occurred during the civil rights movement. Bearing witness to this marginalized history does not negate Richardson's perspective that this could not be understood until the contemporary moment; rather, it shows how ahead of its time the cooperative movement was.

Richardson makes this observation as an academic but also a quilter of Black history and culture. As she pulls together craftwork and southernness as a site of identity formation, Richardson argues that this assemblage generates innovative artistic creativity. We can see this in her own appliqué quilts that range from autobiography to cultural history of Black southern life, including family cotillion moments and memorials to civil rights leaders. Through her quilting, Richardson communicates and creates meaning that cannot be held within academic writing, or even through words. For example, her quilt "The Ties That Bind" displays the trio of John F. Kennedy, Bobbie Kennedy, and Martin Luther King Jr. because Richardson remembers that "numerous households of the 1970s and 1980s had altar-like mantels or tables where either individual photographs of the three leaders were arranged or a collective one of all three was displayed."[54] Even though the trio were never photographed together, Richardson's quilt reflects an imagined photography that filters through the memory of Black households. Like Bambara's posters on the walls of the co-op, the tribute Richardson makes is less a statement about these men as political figures than a reflection of a Black tradition remembered by Richardson. Her play on the word "ties" shows the leaders wearing the same color tie binding them together by Richardson's artistic choice, but it also represents how the visual memory of those portraits binds Richardson to a sense of community. Her quilts perform a relationality to the South that express its complexity through the unique perspective of seeing southerness from one's own home and memory.

"The Ties That Bind" documents a tradition preserved through Richardson's memory in the way that Walker's story about quilting documents embodied knowledges and Varela's photograph documents the preservation and reteaching of that knowledge. These artifacts stand in place of the stories we cannot know of the women who worked in craft cooperatives. We catch glimpses of their lives through their craftwork, the recording of meetings, or from the words and photographs of others. Through this media, we can witness solidarity in labor that has remained hidden behind the surfeit of images of direct action and violence that dominate the cultural imaginary of the civil rights movement, in the way Hartman recovers the "intimate dimensions" of black women's lives in the nineteenth century using a fragmented archive.[55] As Hartman claims, "Every historian of the multitude, the disposed, the subaltern, and the enslaved is forced to grapple with the power and authority of the archive and the limits it sets on what can be known."[56] She continues:

> I searched for photographs exemplary of the beauty and possibility cultivated in the lives of ordinary Black girls and young women and that stoked dreams of what might be possible if you could escape the house of bondage. This archive of images, found and imagined, would provide a necessary antidote to the scourged Blacks, glassy tear-filled eyes, bodies stripped and branded, or rendered grotesque for white enjoyment.[57]

Even though Hartman references an earlier and significantly different time, the desire to find images of joy, love, and intimacy resonates. Derby's and Varela's photography parallels Hartman's mission to create a usable past for an imagined future. As Derby claims, "I wanted to document so that the things that I felt that I was lacking when I grew up that I had to really find out about, I had to look for, I wanted other people to have those visual images and I wanted to show what the average person was doing as well as the leaders."[58]

In this example of ordinary cooperative activity, women work around a stove in a one-room factory for dolls, which resembles a one-room schoolhouse. Here and in other similar photographs of women working, the camera seems intrusive and the subjects look down at their work instead of at the camera. In another photograph not pictured here, a white woman holds an item up to the stove while others look on—a young novitiate and older women gathering around the heat in their workspace. The woman in this photograph is probably Sima Felsen, during her time down South training others on sewing techniques. Many activists acted as intermediaries and teachers. For example, Derby also often acted as an intermediary, learning a skill like candle making from an expert then turning around to teach that skill to an

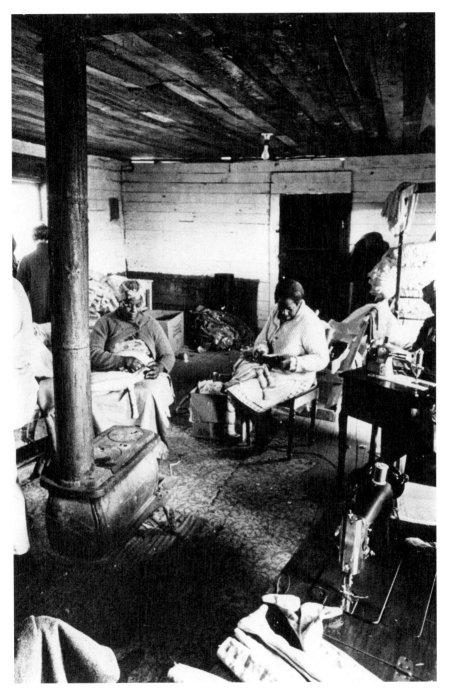

Figure 11. Cooperative women sewing, by Doris Derby. The Doris A. Derby Papers, Stuart A. Rose Special Collections at Emory University, Atlanta.

Figure 12. Filmstrip of Poor People's Corporation's cooperative meeting in Mississippi, taken by Doris Derby. The Doris A. Derby Papers, Stuart A. Rose Special Collections at Emory University, Atlanta.

interested co-op. Even though Felsen claimed she never felt in danger, at one point, when her host family heard news of an inspector coming, they had to hide her to avoid "danger for both guest and host."[59] However, in the moment this photograph was taken, all the women sit relaxed; one drinks a cup of coffee, and another packages a craft object, while Felsen seems to be feeding the stove. The scene reverses expectations of how women should be operating in a domestic space in the Jim Crow South: the white woman in a position of labor while the Black women sit above her. This photograph, in its quiet portrait of activism, documents an interracial, intercultural cross-section. It would seem a utopian vision of labor, obligation, and care, except that Felsen later commented that she was in favor of the program because it kept Black people out of northern cities. Activism is a complex and messy terrain.

In a series of photographs taken by Derby at a meeting of the Poor People's Corporation, cooperative managers show Black women seated together, sharing ideas and making decisions about their work. The table is created by four tables making a large square in the center of a large warehouse, with a backdrop of boxes. The majority of those seated at the table are Black women, with a few Black men. Seated just outside of the table are benches where others sit, including a couple of white people. The empty seat where the photographer sits is closest to the camera and looks like an invitation to the viewer to imagine themselves at the table. The series of photographs visualizes listening and a viewer can follow people's heads turn toward whoever is speaking. Together with the minutes from a cooperative management meeting from December 20, 1969, the archive reveals the freedom with which people complained about the Poor People's Corporation's organizational structure. As feminist scholar Sara Ahmed argues, "The path of a complaint, where a complaint goes, how far it goes, teaches us something about how institutions work," and so, because complaints over financial issues were recorded and listened to, we have a glimpse of how the Poor People's Corporation worked.[60] Mrs. Lea of the McComb leather cooperative threatened to quit, stating that "Liberty House was organized wrong" and they should have "let the group support itself on a 50–50 basis," and Mrs. Woods of Baertown also used the language of strike mobilizing, claiming "that they were not going back to work unless prices have been changed."[61] Beyond the money flow issues and demand for consistent pay, they made known their complaint over treatment. "She said Jesse [Morris] did not have to say what he said he could have said it in a nicer way than he did . . . I thought Jesse was a business man" as whoever recorded the minutes notes, "But I see he is not."[62] In the last two sentences, it's unclear who is narrating the complaint, the speaker or the recorder. Either way, the archive reveals a sense of honesty and directness, including about Derby, who is criticized for her prioritization and not taking direction from management to only focus on problems to which she is assigned. If, as Ahmed argues, "frustration can be a feminist record," here we see that embraced in practice.[63] The scene suggests the power of cooperatives to create enough autonomy for their workers to look at how the system works and fails to work and imagine better methods for themselves. The indignation of the workers encapsulates what Alice Walker expresses in *The Color Purple*, discussed in the following section: that economic autonomy creates the conditions for consciousness-raising and for imagining an improved future for oneself and one's community.

Seeking Intimacy in Alice Walker's *The Color Purple*

I turn to *The Color Purple* to illustrate how the cooperative movement—one of the least discussed aspects of the civil rights movement—finds its way into one of the most famous stories in American literature. I believe that Alice Walker's *The Color Purple*, a novel about Black women who loved and supported each other spiritually and financially, shares a relationship with the cooperative movement archive. Even though Walker has emphasized inspiration from her own family history, she also participated in some civil rights movement activity and had a friendship with Doris Derby. Walker was close enough with Derby to have her take a series of portraits, and whereas Derby's civil rights era photography usually shows people midaction, her portraits of Walker capture the quiet solitude of her activism, which involved the deep listening practices reflected in her writing. In Walker's journal of her time in Mississippi, she notes relief in meeting Derby, among others, as friends in a place that caused Walker much trepidation. Walker's novel *Meridian* directly draws influence from the southern civil rights movement and its relationship to northern activists; however, *The Color Purple* maintains a conversation with the Movement, even though the novel takes place in the decades leading up to the 1960s.

Walker's witnessing of Derby's work and philosophies reverberates within Celie's story of finding liberation through sewing and intimacy with blues singer Shug Avery. The novel offers a view of intimacy between women that the archive cannot. For example, the following passage from *The Color Purple* brings us closer to the dialogue over financial support that comes from within the Black community and from a place of love. In this moment, Celie's sewing business, Folkspants, Unlimited, begins to take off as her lover and investor, Shug Avery, observes her work:

> I sit in the dining room making pants after pants. I got pants now in every color and size under the sun. Since us started making pants down home, I ain't been able to stop. I change the cloth, I change the print, I change the waist, I change the pocket. I change the hem, I change the fullness of the leg. I make so many pants Shug tease me. I didn't know what I was starting, she say, laughing. Pants all over her chairs, hanging all in front of the china closet. Newspaper patterns and cloth all over the table and the floor. She come home, kiss me, step over all the mess. Say, before she leave again, How much money you think you need *this* week?[64]

Both Derby's photography of the cooperatives and Walker's writing celebrate the mess of fabrics; these workshops became spaces where Black women could congregate and learn from each other while working independently of the white economy or political structure—or at least that was the dream. Investment comes from a place of intimacy, as Shug steps into Cooper's imagined scene of a sister leaning in to lend a hand to another. However, even though Cooper, Walker, and Derby ground this in dollars, it cannot depend on money alone. Shug invests in Celie financially but raises her consciousness through sex and love. The financial support cannot be separated from intimacy. Both women perform labors of love: Shug works to support Celie's creative process and Celie sews endlessly to create the perfect pair of pants for Shug. The novel holds within it not only this story of intimacy and craft labor but also the political complexity of cooperative labor and its relationship to Black uplift, an ideological framework that can be as messy as it is productive.

Celie's entrepreneurship is one of the most criticized aspects of Walker's novel, a source of multifaceted debate over authenticity and politics, which has existed from first reviews and continues today. In terms of reading its economics, Lauren Berlant argues, "the mythic spirt of American capitalism [is] the vehicle for the production of an Afro-American utopia."[65] Berlant works to determine why the novel concludes with "the familial model of utopian capitalism" as a reinstatement of "nationalist discourse," which oscillates in a manner that Berlant reads as ideologically confusing:

> Folkpants, Unlimited is an industry dedicated to the reproduction and consumption of a certain system of representation central to the version of Afro-American "cultural nationalism" enacted by *The Color Purple*. But Folkpants, Unlimited also participated in the profit margin: the image of the commodity as the subject's most perfect self-expression is the classic fantasy bribe of capitalism. The illogic of a textual system in which the very force that disenfranchises Afro-Americans provides the material for their national reconstruction is neither "solved" by the novel nor raised as a paradox.[66]

Berlant's reading exemplifies the disconnect between the efforts of the cooperative movement and the public, or at least scholarly, perceptions of what Black literature should do in the wake of the civil rights movement. Both the novel and Berlant's article were published in the 1980s and reflect the following two decades of debate over *The Color Purple* and the ethics of representation. Berlant reads the novel as illogical and unresolved; however, this criticism accurately reflects the broader debates about cooperatives and Black self-help initiatives during the civil rights movement to which Walker was a witness. Walker wrote, like Richardson sewed in "The Ties That Bind," a representation of a complex value systems that may not be legible to those outside of it.

Walker's connection to the cooperative movement offers insight into how Black women sewing and making their own money has always been a controversial subject. Celie's personal liberation depends on capital investment so that she could have the self-sufficiency to gain independence from her husband. Yet Celie's business is Black owned and operated, which questions its relationship to American capitalism, an economic system supported by racist and sexist division of the labor force, especially in the Jim Crow setting of the novel. Rather than being utopian, the harmony at the conclusion of the novel is riddled with imperfections and contradictions as a reflection of what activists in the movement knew: that the small, local changes in communities were an essential part of the freedom struggle. The application of theoretical labels limits an understanding of people's everyday lives, which is something activists struggled to make sense of at the time of the civil rights movement. Yet their commitment to the needs of local people obligated them to move forward with cooperatives, despite their illegibility to others or even impossibility to turn a substantial profit.

The novel parallels Celie's story with an indictment of domestic labor through the character Sophia, who loses her livelihood and spirit to become indentured to service for a white family. After she "sasses" the mayor's wife when propositioned for domestic work, she is beaten, jailed, and forced to serve out her sentence as a laborer in the house of the mayor's wife for the majority of her adult life. Sophia is estranged from her children and loses her mind as a result: "she suddenly sort of erased herself . . . One minute I was saying howdy to a living woman. The next minute nothing living was there. Only its shape."[67] The forced domestic work destroys Sofia's humanity and exemplifies the psychological harm of labor systems that alienate people from their home.

Returning to a key point in Varela's report for the Selma Literacy Program from the previous chapter, she writes this specific goal: "That man should participate in the basic decisions of his [their] society in order to achieve a *fully human life*."[68] Varela connects social decision-making to a full, or holistic, humanity, suggesting that participatory democracy is a basic need. The concept of a *fully human life* brings together Marx's philosophies of estrangement with Cooper's concerns for social wealth. Marx was concerned with the philosophical questions of human identity and how one's relationship to the "act of production" shapes or distorts that definition.[69] Marx's concept of estrangement or alienation argues that because a person labors for the benefit of another, they become isolated from the product they create as well as the means of sustaining their own life, the goods they purchase elsewhere.

Sophia's experience of dehumanization is an incarnation of Marx's description of exploitative labor as a "sacrifice of his life."[70] The novel takes a clear position on domestic labor for white families: it is a sacrifice of a life.

For Cooper, social wealth meant so much more than the flow of money in Black communities. Her theory tied economics together with self-actualization and the restoration of life, whether that be through her vision of the family model, Walker's vision of queer family-making, or cooperative modes of intimacy-making through collective labor. Like quilts, the container of these theories shifts and changes, reflecting the flexibility and imperfections that come from necessity, but what remains is the spirit of beautiful experimentations in how to live. Liberty House and the cooperatives of the Poor People's Corporation engaged with this level of experimentation with mixed success, yet they brought people together to imagine a world based on cooperative labor. In the next chapter, I turn to farming and agriculture, and how beautiful experiments in labor reform inspired independent media in the South as activists searched for new ways to tell the stories of workers. For cultural workers, labor is not just livelihood; it is a story about one's life, and they worked to reclaim those narratives for their communities.

Five

Art/Work

The Independent Media Archives of the South

———

I want to begin with a visualization that describes the object of study for this chapter:

In a small farming town in the South, a group of Black farmers approaches a SNCC activist who works at a local freedom school and asks about opportunities to buy better equipment. They've heard of others applying for money from the government, but they don't know where to start. The SNCC worker writes to the Poor People's Corporation in Jackson, Mississippi, and they respond by sending a script booklet attached to a piece of cheesecloth containing a rolled-up filmstrip. The script is called *Something of Our Own* and was created by the West Batesville Farmer's Cooperative in collaboration with SNCC photographers and illustrators. The SNCC worker holds the filmstrip up to the light and sees the positive images; they realize the specific kind of projector this kind of film requires. The previous year, the local SNCC office received a projector from a foundation grant that helped outfit the freedom school. The educational and literacy materials that came with the projector were irrelevant to the Black community in the southern small town, so the projector has remained unused in the corner for months.

Now, the SNCC worker organizes an event calling together the Black farmers in town for a screening and live reading of *Something of Our Own*. They bring their families and others who are interested or just curious. People take turns reading the script, struggling to make out the words in the dark as the SNCC worker controls the projector. People laugh at the illustrations of "Mr. Charlie" and cheer at the line, "We are tired of working to make him rich." The audience witness photographs of the community coming together and of Black people holding okra and operating large combines and trucks that farmers were able to collectively buy with assistance from the federal government. After half an hour, they turn on the lights and an enthusiastic discussion follows. People crowd around the projector, learning to operate the machine and returning to their favorite images, debating the feasibility of creating their own cooperative. A feeling of hope resonates among them and they begin to mobilize. Soon their cooperative joins the dozens that comprise the Federation of Southern Cooperatives.

In this imagined scene based on archival materials, we can witness the possibilities of cultural activism. The filmstrip, *Something of Our Own*, communicates how to form a cooperative through collaborative intermedia art-making. It creates a material object that reflects an ethos of participatory democracy, promoting nonhierarchical engagement as the path toward social justice. *Something of Our Own* did not use prerecorded audio alongside the projection of the images; rather, the person working the projector coordinated with the reader of the script. While the projector displayed photographs taken by SNCC photographers Bob Fletcher, Ben Jackson, and Maria Varela and illustrations drawn by Claude Weaver, the reader would read aloud lines such as the following: "It's better not to plant at all than to raise okra for Mr. Jacobs to get rich. Let us see can we do something for ourselves. So we decided we would try and sell our okra ourselves and get a better price."[1] The script was recorded and transcribed *as is* in order to communicate their tone and style of storytelling. Because the script is written in the collective "we" of the okra farmers, the reader-performer becomes a medium through which the okra farmers could speak across temporal and spatial distance directly to the audience. Together with the person operating the projector, they enact a choreography between words and their correlating images. In this way, the SNCC cultural workers become cocreators in a new medium that incorporates the oral tradition, even if it relies on technologies of print and visual media. They make possible an embodied performance of story, an invitation for others to tell and retell the victory of cooperative labor in West Batesville, Mississippi.

The other filmstrip-performance, *Farm Worker's Strike*, was also produced by Varela and illustrates the journey taken by farmworkers and the union in

Figure 13. Image of okra from *Something of Our Own*, produced by Maria Varela. The Doris A. Derby Papers, Stuart A. Rose Special Collections at Emory University, Atlanta, GA.

the strike in Delano, California. Through photography, illustration, and collective voice, *Farm Worker's Strike* projects over a hundred images detailing the formation of the union, the strike, and the March to Sacramento in three parts. Even though the script centers on Cesar Chavez as the hero of the farmworkers' movement and elides the roles of Dolores Huerta and Larry Itliong, the photographs visualize diversity and foreground a community of people that includes women, Black and Filipinx farmworkers, and activists. *Farm Worker's Strike* and *Something of Our Own* share this in common: they model modes of relationality, such as cocreation through listening, and prove that these seemingly peripheral activities were central to the participatory actions of civil rights protests.

As a new medium of communication, the filmstrips emerged from the pedagogical activism of SNCC's adult literacy initiatives, as discussed in chapter 3, "A New Lesson in Activism." Varela and other like-minded activists rejected inappropriate educational materials and opted to create something new. Varela remembers, "I wanted to create an adult education program that communicated lessons learned when local people organized successful projects in Black Belt communities."[2] When it came to labor organizing, there had been success with cooperatives, such as in West Batesville, and they became an ideal subject for telling their own story. Such a radical message of everyday living necessitated an independent media structure. SNCC worked to reclaim the right to methods of communication as part of their larger initiative to "tell it like it is" in response to mainstream sensationalist narratives of civil rights activity.[3] As Sharon Monteith argues, "We learn more about the interior dynamics of a social movement through sustained attention to how it forged its narrative and consciously curated a range of storytelling practices."[4] SNCC's new method intersected multiple forms of media to craft their narrative. Their intermedia storytelling process inherently builds in a cooperative structure into SNCC's art-making practice and invites new methods of participation and interpretation.

As a subject, the act of forming a cooperative or insurance fund may seem small compared to the visually impressive protests that make up much of civil rights memory, and yet improving daily life often held more significance to the ordinary people of the Movement.[5] Varela estimates that photographing protests only made up about 15 percent of an average SNCC photographer's time, which evidences the abundance of programming beyond protests.[6] Images of Black and Brown workers upending extant labor systems offered audiences detailed instructions on how to make a freedom dream real. For example, slides from *Something of Our Own* show Black farmers walking through a cotton field to survey the countryside and others from *Farm Worker's Strike* explain how the union organized families to distribute food and clothing according to need during the strike. The slideshows reveal economic and social systems thriving outside of contingent and dependent relationships with oppressive white landowners and buyers. Even though there was direct action against those systems, much of the imagery in the slideshows centers on the community and the alternative economies created within a cooperative or union. Through this media, we get a glimpse beyond the public-facing spectacle of the struggle for equal rights and bear witness to *how* that work was accomplished at the community level.

The independent media initiatives discussed in this chapter—SNCC's filmstrips, Charlie Cobb's mixed-media poetry collection *Furrows*, and the Free Southern Theater's *Nation Time* broadcast—hold an uneasy position within civil rights media, a genre defined through major journalism outlets and Hollywood representations of the Movement.[7] To be clear, the Black freedom struggle has an entrenched relationship with independent media, but the archives receiving the most attention tend to be focused on work being produced in coastal and northern urban centers.[8] The cultural work resulting in the filmstrips has been overshadowed by the cultural memory of a relative handful of images centering on violence against Black bodies, which Leigh Raiford argues have "come to distill and symbolize a range of complex events, ideas, and ideologies."[9] Her study of civil rights photography reveals that the "use and repetition of movement photographs in contexts as varied as electoral campaigns, art exhibits, commercials, and, of course, academic histories have crystallized many of these photographs into icons."[10] Many scholars of Black visual culture, such as Nicole Fleetwood, have shown the extent to which racial formation happens through visual culture "meant to substitute for the real experiences of black subjects."[11] As a response, Fleetwood looks to "*non-iconicity,*" which interrupts the burden of representation by "favoring localized everyday scenes and moments of the mundane and ephemera."[12] As a term, non-iconicity reveals what activist photographers and local people valued in the visual representations of their collaborations.

The scholarly turn to independent media and grassroots storytelling searches for narratives at the fringes of cultural memory, which may in fact be the central story of the Movement. "The camera first offered SNCC a way to intervene in dominant media frames," and as Raiford argues, "the camera would then provide a technology for self and communal expression, a way of presenting and representing rural black southerners to themselves."[13] Independent media experimentation captured the everyday work of social change, distilling the word "social" down to the everyday ways a society functions. Their efforts were not solely to create independent media but also to create pathways to living independently. As Varela recalls, "We all felt the need to develop parallel institutions as it was clear by 1964 that mainstream institutions were not effective in enabling local people's agency to change their lives."[14] Initiatives in media autonomy reflect how other cultural workers felt at the time, especially in terms of Black independent filmmaking, which was seen by writers and filmmakers such as James Baldwin and Toni Cade Bambara as the future of Black cultural expression. In her study of Baldwin's search for "another cinema," Hayley O'Malley quotes Bambara's premonition for Black cultural work: "'How shall a diasporic people communicate?' Bambara asked rhetorically. 'Answer: Independent films.'"[15] Toni Cade Bambara's writing and philosophy frame the following readings of intermedia art activism here and over the course of the book because her perspective on cultural work did not differentiate between community service and art-making.

Documentary activist film comes closest to the intentions of SNCC culture workers and offers what Angela Aguayo calls "participatory media culture(s)." Although Aguayo imagines this as a product of the digital age, the concept can be retrofitted to describe what civil-rights-era independent media was trying to do: "wresting back the means of media production and circulation from the hands of the powerful."[16] But that was only a small part of what was important to these groups, according to Varela. The main impulse behind their labor was "representing black people with agency to change their lives through their work."[17] The "participatory commons" Aguayo describes "uses collective social practices of creating, remixing, and sharing documentary recordings as a means of engaging publics," and furthering this, the "documentary commons is a critical site of intervention where the underrepresented confront the structures of power."[18] To Aguayo's definition, I would add *participatory instruction*, a collaborative approach to creating models for and advice-giving on the *how* of social change. Independent media initiatives prove that participatory media cultures existed before the digital age. It was not technology that created the commons but rather the commons that determined what the digital age would look like. Part of this history, which Aguayo ties into financial funding from the nation-state, should also consider the ingenious ways people have made documentaries happen with few resources.

The development of new forms of communication emerged in collaboration with farmers and local people about *how they wanted to be represented*. By listening, activists embraced the experimental possibilities enabled by independent media and by developing a new communication modality for people of color through intermedia. The term *intermedia* emerges contemporaneously to the production of the filmstrips, even though the circumstances surrounding the civil-rights-era South were very different from those of the art world of New York City.[19] Even though intermedia has its own set of definitions and counterdefinitions in art history, José Esteban Muñoz reclaims the term as an analytic method for queer cultural production of the late 1960s and early 1970s.[20] His definition aligns with the ways in which the SNCC collaborations functioned in the South and in California, because of the potential of intermedia art to disregard the conventions of any singular medium and because of its emergence within relational networks. "This intermedia process," Muñoz claims, "leads to a perpetual unfinished system that is by its very nature antisystemological, and thus analogical to the preidentitarian moment in which I am so interested."[21] The unfinished system does not solely mean incomplete here; it also means that there is no defined circle that closes off collaboration. Rather, the network of collaborations and contributions to a single work of art sprawls out infinitely. Muñoz sees within intermedia art a representation of this network and "a radical understanding of interdisciplinarity" grounded in a "communal vibe."[22] The communality becomes a part of the work itself as a manifestation and reflection of the network that created it.

Muñoz's term also feels apt because it couches intermedia within performance, not only in a literal sense (that intermedia often accompanies performance) but also in a relational one, which exposes the way process can be performative. One example is the process of making the filmstrips engage in performative listening on behalf of SNCC cultural workers. They recorded the farmers telling their stories, so that the narrative could also be their own. Listening became iterative of what Diana Taylor calls "an act of solidarity as in responding to, showing up, and standing with."[23] Taylor's definition of *¡presente!* emphasizes the importance of presence as a "commitment to witnessing," even when that means forgoing narrative control so that farmers could articulate what was important to them. The process was second nature to activists such as Varela, but worth emphasizing because too often documentary efforts begin with a predetermined narrative rather than deep listening practices. Through community-generated narratives, Varela and others created a method of intimate witnessing that presented the stories of local people without overwriting them. The process of witnessing extends to the audience, who listens to a performer reading the script or reads the farmers' words in their booklet. The reader vocalizes the collective "we" in order to make familiar the act of cooperating by performing a shared identity. As a strategy of activism, intimacy-making can redefine one's relationship to work through creative collaboration, in this case, the process of cooperating with others.

In the same way *inter*media suggests a different relationality than multimedia, I use *inter* not as a substitute for multipurpose art, but rather to indicate another approach to purpose or use that brings teaching, protest, and aesthetics into relationship with one another. Emerging from the *aesthetics of obligation*, a term inspired by the creative collaboration between Toni Morrison and Toni Cade Bambara, inter*purpose* art signifies the multilayered uses of cultural activism that are bound together through relationships. Though all art possesses the potential to generate a multiplicity of meanings, interpurpose art serves multiple purposes simultaneously, such as storytelling and job training. SNCC cultural workers repurposed projectors as both educators and artists, combining two intentions: to innovate education through storytelling and, in turn, to innovate art by making visual storytelling instructional, building a relationship between instruction and aesthetics.[24] By nature of its process, intermedia art establishes a network of obligations to others, which opens the door to appreciate how cultural activism centered aesthetic principles around economic uplift for poor people.

The independent intermedia art of the civil rights movement offers evidence of intimacy-making between cultural workers and local people, and their relational network. The intermedia works discussed in this chapter reframe Black southern identity beyond the images of oppression found in mainstream media, reorienting one's consciousness to make new connections between Black and Brown people and how they move, work, and thrive in rural spaces. Aside from the filmstrips, I analyze Charlie Cobb's intermedia poetry collection *Furrows*, published by SNCC's Flute Publications. *Furrows* overlays poetry and SNCC photography to create a dialogue between words, images, and the publication process. The independent publishing collective was founded by Varela, Cobb, and Jane Stembridge, with the title inspired by the latter's poetry collection, *I Play Flute*, in which poems such as "The Flute" and "Mrs. Hamer" created space for reflection amid the whirlwind of activism. The final section describes an episode of the short-lived broadcast *Nation Time*, which emerged from the Free Southern Theater's collective in New Orleans. It was the only episode available to me from their archive and shapes how I imagine their other episodes. The collection of media discussed here imperfectly represents a larger body of work beyond the scope of this chapter, such as Matt Herron's Southern Documentary Project, Highlander Research and Education Center's "media justice," and Appalshop's community-based documentary program. It also stands in for the many unfinished or unpublished media projects of the civil rights movement, including those of Southern Media, which gets an interlude tribute later on in the chapter.

Intermedial Actions: SNCC's Filmstrips

Something of Our Own begins with a petition from Black farmers in Panola County to Mr. Jacobs, the white buyer, asking more money for their okra, hoping for 5–8 cents a pound. Mr. Jacobs refuses, so soon after they decide to try to create a cooperative that releases them from their dependency on white intermediaries between farmers and the market. Even though the slideshow portrays Mr. Jacobs as a real person in a photograph, he is quickly cartoonized as Mr. Charlie, the classic caricature of white supremacy. An illustration shows a farmer throwing off a shackle toward Mr. Charlie, claiming "Freedom Now," while the title below states, "We need to quit depending on Mr. Charley."[25] Rather than the typical image of the violent white oppressor, "Mr. Charley" looks down at the shackle, confused and disappointed. The cooperative challenges the white supremacist tactic to developed during slavery: to keep the workforce uninformed, silent, and invisible. However, rather than direct action against the white buyers, the farmers remove themselves from the equation and instead begin to grow and sell their own okra. Images of white men in the photographs and illustrations show them confused and disgruntled, rather than violent, as the Black okra farmers continue to develop their cooperative.

Something of Our Own and the *Farm Worker's Strike* both center farmers because of the values inherent to both SNCC and the United Farm Workers union. Agriculture represents one of the most oppressed workforces and difficult to organize sectors of labor in this country. If methods of agricultural organizing fail, it is because the entire enterprise of farming was designed to maintain an exploitative work structure that keeps people of color landless, in debt, and unable to organize for better working conditions. The filmstrips resonate in their themes and this message: that economic autonomy is possible and available to all *if they cooperate or unionize*. They celebrate successful labor organization against a system that upheld white supremacy in the form of land ownership in the Delta and the San Joaquin Valley, emphasizing the technological innovations that made mobilization possible. The filmstrips send a powerful visual message that counteracts visuals of poor, Black sharecroppers and migrant laborers, which reify Black and Brown farmers as always being poor and existing outside of modernity.

Neither *Something of Our Own* nor *Farm Worker's Strike* neglects the reality of encounters with white supremacist violent opposition, but the focus remains centered on the technologies of economic reform: How can one build a cooperative? What are the necessary support systems for a strike? If mainstream media coverage of the civil rights movement famously centered on spectacle, the demystification work of the SNCC filmstrips undoes spectacle by clearly explaining how to organize. The resistance and circumvention of white supremacy happens not as a grand gesture but as a noniconic everyday occurrence. In this version of direct action, the farmers work toward self-sufficiency and internal support. Black farmers and migrant farmworkers use technology as part of their skilled labor despite a system designed to fail them. The media design amplified the voices of those trying to reform neglected and exploitative systems of labor while offering visuals to a wider public largely unaware of what okra farming or grape harvesting looked like. These visuals communicated pride and skill in agricultural labor, a counternarrative to the history of agriculture in the United States and its exploitation of Black and Brown people.

Scholars of the U.S. South have repeatedly debunked the myth of an antimodern South, exposing this narrative as part of an overly romanticized vision of the region, or as part of a national project to avoid addressing broader complicity in slavery and the failure of Reconstruction. Too easily, people viewed Black sharecroppers or Brown migrant workers as a natural part of the landscape instead of part of an intentional design backed by policy, such as the Bracero Program. Ben Child traces the "dense and peculiar history of modernization" in the South, arguing that "while tenancy [sharecropping] in the period wasn't exclusive to the South . . . it lingers in the popular imagination as a mostly southern phenomenon."[26] Child cites the photography of Walker Evans and Dorothea Lange as a source of this tenacity, and indeed, those photographers are cited with more frequency in activist photography than SNCC's cultural workers. Raiford argues that at times SNCC also propagated this narrative in some of their photographs, as specifically one by Danny Lyon in which the camera looks down on a Black farmer and another photograph of a lynching with the title *Mississippi*, both of which were turned into posters.

The filmstrips center the details of labor, such as the perfect shape of a marketable okra and workers' daily life. Inspiration comes from the incredible stories of these farmers but also from the teachable skills communicated through the medium. The series on film reveals images of agency and joy that act as a counternarrative to mainstream media's denigrating portrayal of agricultural workers, poor people, and rural life. They project an image of rural modernity beyond the Delta in two ways: through farm machinery and by harnessing media technology. Moreover, they present rural modernity as Black owned and operated. For farmers in *Something of Our Own*, this includes the combines and pickers that they were able to buy collectively as a cooperative rather than purchase as individual farm owners. Claude Weaver illustrates this message of collective power in a slide showing a sole farmer buckling under the weight of a machine with the script stating, "They say farmers are independent and hard to get together. Well, there comes a time when you're too small to stand alone."[27] In the following slide, the farmer is joined by other farmers and is able to lift the machine, while the script claims that now is the time for cooperation. *Something of Our Own* makes clear that the path toward empowerment requires collective action and that economic uplift cannot be an individual endeavor—busting the capitalist myth that any single person working hard enough can accrue wealth.

Farm machinery marks a pathway for uplift and possibility as the farmers exclaim, "When we put our first picker in the field it was something

Figure 14. Farm machinery from *Something of Our Own*, produced by Maria Varela. The Doris A. Derby Papers, Stuart A. Rose Special Collections at Emory University, Atlanta.

to see. No more crawling for us—we're riding now!"[28] In the sequence of images, the farmer moves from the position of picking cotton to operating a machine high above the fields. The images welcome technology as an agent in the cooperative: combines and pickers make farming more profitable and sustainable, photography and projectors enable farmers to communicate their message on their own terms, and the economic technology of forming a cooperative challenges white economic dominance. However, farm machinery carries a complicated past because of how it rendered jobs obsolete and acted as one of the forces that produced the Great Migration to the North for job opportunity. Rather than trying to uproot or change the entire system of agriculture in the U.S., cooperatives such as the West Batesville Farmer's Cooperative were adopting methods to build capital within the okra and cotton markets that could have a "communal vibe," to use Muñoz's phrase. The economics of cooperatives were complex and provocative, as they encouraged a Black and Brown separatist economy that would challenge white supremacy while participating in the market. However, from a community basis, the sharing of equipment, information, and money required a degree of intimacy and trust that operates directly against individualistic capitalism. The farmers reference individualism in the slideshow as something they've overcome.

Through collaboration, farmers creatively used the technology initially designed to render them obsolete as a pathway out of exploitative labor. Similarly, in the second part of *Farm Worker's Strike*, the script explains how farmworkers used cars and SNCC-donated two-way radios: "We wait for our scout cars to radio back to the office when they find scab workers."[29] Even though they explain how radio acts as a tool of protection, they also use the same modes of transportation, communication, and surveillance as the police and ranchers. In the image, the farmworker holding the radio stands high above a field with images of scab workers in the distance. Instead of using weapons of coercion, the farmworkers project their voices to convert the scabs to the union, appealing to their conscience. A photograph of a striker on the roof of a truck shouting through a bullhorn accompanies the text: "Our work every day is to move around from field to field, trying to talk the workers out of the field to come join us in the strike."[30] The interplay between uses of technology emphasizes the repurposing of tools of oppression as a step toward liberation. These tools might not dismantle the master's house, but they opened the creative potential to make a house of one's own.

Beyond the practical uses of combines and radios, farmworkers were also reworking the economic technologies of sharecropping and migrant labor that dominated the Mississippi Delta and the San Joaquin Valley. Again, this comes up against a complex history of race and labor: as Leigh Anne Duck argues, "While blackness is mobilized by governments as a technology for dividing a population and disenfranchising a labor force, it also serves to assemble people with experiences and memories that attune them to local and global injustice."[31] For farmers in the South, the cooperative structure reimagined labor through Black ownership, innovating how people worked in relation to each other. The script and images instruct the viewer on this history: "The rancher pays maybe 50 cents a box. But he doesn't pay it to us. He pays it to the contractor. The contractor gives only 20 or 35 cents a box and keeps the rest for himself."[32] And with *Something of Our Own*, Weaver's illustrations walk the viewer through the dynamics of selling okra on the open market and the benefits of getting early contracts from buyers. By simplifying the complex, illustrations dismantle one of the main tools of white supremacist capitalism: the confusing economics of the market and the strategy of keeping workers ignorant of their potential collective power. In *Farm Worker's Strike*, unraveling these systems of exploitation still remains secondary to a joyful emphasis on skilled labor as they developed a consciousness-raising

Figure 15. Child jumping from *Farm Worker's Strike*, photo by George Ballis. Produced by Maria Varela. The Doris A. Derby Papers, Stuart A. Rose Special Collections at Emory University, Atlanta.

technique that highlights practices such as correct pruning: "If you don't cut the vines in the right places, they will die."[33] The use of "you" as a directive suggests the teachability of the narrative, and the series of photographs in this section on labor contain close-ups, which illustrate their lessons and showcase the care of their work, as in one frame where a worker bends over barbed wire to prune in just the right spot.

Both filmstrips engage with the impact on children and how they are incorporated into labor at the expense of their education. The West Batesville farmers see this as an investment not necessarily for capital returns but in their children's future. Formerly, their children had to go to school "split session" in order to pick cotton during the harvest: "Knowing that our children would be in school and that probably just one or two people would be home to pick the cotton—that was when we thought about going together and buying some cotton pickers and combines." The farmers communicate lesser-known obstacles to equality such as access to advanced farming equipment. This broadens the scope of what we think of as barriers to education, revealing how deeply systemic racism can be. *Farm Worker's Strike* discusses the generational cycle of migrant labor within the same process of awareness, claiming, "The children we have now will never have the education they need to have a better life than we had. They'll have to drop out of school and help support their families."[34] However, rather than an image of a child being exploited for their labor, George Ballis's photograph shows a young person performing a high jump over some makeshift equipment. The pole is held up with nails in posts, and the child clears the pole shoeless onto a dilapidated mattress. We witness a very American scene of collegiate competition in the unlikely place of a labor camp. The image offers a message of hope and carries with it a subtle suggestion that the children of farmworkers could outcompete others through their innovation and resilience. What holds back poor children, the photograph argues, is circumstance rather than lack of skill or talent. Unlike the exploitative images we associate with photography of migrant labor, both filmstrips prove that images of joy and hope can still be effective vectors of consciousness-raising.

The photograph of the jumping child is symbolic of the creative potential of repurposing, a value integral to the cultural activism of SNCC workers. Their intermedial experiments with filmstrips repurposed projectors into an artistic medium, while also improving their capacity to educate others. The collaboration between activists and local people transformed a projector from a machine designed to standardize education into a tool inviting audiences to be cocreators. Their repurposing better aligned with Varela's teaching values by transforming farmers into visual-oral storytellers through their collaboration with photographers. By not including audio, the collaborators invited audiences to be active, not passive, witnesses by reading the script. This was an economic necessity before it ever could be an artistic one—they did not have the right audio equipment. Yet, as I've argued throughout this book, economic constraint does not override the possibility for artistic analysis. Their process signifies a larger improvisational and aspirational imperative: doing what they could to document the lives of others and in the process creating a new method of documentary.

SNCC's filmstrips have not yet been considered within the artistic innovations of performance art in the 1960s in which the projector was used as a method to combine visual media with performance. In this emerging scene, visual artists collaborated with dancers, such as Dan Graham and Simone Forti, to create intermedia experiences that brought the projected image together with the body. Chrissie Iles, writing about Graham and Forti's collaboration, claims, "The presence of the body as a major component of projective installations of the 1960s and 1970s emerged in part from the breaking down of boundaries between disciplines that has occurred in stages through-out the twentieth century and reached its apogee in the 1960s," which con-tributed influences to the now-canonical Fluxus and Judson Dance Theater.[35] Multidisciplinarity has multivalent roots in the worlds of art and perfor-mance, of course, but shares a history with activist strategy, from which many of these innovations emerge. Rather than Graham and Forti, there is a stron-ger connection between the SNCC slideshows and Nan Goldin's *The Ballad of Sexual Dependency* slideshows of the 1980s, made in collaboration with a community of queers, misfits, and sex workers who through Goldin's camera understood how their lives and stories could be art. *Something of Our Own* represents the same quick and dirty assemblage of equipment access, innova-tion, and collective curation as Goldin's slideshows and also challenges the divide between the base reaches of "low" politics and "good art" that Aguayo observes as a tension dismantled by activist documentary.[36] The aesthetics expressed within SNCC's projects present something as common as dirt as valuable and beautiful when for so long it had been coupled with oppres-sion and trauma. The interpurpose of these projections seeks to document a community *while also* offering the community they document the joy of self-witnessing. In *Something of Our Own* the reenvisioning of agricultural life as desirable and progressive takes equal importance to the need to communicate a political message—care for community becomes part of artistic intent and the message itself.

As a point of departure to other experiments in projection art, the work done in the South confronted the reality of their environments and the expenditure of labor undertaken by activists who were already stretched thin. In her recollection of the making of the filmstrips Varela details the barriers that made the booklet versions of the stories (without the filmstrip compo-nent) more popular:

> The whole front end took probably weeks if not months to do. The images for the strip had to be collected and/or shot or drawn. Then using a copy camera, the images had to be shot in order. If we messed up, we had to start all over again. But once the negative was made, we could produce 20–25 strips in a day at a cost of roughly $1.00 apiece. The other advantage was that with the books, we had to hand-deliver them all over the Black Belt. With filmstrips, we could simply drop them in the mail. What we hadn't anticipated was that not every com-munity could lay their hands on a filmstrip projector. We assumed that schools had them: some did and some didn't.[37]

Cultural work cannot assume a ready and available audience, such as art made in urban areas within artistic communities. So often what shaped the art practice and its product for media experimentation was the distribution of material and creating encounters in rural spaces. Access-oriented art makes access equal to innovation, but so often that means extra labor and logistics. It also means adhering to the desires and needs of their storytellers. When Flute Publications was ready to publish Fannie Lou Hamer's autobiography—created from a recording of her own words—they had to abort the distribution because Hamer did not like the final product.[38] At risk of understatement: true collaboration, built from mutual respect and trust, is hard to do.

When we discuss civil rights art activism next to more canonical works of intermedia, the meaning of art expands to encompass a better range of intents and purposes. Intermedial approaches expanded what art could be, and part of this history includes SNCC's necessity to invent new modes of storytelling as part of nonhierarchical and intimate collaborations. The collaborative art of SNCC activists and farmers would always be interpurpose because it reflected a community of care at the same time it centered getting resources to poor people. The filmstrips evidence how improvisational creativity emerging from necessity could shape the history of art as it serves to raise people's political consciousness. From the constraints of navigating scant resources came an effective way to communicate that reflected the intimate bonds people had with one another.

Southern Media Interlude: A Tribute to Unfinished Projects

The production of the filmstrips happened in a darkroom in Tougaloo Village in Mississippi by Varela and SNCC photographers and Varela had made agreements with Jesse Morris of the Poor People's Corporation, the Cooperative League of the USA, and other SNCC organizers to distribute the booklets and filmstrips. As discussed in the previous chapter, the Poor People's Corporation was founded by Jesse Morris in Mississippi in 1965 and supported by Doris Derby and others. They asserted a vision of an autonomous economy and culture in the South that could exist independently of the mainstream. Like the SNCC photography and communications unit, one of the Poor People's Corporation's units, Southern Media, aspired to find more egalitarian forms of communication, confront alternative forms of literacy, encourage a more positive "self-image," produce a more effective means of instruction, and enable self-expression. In their information pamphlet, they argue that "movies will not save the world, nor even white and black Americans, but they can help in the long task of forging a new image for oppressed men and they might help link these men together."[39] The spirit of newness reflects the similar ideas of other independent media organizations and speaks to the way similar avant-garde practices emerge independently based on a set of necessary conditions.

Southern Media began as an initiative in San Francisco between two activist filmmakers, but quickly transitioned to Jackson with a new staff of Derby, Lary Rand, Richard Skinner, Lillie Vaughn, Robert Boyd, Georgia Taylor, Nayo Neyonu, and Shirley Ann Johnson and others who contributed their labor at different times. Similar to the language of SNCC's photography unit, they state, "The basic goal of Southern Media is to create a comprehensive communications channel within the black communities in the South" and "to train local black-folk in the use and operation of these tools in order to spread and maintain the network."[40] The archive exists as a series of small-scale and incomplete projects and seems to have been a passion project of Derby's. They attracted initial success for their portrait photography and activist media work, such as a filmstrip for the Delta Ministry of the National Council of Churches and a silent film on sewage issues for the NAACP Legal Defense Fund. The rest of the projects exist in fragments, such as "A Day in the Life of the USA" filmed in Chicago and featuring Bill Walker's mural *Wall of Truth*. In the archive, this film exists as a few dope sheets and a series of photographs. Another project, which operated at a loss for Southern Media, was a film about the craft cooperatives of the previous chapter with a focus on the Grand Marie Vegetable Cooperative. This exists as a prospectus and some photographs, including one that I used as the cover of this book. Other projects, such as documentaries about the Jackson railroad switching yard, the 1967 Freedom Democratic Party, and hunger in the Delta, would all remain as dreams.

A look at the projected budgets of Southern Media reveals how expensive media projects can be; they range from an undated budget of $76,280.00, with equipment costing over $15,000 and supplies and lab costs at $10,000, to another estimate from 1967–68 for $18,472.50.[41] This was then revised to a more realistic budget from May to December 1968, which came in at $25,580 and seemed to concentrate specifically on the film about the Grand Marie co-op. The numbers tell their own story about cultural work and the price—both literally and in mental labor—of independent media. Lary Rand attributes the inability of Southern Media to complete their projects to the difficulty of "attracting sufficient full-time people to the program."[42] In the interim, they screened entertaining cartoons for children in the morning, which was popular, and educational films in the evening, which did not attract the audience they desired. Rand suggests they wanted to move into filmstrip making and make educational filmstrips about Head Start. The story of Southern Media speaks to a lack of resources that hindered the ability for ideas to flourish into finished products, but their existence proves how important independent media was to the Movement. Funds may have been scarce, but the number of stories needing to be told were unlimited.

Poetic Media and Media Poetics of the Civil Rights Movement

Poetry has always accompanied revolution, and SNCC organizing was no different. Varela, reflecting on the publications of Jane Stembridge and Charlie Cobb, describes Movement writing as "poetry of desperation," reflecting how central necessity was to art-making.[43] Toni Cade Bambara's short story about a cooperative, "The Organizer's Wife," offers a theoretical vision that describes poetry as necessary to organizing in rural areas. Everything Bambara describes in the story comes from a place of desperation, especially keeping up morale through the difficulty of organizing in the rural South. The narrator of the story describes a sound truck that travels throughout the area reading poetry over a loudspeaker. Bambara is acutely aware that politics alone cannot hold a community together, and so the narrator gives credit to a young poet orator "whose poems and tales and speeches delivered from the sound truck had done more to pull the districts together, the women all said, than all the leaflets the kids cluttered the fields with, than all the posters from the co-op's graphic workshop masking the road signs, than all the meetings which not all the folk could get to."[44] Poetry resonates in a way that other political ephemera cannot. Because people cannot always physically gather, poetry must come to them in a manner that rejects institutional art spaces in favor of something mobile, following the example of moveable protests. The sound truck valorizes access, reflecting the aesthetics of obligation as the determining factor for how art gets made and communicated to the people.

Cobb's *Furrows* combines poetry and SNCC photography, detailing the experience of civil rights organizing across many years and locations.[45] *Furrows* carries many stories: the stories of the subjects of the photographs, of photography's importance to SNCC activists, of the need for Black-owned publishing, and of Cobb's experience as a Black, college-educated student from the North living and working in the South. Varela describes the main theme of *Furrows* as "the growth of black identity and a call to move together in that identity" and emphasizes that Cobb's poetry reflects the "coming of age through movement encounters, setbacks, and the reaction of white America."[46] Here, I focus on Cobb's poems in dialogue with images of people in the South and its landscapes and analyze how they dismantle connotations between Black agriculture and disempowerment.

The collection opens with a photograph of a woman standing in a field leaning on a hoe surrounded by others holding farming tools. The photograph taken by Bob Fletcher attempts to form a new connection between Blackness and the southern landscape that suggests autonomy and power. Her body posture suggests impatience, and her look down at the photographer communicates defiance, a performance for and against the camera. Instead of images of destitute poverty or backbreaking labor, we are presented with a body pausing in stillness and a camera perspective that looks up at its subject, who demands respect and acknowledgment. This photo appears twice in the collection, once as one of the title pages alongside an excerpt from "In the Furrows of the World," and then again later in the collection as a full page before the poem in its entirety. The twice-positioned coupling of poem and photograph interlinks them as one, which suggests an intermedial dialogue rather than a privileging of either poetry or image. The poem places agriculture as the nexus of the "black yellow brown / around the world," and the photo places the farmer above the viewer, uplifting the image of the laborer, who looks down at the camera with a smirk of confidence. The poem's present tense, "backs unbend / and bodies stretch," suggests bodies rising in revolution, but the image shows people already standing as if to say: there have always been farmers upright and ready for action, and SNCC has merely showed up to document it.

The photographs connect the poetry more intimately with persons, landscapes, and the photographers who become visual poets when placed alongside Cobb's words. When the narrator uses "we," a bridge forms between Cobb as an educated, middle-class poet and the anonymous subject of Bob Fletcher's photograph. We emerge from dirt, the furrows that indicate a Global South identity based in agricultural economies; "WE / can only be / do / from what we are" because of soil and the growing of food, which is reflective of the movement's emphasis on cooperative farming and food justice.[47] The visual image reframes the Black farmer, and the poetry does not romanticize her experience, but contrafacts agrarianism into a *useable pastoral* for Black folks, what Riché Richardson refers to as "linkages to the Africana South," discussed in the previous chapter.[48] Cobb complements this countervisual with his poetry, offering the reader alternative perspectives on the pastoral: the ties that bind Black identity to the South need not stay fixed within one narrative but are rather a vector for multiplicity that invites an intimate reconnection with place. Later in the collection, we get the full poem that completes the stanza: "we can only be / do / from what we are / what we see," intensifying the verb *to see*, making clear the need for representation of empowered Black agriculture.[49] If what "we" are begins with farming, and if the origins of Blackness in the United States remain tethered to working on Southern land, then those images matter.

As with the filmstrips, countervisual narratives of agricultural labor offer a reminder of the dignity of farming so that a necessary coalition could form between middle-class activists like Cobb and poor sharecroppers. The images, such as that of the farmer leaning on the hoe, conflate with the narrators of poems—not in a way that speaks on behalf of a silent subaltern, but rather crediting the invisible collaborations of *Furrows*. The poem "Starred-Dark Night" (1966) juxtaposes images of people working and intimate portraits taken by Fletcher and Rufus Hinton, and on the last page of the poem appears an image of a dirt road and two people walking, one wearing a handmade Black Panther shirt photographed by Varela. The images alone tell a story that moves from a person bent over picking cotton to marching upright together, complementing the progression of the poem from "where backs / bend / down" to "as backs unbent" on the final page of the poem.[50] Fletcher's photograph of the person picking cotton—which also appears in *Something of Our Own*—accompanies Cobb's words, which almost seem to fall into the trap of romanticizing the oppressed worker, "the pain / of black / Mississippi," where people suffer through winter with "clothes stuffed in the shanty's pores."[51] However, the following page complicates this view with two portraits by Hinton that bring us in closer to the perspective of their subjects, which uses chiaroscuro to obscure their faces, just at the moment in the poem that we begin to hear their thoughts toward social change. The viewer sees mostly shadow on their backlit faces, with minimal highlight. We are reminded—as the poem switches to a more intimate "we" tense—that there is much we do not know about the subjects of this poem and that the collection offers both intimacy and opacity. The second portrait is dark and blurry, and the quality of the photography serves as a reminder of Flute's printing budget and the wear and tear of time in the archive.

In thinking of the duration of image manipulation through media and Blackness, Tavia Nyong'o claims, "I derive my concept of liveness, which I do not consider to be apart from, but rather entangled with, the material qualities of the recording apparatus."[52] While Nyong'o mobilized the cinematic term "crushed black" to bring attention to time and the way Black art comes to be in the world, I see in the material mediations a means of tracing artistic dialogue and intimate exchanges of resources, asking, *how many hands handled these photographs? How many prints and scans and screens stand between us and the original?* As Nyong'o argues, "Instead of gradual revelation, perfect restoration, or the trope of what Heather Love has termed 'emotional rescue' . . . these strategies offer us an alternative I want to call—invoking a long, subterranean tradition of black escape and fugitivity—'dark fabulation.'"[53] Dark fabulation stands in for what can never be truly known or understood about the collaboration that produced *Furrows* and the relationships between the photographers and their subjects. The obscurity of the pair of portraits serves as a reminder about the opacity of the anonymous subjects of the photographs, even ones that *are* clear. Because of its collaborative nature, intermedia art raises these questions about process, the exact kinds of questions SNCC wants us to ask, specifically, *how* things come into existence and whose stories get told.

As the photograph recedes from legibility, the viewer turns to the poem for understanding, but Cobb writes a vague call to action to prepare for what appears to be something impossible. In the poem, a set of parents in the "tremble of ready" say in quotes, "We got to get together," a line resonating with the West Batesville farmers' narrative. That line marks the break in the poem to the block between the two portraits. It's not obvious whether the narrator changes, but the lines are shorter, snippier as the narrator begins: "get a plan / find a way," then Cobb returns to a collective "we" in his narration— "an you / an me / we"—but the dialogue expresses the limits of this coalition as it concludes with a deflating admission "cause everything / that is / is / his / already."[54] It's unclear who owns everything. Is Cobb writing a freedom dream made real and the sharecropper in the poem already owns the world and doesn't yet realize it? Alternatively, "his" could refer to the white power structure, who already owns it all, making a revolution feel futile and all the energy of getting together and ready seem exhausting. We encounter a moment that expresses both a sense of hope and an undercurrent of futility. The ambiguity leaves room for people to work through feelings, even feelings of hopelessness, which of course existed within local people and organizers even if that has not always been represented in the cultural memory of the civil rights movement.

If the cultural worker's role is to bear witness rather than impose change, these collaborations reflect SNCC workers as they reconfigured their role from direct intervention to documentarists in word and image. In their obscurity, the portraits and the poem ask: *What is the point of being seen or understood?* I return to Diana Taylor's "commitment to witnessing" and the question that drives her inquiry: "What can we do when apparently nothing can be done, and doing nothing is not an option?"[55] SNCC's witnessing through intermedial processes, therefore, gestures to the unwitnessed knowledges, strategies, and intimacies of social movement activism. The poemimage relationship calls on its viewer to witness what they can neither fully see nor know.

For Bambara, obligation to others was a philosophy to live out in one's life, and the aesthetics emerging from art produced within this network of care always reflected it. The sound truck she creates in "The Organizer's Wife" symbolizes how outreach and obligation innovated artistic production, a quality that defines cultural work. Intermedia art—whether that be a sound truck in fiction, performance slideshows, or photographic poetry—reflected dialogues between cultural workers and local people. Even though the following section shows how Black independent media aspired toward film and television, Charlie Cobb's collection of poetry and photography and the SNCC-produced collaborative filmstrip performance pieces are intermedial works of their own and represent the new means of communication to which SNCC was truly aspiring toward. As a medium, television offered both a powerful tool of communication and a difficult collaboration to navigate, as I show in the Free Southern Theater's *Nation Time* broadcast and the tension created between independent media content and the expectations of what was supposed to be on television.

Broadcasting Community with *Nation Time*

In 1972, the Free Southern Theater produced a television series called *Nation Time* in collaboration with WYES TV in New Orleans, which aired every other Wednesday night at 10 p.m. and Thursday evenings at 6 p.m.. The Free Southern Theater wanted to communicate to a larger audience and amplify Black-controlled television. *Nation Time* oscillated between entertainment and educational television, and the thirty-minute episode available in the Free Southern Theater archive follows the educational tract, "African Slave Trade to the Civil War," which aired on December 20, 1974. The episode documents the racist foundations of the United States, seeking to contextualize contemporary issues for the Black community of New Orleans and the United States.

Part of *Nation Time*'s method emerged from the struggle to financially support and sustain programming, a saga that unfolds like many other endeavors and shows how thin the Free Southern Theater stretched itself in the late 1960s and '70s. In a 1970 grant proposal to National Educational Television, a suggested pilot showcases their depth of community involvement. Here is a list of what they wanted to film for the pilot: a BLKART-SOUTH tour of Black New Orleans; a segment to showcase their newspaper, the *Plain Truth*; Tom Dent talking about the *Nkombo* journal and "why use and explore all of the arts communication devices"; then Bob Costley discussing his involvement and the writer's workshop; the writer's workshop; a poetry reading with visuals of the city "illustrative of the poems"; then the actor's workshop, theater philosophy, a play, the play's discussion; then the Golden Agers rehearsal at the Guste Homes for seniors; a segment of the theater on the road, then back to New Orleans and "perhaps a final poem."[56] All in a single television show! At this point the author of the proposal makes a direct address to the reader:

> Will the television program be structured just like this? No, man, no. This is FST's FST, and what happens when we shoot the street footage, what happens on the road, what happens when we listen to the crowd in New Orleans and in Mississippi can change it all.[57]

In their vision of what television could be, the Free Southern Theater desired to hold on to the improvisatory and makeshift process of art-making, with a "heavy stress on relation to their community."[58] Their vision was to make recorded television a live process and communicate the *feeling* and *atmosphere* of the Free Southern Theater to a wider audience, rather than any specific political message.

Their lofty aspirations were realized a couple of years later, when WYES, a public broadcasting station in New Orleans, aired the first episode of *Nation Time* on October 11, 1972, hosted by Bill Rouselle, associate producer for the Free Southern Theater. Aside from news analysis by Dick Beverly and cultural reviews by Kalamu Ya Salaam, the show included the band the Meters, interviews with activists, and a poetry reading by Sister Omedele Ra. The change between the proposal and its realization is significant. As the idea moved into fruition, not only did they scale down their ambition, but they also shifted to more expansive representation of the arts community in New Orleans, rather than spotlight Free Southern Theater programming. The Free Southern Theater newsletter article solicits audience feedback, suggestions, and community support. Directly, Rouselle asks, "All too often, Black produced shows suffer from lack of audience response. We are an oral people and while we tell our friends how much we 'dig' this or that, what is really important is that we tell the stations."[59] Rouselle claims the moment as being "on the threshold of a communications revolution," and reminds the community of their responsibility in maintaining the momentum.[60]

In a summary of the inaugural meeting of the "FST Production Staff Group" meeting in December 1973, there is a definite shift from focusing on theater to media: "The concern is centered in the production activities because these are the primary means we have of reaching the public."[61] One of the main focuses included a special events program for "Black musical expression" where they could merge political content with music. *Nation Time*'s goal was to "use T.V. magazine format to provide information and direction to Black folk in the region, based on our analysis of present conditions and possible solutions," but then they revised this to better articulate their main purpose: "To use T.V. magazine format to clarify the class nature of the problems confronting Black people in the region, and to heighten awareness of the leadership role we must play in finding and implementing solutions to these problems" and feature "the most dominant aspects of class struggle & efforts toward national liberation."[62] As they moved toward fulfilling those ideals, the show leaned into educational programming and consciousness-raising.

In "African Slave Trade to the Civil War," *Nation Time* detailed a critical approach to American history with sources from John Hope Franklin, William Foster, and Joanne Grant to compile a history of the foundation of the United States from a Black Marxist perspective. This episode is the second in a series of educational lectures about Black history, informing audiences about stories not covered in traditional schools. Opening with Frederick Douglass's "What to a Slave Is the Fourth of July," hosts Bill Rouselle and Jeannette Williams conclude the lecture-style show by redefining the Civil War as "the final stage of the American bourgeois democratic revolution."[63] Rouselle and Williams offer a direct and somewhat dry and monotone delivery of the historical information. Even though at times they intersperse images, the majority of the episode displays Williams and Rouselle in their seats speaking directly to the camera or reading from a script as they deliver the lecture.

This episode deviates from the magazine-style format the Free Southern Theater discussed in their proposals and earlier episodes and their desire to have the camera out in the streets, rather than in the studio. In a memo introducing *Nation Time*'s third season, Rouselle states that the past two years of

Nation Time "fell far short of the type of programming we fought for in the community participation in the media struggles of a couple of years ago. This year, I feel, we can present a television production which serves a concrete need."[64] While Rouselle's language is vague, it seems that *Nation Time* made an intentional change in their formatting. Despite the memo's enthusiasm for the change, on the actual episode, the concluding segment addressed criticism from the public that the show was "too intellectual," and its hosts were "too much like school teachers and professors."[65] In addition to complaints from the show's audience, they also mention that the station suggested a "less consistently political program."[66]

While Williams agreed to offering a less pedantic approach, she defended the more serious and sober nature of the revised format for the show, stating, "We feel Blacks have been entertained and have entertained up to here [holds hand up to neck]."[67] *Nation Time*'s producers decided to slow down and educate, making a political statement in their decision to *not entertain*. In their serious delivery, Rouselle and Williams engage with the Black performance tradition of inexpression, what Tina Post refers to as the "the realm of deadpan aesthetics," and describes as embodying "artistic gestures that trade in a combination of visibility and withholding, especially but not exclusively, the withholding of facial expression."[68] Through their deadpan delivery of the lecture, they grated against the expected format for the medium of television and subverted what television is supposed to do and be. They commit to a plain, straightforward delivery that places knowledge above style and deliver a "restorative performance," one that reframes television with unsmiling faces, looking into the camera and telling the truth.[69] It bears the right to be unadorned, quotidian, and noniconic. Once we learn that the station has complained about *Nation Time*'s programming, Williams and Rouselle's discomfort and their stoicism also becomes a resistance to WYES and the ways in which they are asked to move, smile, perform, and entertain.

The moment reaches back toward the earliest iteration of the theater, when they staged Samuel Beckett's *Waiting for Godot* and contrafacted Beckett's script to push back against images of Black minstrelsy and the expectations of how Black bodies should perform through their serious delivery of the play. *Nation Time* continues this tradition by making television an educational and revolutionary platform and creating public education coming from the community. Rouselle offers his own response, detailing three phases of Black media: being overlooked, being ridiculed, and being regulated. He claims on the show that they are currently in the third phase and that they intend to push back on this regulation. They directly address the issue of media and communication, quoting a recent article in *Black Scholar*, which states: "It is not in the interest of the U.S. ruling class to allow a true picture of the lives of the masses of people: Black, Asian, Chicano, Native American, Puerto Rican, or white to be presented to this country. Such truth would provide too great a push to the already ongoing struggle of the people to end their exploitation and oppression."[70] Rouselle and Williams justify their position to continue educational programming with the hope that recounting a direct and honest history of the U.S. might be the great push needed for liberation. Their experiment in media doesn't push technical innovation or visual effects forward artistically, but, rather, asserts their obligation to their community as more important than conventions of format or the expectations of the station. Television, thus, becomes part of the interpurpose nature of art activism: it is for joy and pride in community, it is for history told by Black people, and it is a means for open dialogue with the people of New Orleans. The episode ends with another call for feedback and commentary, asking people to contact both WYES and the Free Southern Theater. Following the tradition of their theater, the television show invites dialogue and active participation; it is not a passive medium for being entertained.

In the middle of a twenty-six-week production schedule, WYES cancelled *Nation Time*. In a press release, the Free Southern Theater comments, "We contend that the cancellation is an effort to censor information and to eliminate a point of view which is in the interest of the broad masses of working people, the poor and particularly oppressed Black people, and not the narrow interest of the WYES board of trustees and station management."[71] Their statement places fault on the station and not the public, suggesting that the public was in favor of the programming, for both entertainment and education. The memo deconstructs the board of trustees and station management to show how they do not in fact represent the public, because their composition does not reflect the public, which in New Orleans, they write, is "predominantly poor, working people and at least 45% Black." After indicting the station's leadership, they contextualize the cancellation as "part of the general trend in the electronic media to eliminate programming which seeks to present the truth about the present crisis in American society" and the media's continued support of situation comedies, such as *The Jeffersons* and *Chico and the Man*.[72] In the memo, they do not reject these comedies, but remind viewers of their ability to "detour our minds off sincere efforts to bring about progressive social change." They argue for an actual diversity of programming that can hold space for Black entertainment and Black-centered education. *Nation Time*'s struggle with WYES and inability to stay on the air reveal the limitations of media activism to collaborate with mainstream broadcasting efforts, even public stations.

Independent publishing of intermedia intermedia art proved that there was an audience for such works, and had better funds and support been available, there would have been a flourishing of experimental and independent media in the South. The fact that Charlie Cobb's *Furrows* sold out its first printing proves the desire for a community to have access to independent publications. Perhaps if organizations such as Southern Media could have been supported enough to thrive, *Nation Time* might have been able to be hosted independently under their own auspices. The archives of cancelled programs, incomplete films, and unpublished projects call on us to continue the imagination work of what could have been possible, so that we might look at the contemporary landscape, currently undergoing its own media revolution, and ask what could be different. However, in the following conclusion to this book, I do not have to imagine an alternative future of activist art because contemporary organizations have proven the longevity of art grounded in social justice. Instead of concentrating on genealogies of influence, I mobilize *emergence*, a term adapted from adrienne maree brown's *Emergent Strategy*, to trace evidence of carework that has sustained networks and spaces over time so that, even without direct connection to civil rights groups, the tenets of cultural activism—improvisation, intimacy-making, and community collaboration—continue to flourish.

Conclusion

The Open Channel of Cultural Activism

> This is not ancestor worship, it is the lineage of art.
> It is not so much influence as connection.[1]
> —Jeanette Winterson

Regeneration and Emergence

In late November 1985, the Free Southern Theater staged their final performance, *A Valediction Without Mourning: The Role of Art in the Process of Social Change*,[2] in the style of a New Orleans funeral. Theater groups from around the country, artists, writers, community activists, and people from the neighborhood took it to the streets to commemorate the Free Southern Theater's "death" with a multiday series of performances, talks, and strategies for the future. For the funeral procession, an empty coffin with a mirrored bottom was brought in, and participants were "instructed to bring things signifying their relationship to the role of the arts in the process of social change to put in the coffin."[3] The body of the Free Southern Theater became a collective memory for living groups around the country. The band played "We Shall Overcome" while performers acting as pallbearers lifted the box to carry it across Congo Square and Louis Armstrong Park. Using the process of a second line, which celebrates life in the process of mourning death, they invited the audience to witness continuity through regeneration. This ritual did more than mourn the end of the Free Southern Theater; it celebrated the continued life of the other activist theater groups and organizations that gathered together around the conference and performance. *A Valediction Without*

Mourning recognized not death, but the future of cultural activism, inviting us to celebrate the dying out of organizations as an act of necessary growth.

In this book, I have traced intimacies shared by cultural workers in their artistic processes with attention to the *aesthetics of obligation*—the commitments cultural workers hold to each other and their communities, which shape their art and transform their lives. Through my analysis of cultural activism, I've expanded the aesthetics of obligation beyond Toni Morrison's description of Toni Cade Bambara's cultural work and toward a framework that unfolds the *interpurpose* nature of civil-rights-era art activism. And now I turn to what obligation looks like across generations and between organizations on a scale encompassing the decades after the civil rights movement. Cultural workers of the Movement built the foundation for future cultural activism in the feminist practice of carework, which nurtures the conditions for sustainability and allows organizations to dissolve when the moment calls for it. The Free Southern Theater thrived for as long as it did due to the active and often invisible labor of its participants, efforts that overlapped into other organizations and created an organic transference of ideas and strategies that could adapt to different contingencies and communities. Because of those sustained efforts, the spirit of the civil rights movement continues into today's organizations, collectives, and communities, especially in the South. Through the second line, *A Valediction Without Mourning* honored and celebrated the carework of cultural activism, which included letting their organization die so that it might regenerate in a new form.

In *Emergent Strategy*, adrienne maree brown describes the evolution of organizations as naturally derived, arguing that, because nothing in nature is disposable, "the cycle of life ultimately makes use of everything" and invites humans to participate in the cycle of destruction and regeneration by making use of the past.[4] Her definition of resilience starts with what's already been happening in nature and extends to the possibility for activism to reinvent itself over time. The spontaneous regeneration of patterns and textures of cultural work are *emergences* from what has come before, and, like in nature, networks and pathways siphon resources to nurture fledgling forms to fruition.

Paradoxically, emergences are both organic occurrences and strategically designed tactics. In her essay on Black Lives Matter protests and performance, Daphne Brooks theorizes on the continuity of activist forms by excavating Movement-era civil disobedience with the contemporary protests in the wake of Oscar Grant and Trayvon Martin. Brooks observes how the prone bodies of both young Black boys and the Black Lives Matter protestors resonate with the tactics of civil rights movement activists and the long history of laying one's body on the line in the name of civil disobedience. Channeling Imani Owens, Brooks brings in Zora Neale Hurston's reading of Black dance as "dynamic suggestion" and bridges the "compelling insinuation" of Black dance with the way others have answered or contributed to the suggestion over time. This reading calls attention to the *gestures* of protest as a vehicle for meaning and dialogue. Reading across time, Brooks quotes Hurston, who says, "That is the very reason the spectator is held so rapt. He is participating in the performance himself—carrying out the suggestion of the performer."[5] In her writing, Brooks inhabits "the realm of non-standard, civil disobedience time" by carrying a through line of emergences from the Harlem Renaissance, the civil rights movement, and Black Lives Matter protests.[6] In an intellectual dialogue with Fred Moten, Brooks opens channels of "sonic resonance" in the civil disobedience timescape and brings together crossover between sound and poetics, between then, now, and future.

In a way, *A Valediction Without Mourning* centers death in response to the proliferation of rituals with which Black communities confront grief, which because of the historical continuities of being "in the wake" of colonization and slavery bear the weight of injustice.[7] Through the sonic resonance of the second line, the inequities of how people live and die reverberate. Without disrespect for human life, the Free Southern Theater contrafacts, or radically adapts, this format as a new way to pay tribute to an arts organization, one that could also emotionally process the grief around transitions and the bitter knowledge that conditions of loss are too often brought about by systemic underfunding and devaluing. In the middle of the 1980s, the Free Southern Theater bridges past and future through the combination of joy and grief that accompanies cultural work. Honoring the death of a single organization could reaffirm the ongoing cyclical life of civil disobedience and cultural work. The performance's dynamic suggestion calls on future generations to reimagine the methods and processes of the Free Southern Theater, not through repetition or replication, but through the growth of new ideas. What endures, therefore, does not have to be about direct influence, but continuing that initial energy that searched for new forms and aesthetics that could bring about social transformation.

With what method do we discuss artistic *afterlives* in "civil disobedience time"? In writing about activism, it's tempting to assert a value-based assessment between then and now and argue that today's organizations should learn from the past or that the civil rights movement was merely the groundwork for a more evolved approach to mobilization. However, people were then, as they are now, imperfect, and even though there have been obvious improvements in, for example, approaches to gender equality and sexuality, there are many ongoing issues with funding streams, identity, and equity that feel timeless in the narrative of activist organizations in the United States. Rather than a comparative approach, this conclusion traces the patterns that emerge from the falling apart and coming back together of social-justice-oriented arts organizations. Emergence asks us not to trace lineage through direct connection, but rather through gestural impressions that have survived historical erasure and forgetting, what Diana Taylor calls the repertoire. This means tracing methods of cultural work that reappear over time, even if they have little direct connection with any specific civil rights movement organization.

Doing so better reflects a decentralized, abundant movement of living ideas that reveal the intricacies of the network from which they came. Through the archive of finished and unfinished artistic expression, we can trace fragments of a network and honor the labor of cultural workers, even if it's impossible to make direct connections. The invisibility of this kind of work makes emergence look like happy accidents or spontaneous convergences, yet, even without a direct genealogy of influence, we can still honor the many cultural workers who have sustained spaces where both social justice and creativity can flourish.[8] Just because it's untraceable doesn't mean a network didn't exist that could connect methods, ideas, and resources.

By moving away from the genealogy of influence as a method, *emergence* emphasizes a set of conditions from which certain strategies become necessary. The historic continuity of resource scarcity for artists in historically marginalized communities demands a resourcefulness, which seems to emerge organically, but actually points toward social inequity. For example, the history of theaters that communicate current events to their audiences—such as the Living Newspapers of the 1930s or El Teatro Campesino's acto *Governor Brown*—emerges from the lack of news media that speaks to the community, more so than a chain of artistic influence from the Soviet Blue Blouse theater. The jazz aesthetic of improvising and repurposing reveals a framework of underfunding as much as it argues for creativity. Their brilliant workarounds emerge as a necessary reaction to a society that has devalued or exploited the lives and communities of artists of color.

The temporality of civil disobedience moves art away from paradigms of influence and, as Jeanette Winterson claims in the epigraph to this chapter, focuses on connection. Among the many organizations that have emerged in the wake of civil-rights-era art activism, I listen to the sonic resonance of method and practice across three. The first is a Texas-based performance collective, the Austin Project, whose *jazz aesthetic* method manifests the Free Southern Theater's "dynamic suggestion" to create transformative theater modeled after jazz structures. The second is another Texas-based performance collective organized by Irma Mayorga and Virginia Grise, who produced *The Panza Monologues*, a piece created in collaboration with the San Antonio Chicanx community. They developed a method of collective storytelling grounded in social justice, building on a world envisioned through El Teatro Campesino's practice, but committing to processes of protection for the women sharing their life experiences. The third and final organization is not a theater or performance group, but a social justice-oriented farming collective, Soul Fire Farm in upstate New York, which centers on cooperative farming and food justice. Like the Poor People's Corporation and SNCC, Soul Fire Farm brings together cultural work, education, and cultivation as necessary parts of its mission. Each of these examples opens channels of resonance across time based on the aesthetics of obligation and intimacy-making central to this book. They bring together the "compelling insinuation" of performance and the responses of people who heard the message and carried it out without missing a beat. As artifacts, such as songs, ideas, and performances, are reprised, adapted, and contrafacted over time, they reveal imprints of the relationships formed through art-making.

The Unbroken Circle and the Jazz Aesthetic: The Austin Project

In the years of their production and transformation, the Free Southern Theater inspired cultural organizations that experimented with democratic practices and wanted to tell stories of their communities, culminating in organizations such as the Southern Black Cultural Alliance and BLKARTSOUTH, and literary collectives such as *Nkombo*, a black owned and operated literary journal, and the Blk Mind Jockeys, to name a few. Their endeavors were Black-focused, but not exclusively so. John O'Neal founded Junebug Productions, a theater group that continues the vein of social justice performance practice in present-day New Orleans. Junebug Productions has collaborated with a plethora of theater groups claiming a variety of regional and ethnic identities. A long-term collaboration with Roadside Theater, an Appalachia-based theater and media collective, worked on productions designed to combat racism and continue the civil-rights legacy of interracial cultural activism. Alternate ROOTS, which previously stood for Regional Organization of Theaters South, was founded at Highlander Center in Tennessee and continues to fund and empower creative work grounded in social justice in the southern region of the U.S. James Smethurst recognizes the work of the larger southern network as providing "influential arts elders in their communities and across the region long after the heyday of the Black Arts."[9] Even though many other organizations in the lineage of the Free Southern Theater did not survive into the twenty-first century, Smethurst calls attention to impact *beyond survival*, claiming, "there is a certain sense in which Black Arts, the communities it nurtured, and its sensibilities endure in New Orleans to the present."[10]

Within Junebug, O'Neal established the Story Circle, a methodology emerging from community-based practice that creates space for intimate connection through storytelling. Participants hold space for each other's stories, while also listening to and building off the previous story. Through this improvisational technique, the group becomes more intimate with one another as their stories knit together a connected narrative unique to that moment and group. This practice combines the egalitarianism of participatory democracy and generative collaboration. On the Junebug website, O'Neal describes the method as a way of being in the world, claiming, "The rules of the Story Circle are the rules of civil participation in society. You agree to listen. You agree to respect."[11] Listening and improvising emerge from the civil rights ethos of participatory democracy; however, they evolve into their own tactics in the world of artic collectives that want to challenge hierarchies in the creative process.

Bearing this in mind, the Austin Project, a collective theater group founded in 2002 by Omi Osun Joni L. Jones, exists just beyond a direct connection to the Free Southern Theater. Yet they developed a similar method with their Finding Voice circle, a closed-group gathering for vulnerability and generative sharing. Like the Story Circle, the Finding Voice circle creates a space for intimacy-making between participants and, because the participants of the Austin Project are majority women of color, the Finding Voice circle finds kinship with the consciousness-raising power of the rap sessions of the 1970s, such as recorded in Toni Cade Bambara's *The Black Woman* anthology. Yet, as a theater practice, the Finding Voice circle also shares the generative possibilities of the Story Circle and the jazz methodologies of the Free Southern Theater, leaning into the workshop model as "a training ground and method rather than a space specifically designed to raise questions and showcase art."[12] What emerged in Austin was more a process-oriented theater to which the Free Southern Theater aspired and helped pave the way for. The Finding Voice circle opens spaces for artistic experimentation through intimate sharing and trust. The intention of the theater is to engage in social transformation, both in the community and on the campus of the University of Texas. The Austin Project cites contemporaneous projects such as Anna Deavere Smith's Institute on the Arts and Civic Dialogue, June Jordan's Poetry for the People, and the Animating Democracy Initiative, which supported work "stimulating meaningful dialogue between audiences and art makers."[13] Smith's and Jordan's initiatives were aligned with institutions of higher learning, and as a point of differentiation, the Austin Project sought to embed itself in the community of Austin beyond the University of Texas, seeking out their ideal audience where they lived.

Sharon Bridgforth describes the Finding Voice circle as "based in a (theatrical) jazz aesthetic . . . an African American art creation," which she describes as "an ongoing experiment in the structures of jazz as applied to writing, theatrical performance, and daily life."[14] The Austin Project's method is largely inspired by that of Bridgforth, whom Jones calls their "Anchor Artist," and approaches facilitation with the knowledge that "the body is the instrument through which group transformation is possible."[15] With this instrument the group improvises together, and the piece unfolds over time, with rehearsal time barely distinguishable from the final product. The jazz aesthetic adheres so deeply to process that it undermines the concept of a final product. In their manifesto, they note that their inspiration comes from the Combahee River Collective Statement on the liberation of women of color. Liberation and creativity meet in structures of jazz described as follows:

> The body-to-body presentness, the immersion in individual artistry though a strong community ethos, the necessity for and valorizing of multiplicity, the activism inherent in moments of choice and empowerment, the reclamation of what Katherine McKittrick calls "geographies of domination" and the use of safer geographic and psychic spaces all work to create the method for social reconstruction known as the jazz aesthetic.[16]

The Austin Project's method converses with one of the Free Southern Theater's earliest visions: a style of theater inspired by jazz. The Free Southern Theater contrafacted material, changing what was possible within adaptations, by inviting audiences and local communities as collaborators of interpretation, so that the original intent of any given piece could transform in the atmosphere of the Movement.

The Austin Project's jazz aesthetic transformed this practice into a collective-based structure for creating original content. In the printed script of *Spoken Word Orchestra*, a 2005 Austin Project jam session inspired by the jazz aesthetic, they write that the text attempts "to do the impossible" by "documenting the ephemeral, improvised, imperfectly remembered, in-the-moment experience of one evening of performance."[17] The twelve voices overlap as variations on a theme. Like the Story Circle, a thought or memory, for example graffitiing on a bathroom wall, slides into other voices repeating the incident and building on it with their own memories of police interactions and arrests that blend into the original and deviate from it into other memories. One person's story becomes everyone's story as other voices weave together. Because the polyvocality is near constant, the performances of *Spoken Word Orchestra* are more about sound and feeling than narrative. The impressionist style recalls Amiri Baraka's *Slave Ship* and other performances of the Free Southern Theater and El Teatro Campesino, where comprehension of the dialogue is secondary to experiencing the atmosphere. The printed version of this jam session opens channels of sonic resonance so that we might better understand what a performance would have sounded like or imagine what the loud and interactive rehearsals and performances of civil-rights-era theater were like.

The Austin Project opens a channel to witness adaptations of jazz methods within specific communities and how they speak to moments in time. During the civil rights era, the theater groups engaged in public, live interactions with their audiences, whereas with the Austin Project, audiences witness what has already happened in a more private environment. During the *Spoken Word Orchestra*, audiences do not have access to the off-stage experience of the Finding Voice circle insinuated by the onstage performance. As opposed to civil rights movement protest theater, the members of the Austin Project create the safety necessary for women of color to express themselves and find themselves at home with each other. Their approach to social-justice-oriented theater protects the process of intimacy-making through privacy, so transformation happens in collaboration before it goes out into the world.

The Austin Project and the Free Southern Theater intersect at the point of social transformation: the practice of theater influences daily life and interactions. Bridgforth claims that "the jazz aesthetic trusts the process of 'embeddedness' in which the women of [the Austin Project] take their discoveries of clarity and authority and insinuate them into their homes, workplaces, and gardens."[18] Jazz methodologies, from the practice of contrafacting to the process of embededness, cannot be separated from the quotidian realities of economic constraints, access to resources, and time. As Bridgforth reminds us, the portal opens both ways for improvisation to help participants thrive beyond the theater. The symbiotic relationship between the creative space and one's daily life makes a case for the necessity of making art for humans to thrive, especially when their methods reflect the values of the persons practicing.

Hearing the We as an I: *The Panza Monologues* and the Community Dialogues

In the introduction to *The Panza Monologues*, a documentary book about the titular performance piece, artists Irma Mayorga and Virginia Grise discuss working alongside Sharon Bridgforth for the premiere of the play, claiming, "We, like Sharon, are searching for the power of new aesthetics." In a moment of convergence, the sentence echoes the Free Southern Theater's desire for a new aesthetic, a "new idiom, a new genre, a theatrical form and style as unique as blues, jazz, and gospel."[19] During the time of the Austin Project, one of its performers, Grise, was also developing a collaboration with Mayorga and a group of Chicanas in San Antonio at the Esperanza Peace and Justice Center, a nonprofit community center where they worked. As they bantered over lunches and between tasks, the conversation kept returning to the *panza*, an informal Mexican word for belly. Some of this conversation became so rich and poignant—and so funny—that Mayorga started collecting dialogue. Soon they began soliciting other Chicana women to send in writing about their panzas. Their search for new aesthetics emerged from a desire to listen to voices in their community and for those voices to shape the process and product of creating a performance.

Like the actos of El Teatro Campesino, *The Panza Monologues* is a collaborative work of cultural activism emerging within an activist space. Mayorga and Grise found a way to document San Antonio Chicanas, explaining, "We didn't want to look outward for our stories but rather inward, to the history held on the tongues of San Antonio Chicanas—something we believed was not in the public sphere."[20] Looking within, they found the panza, defined as the belly/womb/life force, as a unifying topic for identity—not because everyone's experience of the panza was the same, but rather *because* the word brought forth diverse stories and reactions. Some were shamed by both men and doctors and their adherence to specific body standards created within a white supremacist framework; yet one woman's story laments how her lack of a robust panza makes her feel inferior. The panza is both a source of feminine power—"I must have worlds inside me"—and a reminder of the prevalence of diabetes in the community.[21] Through this set of diverse reactions, panza does the work of unifying a Chicana identity while also subverting it, reflecting the paradox of any label or identity.

In response to the complexity of this issue, Mayorga and Grise developed a community-based performance piece, *The Panza Monologues*, replacing V's (formerly Eve Ensler) original term *vagina* from *The Vagina Monologues*. Their play is a contrafact of V's play—they keep the structure but change the concept until it's unrecognizable except by name. The contrafact transcends adaptation by becoming a product of the community from which the original play enters. It reflects the economic conditions of a place and time, and the spirit of those making the play, specifically people of color adapting white material to make it their own. Because, as Mayorga and Grise argue, talking about vaginas is considered taboo among members of their community, they enter through the panza, which carries a unique significance to the women with which they were in dialogue. By soliciting writing and work from the community, they created "[a]n assemblage of women's writing and voices," and transformed the collective we into a singular performer, a collective-autoethnographic project resonating with the jazz aesthetic of the Austin Project.[22]

The Panza Monologues draws from Grise's work with the Austin Project, as well as key texts such as Gloria Anzaldúa and Cherríe Moraga's *This Bridge Called My Back*. As Tiffany Ana López remarks in the book's foreword, the performance finds a home in the history of Chicana theater, especially Teatro de las Chicanas, founded in the 1970s. *The Panza Monologues* was not improvised like El Teatro Campesino's early actos, but their method of drawing from lived experiences and collective creation keeps the spirit of those actos thriving in their play. As performances, both El Teatro Campesino and Mayorga and Grise drew from improvised exchanges in their respective workplaces and created narratives from the intersection of political and cultural expressions. For El Teatro Campesino, performance enabled participants to explore the contradictions between a burgeoning Chicanx identity and a multicultural labor movement. In the same spirit, *The Panza Monologues* builds contradiction into their performance and adopts a collective *we* that commits to complexity over a unified or consistent message. They both invite audiences to laugh at the illogical landscape of medicine and labor in this country and debunk racist stereotypes and statistics.

Essentially, words and concepts such as "union," "huelga," and "panza" become entry points to explore the nuances of collective identity. The word panza "quickly springboarded discussions of body image, obesity, diabetes, identity, place, and history" and acted as a means of exploring chicanidad from an angle that incited creative energy around shared experiences.[23] Mayorga reflects in her introduction, "I may have felt like a Tejana; she [Grise] felt like San Antonio," when describing Grise's improvisational code-switching that "could not be taught in professional training."[24] The work, as they describe it, surpasses the difficulty of staging a play; it must also translate a *manera de ser* or *way of being* into stage performance. Thanks to the popularity of El Teatro Campesino and its theatrical antecedents, exploiting and exposing stereotypes have become a mainstay within Latinx performance art with infamous performances such as Guillermo Gomez-Peña and Coco Fusco's *Couple in a Cage*, Carmelita Tropicana's stereotypical Cuban man, Pingalito Betancourt, and Xandra Ibarra's *Spictacles*. Drawing on the stylistics of El Teatro Campesino's *Los vendidos* and *Las dos caras del patroncito*, the stereotypes refuse to remain stable and, in their often-hilarious antics, invite audiences to laugh at the absurdity of racism.

The Panza Monologues place a Mexican slang word at the center of the food justice movement in San Antonio. Like El Teatro Campesino's constant play with identity in their improvised actos, *The Panza Monologues* takes an approach to the panza that feels both reverent and irreverent at once. It is through *relajo*, this cheeky style of humor, that the play invites the audience to laugh while making obvious the systems of classism and racism operating underneath. For example, the story "Sucking It In" is an ode to a pair of "panza pliers" that the narrator uses to close the button of her jeans. Even though this struggle is a humorous moment in the play, there is pain, physical and emotional, in trying to conform to a beauty standard determined by whiteness, as Grise struggles on stage. Some of the material emerging from women's stories was so heartbreaking that they had to revise the play in rehearsal in order to conserve both Grise's and the audience's energy. In its final version, the play reflects the dark humor unique to their conversations and storytelling.

This dynamic intersects with issues of medical care and access to quality food as one of the major problems plaguing the San Antonio community, resulting in increased levels of diabetes, which Mayorga and Grise had long understood as activists. In the play—and in the community—statistics of medically diagnosed obesity contend with scenes of women struggling with body image dysmorphia. Even deeper, Mayorga and Grise intersect U.S.-based medical ideas of health against cultural approaches to food, where traditional ingredients and abundance of food and panza is a sign of good health. The play and its introductory material confront the hypocrisy of doctors telling Chicanx people that their food was the problem when the U.S.

contained a proliferation of fast-food chains in food deserts where Chicanx people lived. Many people in the community, including Mayorga and Grise themselves, unwillingly traded in their food traditions for the convenience and cheapness of fast food. All of this material emerges in the play, showing the audiences that food justice is an intersectional issue where radical wellness practices grate against a white, patriarchal beauty standard of what a woman's body *should* look like.

Even if women were not sharing stories about their vaginas, the content was still sensitive and even painful to discuss. Rather than soliciting community members to expose their bodies to audiences, Mayorga and Grise asked women for their narratives as a gesture of trust. Arguably, all theater emerges from lived human experiences; however, the method behind *The Panza Monologues* depends on trust to create a performance centered on the lived experiences of people without a voice in mainstream theater. This is best articulated through the words of El Teatro Campesino participant Olivia Chumacero, who claimed, "You had to draw from yourself, from where you were coming from. Things came out of you, from what you thought, from where you were coming from, from what you had experienced in life. . . . it was not a mechanical learning of lines. . . . It was your life."[25] *The Panza Monologues* engages in the tradition of elevating personal experience over the script, but like the Austin Project, its off-stage processes are evident to their audiences. Grise uses her role as a performer to stand in for the voices of those who contributed to the play.

Grise's performance resonates with E. Patrick Johnson's "Pour a Little Honey in My Tea," a creative reading of his collection of stories from *Black Queer Southern Women*.[26] Johnson presents his presence as proxy for a series of interviews and conversations, many of them anonymous. The method they share is both vulnerable representation and a representation of vulnerability, as they put their bodies on stage in place of those who could not or do not want to be there on stage or in public. In Grise's performance, as in Johnson's, the single actor changes character, reminding us always who is *not present*. The actor always reveals that they are a symbol, never letting the audience forget, in a way that contrafacts Brecht's alienation effect through intimacy-making. As Grise and Johnson continue to change character, they remind the audience of the fact that they are standing in for real people and true situations. This distancing does not result in emotional detachment; rather, it makes a case for emotional investment in another's story as a path toward social change.

Johnson's and Mayorga and Grise's method revises ethnography through their intimacy with their interviewees. They are so close that they integrate them within their own performing body. They contrafact ethnography by keeping the structure of interviews as a method of gathering information about a group, but deviating from traditional modes of scholarship, opting for performance as documentary strategy. They eschew the neutrality or distance between the interviewer and the community of interviewees and bring forward their intimacy as material for the performance. As they play with scholarly methods, Grise and Johnson reveal a complex relationship with academia, by pushing against institutional support. At least three universities supported the project that would become *The Panza Monologues*, which was created outside the institutional space in collaboration with the community, including funding the publication of their book. However, Bridgforth facilitated the world premiere outside of a university setting, supported by the Austin Latino/Latina Lesbian, Gay, Bisexual and Transgender Organization. The story of production emerges from community organization and is inseparable from it:

> [*The Panza Monologues*] was first picked up as a "show" by a radically queer people color-centered space, a non-profit political-cultural organization, as opposed to a more traditional *theater* space of company. Yet again, we believe this invitation demonstrates that for the majority of people of color artists in theater, the paths for our work's development do not always follow the models of traditional American theater and most often works such as our own find their best allies in organizations and venues that directly open out or have dug deep into people of color communities through self-created spaces—the same spaces and people so many theater companies want to garner as new audiences.[27]

Mayorga and Grise bring together theater by people of color under an alternative framework for theater production and even an independent history, which emerges from their obligation to their communities.

For Grise and Mayorga, the decision to perform solo "to make the project manageable" reflects the lifestyle of the creators and storytellers, who create alongside working full-time, serving their communities, raising families, and "unemployment blues."[28] Their obligation meant taking on the challenge of a solo show and learning the skills and stamina required to honor the stories of their community. As Grise performs the women's voices, she embodies the intimacy of becoming a vessel or a medium for collective identity of San

Antonio Chicanas, while also challenging a sense of unity as she continues to shift perspectives. The play embodies an approach to identity that allows for dissent, difference, and uncomfortable truths. *The Panza Monologues* can say things that for others would be unsayable in public—for example, about abortion in "El Vientre" and domestic abuse in "Praying"—because Grise is willing to be the public-facing persona. The trust building that happens through this layer of protection enables a greater veracity to peek through. Grise's decision offers insight into how we can better understand how a theater group could express unpopular, radical, or controversial ideas that people might not want to go on the record about.

The play exists through intimacy and trust, as well as a willingness by Mayorga and Grise to take on the work so that their contributors could continue their daily lives. The divergence between Mayorga and Grise's method and Luis Valdez's directorship of El Teatro Campesino is notable and speaks volumes about feminist approaches to community care and how that shapes art-making. Reflecting back on the approach taken by El Teatro Campesino, we can appreciate how people such as Augustin Lira put their bodies on the line, representing ideas of power and identity, while also recognizing how El Teatro Campesino's lack of protective layer between performer and public influenced which kinds of people felt safe enough to get up on stage, and how that has shaped the cultural memory of the actos in their historic moment. In the unique history of "people of color artists in theater," as Mayorga describes it in the aforementioned quote, theater must conform to the needs of the community from which it emerges—meaning it must confront the time constraints and geographic specificities of the storytellers. If they move, the theater must move; if they cannot access theaters outside their neighborhood, the theater must become part of the neighborhood, and so on. However, beyond logistical constraints, *The Panza Monologues* and the Austin Project devoted energy toward welcoming in those who did not feel a sense of themselves as artists. Through letter-writing and the Finding Voice circle, theater holds space for the process of intimacy-making so that contributors come to a sense of belonging as artists.

The Panza Monologues begins with an obligation to their community, women living and working in San Antonio, and their stories are transcribed by Mayorga and Grise's curation. The play creates a complex terrain that challenges fast food consumerism while understanding the systemic forces that result in the limited options for working-class people trying to access a quick meal. They raise awareness of health issues, while loving and respecting the panza as a life force and honoring traditional comfort foods. As they traverse so many economic and sociological issues, they discuss health without falling into the fatphobia traps designed by the medical industry to shame individual people. In "My Sister's Panza" the narrator tells the story of the narrator's sister's diabetes diagnosis, claiming that the worst part was that "they made mamí go to a nutritionist to learn how to cook out her love."[29] The story parallels the erasure of her sister's cultural diet and the shrinking of her panza with depression, thinly veiled as medical compliance. In the final piece, "Panza Girl Manifesto," the narrator responds by asserting her food culture, "Don't fuck with our *chicharrones*, the lard in our *tortillas de harina*, the gravy of our *enchiladas*, the ooze inside our *barbacoa*," and by encouraging intuition as a rule for diet and existence: "Let your *panza* be your guide."[30] The stories pull together the need for a healthier San Antonio with the equally important need to eat with love and feel at home in one's diet. One story beckons us to eat healthy, saying, "If our body breaks down, then how are we going to do all this work?," while another says, "don't mess with our processed cheese!"[31]

By using a jazz-inspired methodology, Mayorga and Grise design a play that holds space for these contradictions to coexist. Theirs is a blues methodology, the *changing same* of stories that repeat, "but the repetitions are never self-same; driven by a propensity toward deviance, their responses are always reformations, deformations, and interruptions," as Fumi Okiji claims.[32] Grise and Mayorga become the first to create this story, while also claiming the story belongs to no one. Okiji describes this process: "The gathering of contribution that makes up a standard is a celebration of aberration. Within this understanding the communal quality of the blues is self-regulating: it belongs to no one, and neither will it congeal around common interests."[33] Grise shifts between modalities and voices, playing with stereotypical images of abjection and its un-Americanness: "The u.s. of a.'s did not want me / güera / alta / y gorda / any more than it wanted my mother / pieta / baja / y gorda."[34] The opposing descriptions reveal the contradictory nature of stereotypes, but the consistency of *gorda* remains a point of disgust. That is until Grise becomes a *flaca* in "Political Panza" and deals with another form of disgust from her community who critique her lack of panza, claiming, "men want something they can grab."[35] The stereotypical image of a Chicana falls apart into a complex web of pride and abjection.

Every time Grise slips into another voice and narrative, the audience engages with a process that opposes that of reduction: Grise expands the voices out like an accordion across the length of the play, inviting audiences to always be seeing polyvocality within the single person, so that "the 'I' voice of the actor speaks to the 'we' of the community."[36] Grise tells us this through direct address to the audience, "I share them with you cuz they're not just her stories [*points to a woman in the audience*] or her stories [*points to another woman in the audience*] or my stories anymore. They are us. They are our stories."[37] Through stage directions, the play couples the panza with womanhood, assuming an audience of women. Like El Teatro Campesino's use of symbolism, such as the way La Virgen became a symbol for a diverse community, *The Panza Monologues* invites us to witness how strategic essentialism can sometimes—not always—be the beginning of a conversation. As I argued in chapter 2, these symbols can be both sacred to those who believe and a tool of political disruption for those who don't and calls upon audiences to hold contradictory meanings together. The conversations that formed *The Panza Monologues* included men, but the final piece intentionally left them out to create a universal feminine figure (rather than the typical universal man) from which to theorize on identity. They start with those socialized as women who have been taught to be critical and self-conscious of their bellies, so that "the body as a personal storehouse of knowledge and a source of cultural memory" could start the conversation.[38] There is no mention of people with panzas who do not fit into the binary and yet have their own stories to tell. Narrowing the scope to a particular gender or identity pulls the audience into the thicket of essentialism, allowing some people to feel at home at the painful exclusion of others.

The Panza Monologues contributes a particular place and moment to the ongoing dialogue Grise and Mayorga have continued from others before them about ethnic and cultural identity and U.S. racism and sexism. Within a framework of emergence, the play becomes a "dynamic suggestion" from which others will consider what more could be done and where else it could go. Mayorga and Grise invite us to take up their suggestion by looking within our own community and representing its complexity.

Media Experimentation and Food Justice

This final section extends the themes of food justice and artistic expression to include farming practices grounded in social transformation, continuing SNCC and the Poor People's Corporation's relationship to agricultural activism. Maria Varela and members of SNCC's photography and communication department brought together experimental methods of filmmaking, performance, and labor reform, and their work lives within the larger visual culture of the civil rights movement in which photography and documentary flourished. The afterlives of the media experimentation of the civil rights movement emerged into documentary forms, including media programs, such as Appalshop founded in Kentucky in 1969, which puts cameras and production knowledge in the hands of people local to the region to "tell stories the commercial cultural industries don't tell."[39] Traces of civil-rights-era experimentation appear in the editing and directorial practices of Madeline Anderson and Toni Cade Bambara, both of whom display aesthetics of obligation in their filmmaking practices. For example, Anderson's film *I Am Somebody* (1970) has no traceable or obvious connection to the independent media activism of the South, yet resonates with the methods of intimacy-making and how that effected Anderson's editing of her documentary on the Charleston Hospital Workers' Strike of 1969. Anderson put the perspectives and feelings of the women she worked with above the popular vision that the strike failed to form a union.

The most powerful example of independent documentary happened decades later in the late 1980s and early '90s, *Eyes on the Prize*, which was produced by a black-owned production company, Blackside Film and Video Production, founded in 1968. This fourteen-episode, two-part documentary emerged from the experience of its creator, Henry Hampton, in the civil rights movement and featured archival footage and interviews with people involved in the Movement. Beyond the interviews with iconic figures, such as John Lewis, Rosa Parks, Andrew Young, and Coretta Scott King, the series features lesser-known activists, such as Bob Moses, Amzie Moore, and Robert F. Williams. Like the SNCC filmstrips, the camera for *Eyes on the Prize* documents civil rights movement stories from the voices of those who lived the experience, bringing the camera into the homes of local people such as Rutha Mae and Willie Hill Jackson, cousins of Emmett Till. The footage of noniconic local people records the unpolished and uncomfortable delivery of those not used to being asked to tell their stories on public record. The media initiatives emerging in the wake of the civil rights movement parallel the hopes of community-based theater: that representation would extend beyond politics and encompass all areas of people's lives, including economic participation, cultural expression, and the recording of history.

The development of Black independent media is a robust history that at moments converges with agricultural organizing and the cooperative movement. The work done by SNCC's photography unit and the unfinished projects of Southern Media existed at the intersection of these two initiatives. Today, Soul Fire Farm, a Black owned and operated social justice farm cooperative in Rensselaer County in upstate New York, continues the tradition of grounding their practices of cultivation and community-building in social transformation and activism. Established in 2010, Soul Fire Farm has always placed cultural work as integral to agricultural labor. Their documentary book, *Farming While Black: Soul Fire Farm's Practical Guide to Liberation on the Land* (2018), records the long history of African and indigenous farming practices, and their commitment to cultural education initiatives on the farm. Author Leah Penniman collects stories, photographs, data, history, an excerpt from Octavia Butler's *Parable of the Sower*, poetry from Margaret Walker and Ross Gay, and works of art from people in their family, just to name a few. Together these artifacts tell a holistic story of social justice farming in the U.S. and its Global South connections. The Poor People's Corporation and Liberty House are notably absent, even though the book details the history of Fannie Lou Hamer's Freedom Farm and the Federation of Southern Cooperatives—an omission due to a lack of public knowledge about the Poor People's Corporation. Penniman's efforts evidence a recent surge in the twenty-first century to return to the civil rights movement and emphasize the stories of activists other than Martin Luther King Jr. and Malcolm X.

As *Farming While Black* details histories of Black and Brown people working the land from Egypt to now, the narrative around agricultural liberation integrates with creative expression. "We believed that to free ourselves, we must feed ourselves," Penniman claims, and *Farming While Black* argues that nourishment means both food and art, both economy and culture, both the material and the spiritual.[40] This documentary book was written by Penniman, but it is a collectively produced work and guidebook for others wanting to grow their own food. The photographs taken by their child, Neshima Vitale-Penniman, are beautiful in their own right and the historical facts are informative; however, the book is meant to mobilize people to start their own farm. It serves as an instruction manual, such as *Something of Our Own* and *Farm Worker's Strike*, that honors the community through dedicated aesthetics, so that the educational experience can intersect with cultural awareness. As an interpurpose text, it pulls together different initiatives without privileging one over another. The literary references, the singing and dancing are not decorative filler for the hard work of agricultural labor. The farm can only sustain itself through cultural and artistic engagement as a healing practice and the community necessary to bring people together to labor with joy and love. Intimacy-making is the carework of sustainability, for land and community.

Images of Black and Brown people working their own land visualizes the economic possibility of autonomy and sustainability. Their journey of making *something out of nothing* by following no-till practices and indigenous farming methods creates topsoil where the land was previously rocky and difficult. As they worked to hone a multitude of farming skills, which included modern and ancient practices, they've integrated personal and social transformation through workshops, where, as Penniman notes, "We used drums and song to encourage seeds to grow, and we filled the moonlit sky with the sounds of our dancing to Kendrick Lamar and Nicki Minaj."[41] Their embrace of sustainable farming practices that eschew the tools of Big Ag monoculture requires improvisation and creativity. Alongside the visual work are concrete instructions on where to apply for funds and the best conditions for planting.

Their third chapter, "Honoring the Spirits of the Land," rests between the chapters "Planning Your Farm Business" and "Restoring Degraded Soil," and its position signals the importance of the spiritual as well as the pragmatic. "Honoring the Spirits" guides readers through planting and harvest rituals by informing readers about millet festivals in Ghana and offering advice from Zora Neale Hurston for joining in chants and songs: "I just get in the crowd with people as they are singing and I listen as best I can [. . .] Then I carry it in my memory."[42] Penniman collects songs from Igbo and Haitian Vodou traditions as well as songs that evoke spirituals and protest songs from the civil rights movement. The section includes a chant written by Assata Shakur with the line "We have nothing to lose but our chains" channeling both *The Communist Manifesto* and the struggle for Black liberation.[43] As the workers on Soul Fire Farm chant Shakur's words, they participate in Brooks's open channel of sonic resonance, where they inhabit a song with words from another context, adding a layer of meaning for food justice for people of color and elevating original intent about the distribution of land.

Soul Fire Farm continues to share knowledge and host workshops, while proudly participating in Black entrepreneurship and (they hope) profit to continue the farm in the next generation. They live in the contradiction of privately owned land (owned by Penniman) with a cooperative-farming spirit, contending with the dissonance just as those in the 1960s cooperative movement also did and by making the best of what's available to them. Soul Fire Farm takes a step toward liberation, making a dynamic gesture toward a future that might realize Land Back and reparations. The farmers become their own archivists, taking part in the tradition of cultural activism's documentaries, guidebooks, and tools of communication that emphasize recording and remembering as essential to the vision work that imagines better futures.

In addition to their on-site programs, they spread their message and inspiration on social media. Watching their content on Instagram reveals how futuristic SNCC was in developing visual-participatory teaching tools such as the intermedia filmstrip collections. The *Liberation on Land* video series shows the farmers singing and enacting the rituals from the book and teaching others. One reel, released in 2023, shows clips of Soul Fire participants working the land and harvesting, while Mumu Fresh's song "Reparations" plays as a soundtrack. Soul Fire's words say: "Did you know . . . / Our ancestral farming practices / increase topsoil depth / sequester soil carbon / and increase biodiversity / Gratitude To Our Beloved Community / for helping us care for the climate, land, and all living beings."[44] At the same time, Mumu Fresh sings about the healing practice of growing one's own food, asking, "What you going do when you get your reparations? Oh, I'm going to have some fun, pass down to my young" as a young child waves at the camera.[45] The image of the child in the short reel resonates with the images of children from *Something of Our Own* and the okra farmers' call to build generational wealth, not as an expression of capitalist greed, but for the security needed to thrive and continue the conditions for autonomy. They hold hope for a future where reparations have been given to the community, while at the same time they are making that future happen themselves, skeptical that the powers that be will ever pay that debt.

In *Farming While Black*, Soul Fire Farm honors the Combahee River Colony of South Carolina founded by Black women during the Civil War and the Combahee River Collective founded in Boston in 1977 as a Black, lesbian, and socialist collective. The former group represents the Black autonomy primarily agricultural Gullah/Geechee communities holding onto ancestral roots and sustaining cultural autonomy. As Penniman writes, "They found and occupied abandoned farmland, grew crops and took care of one another. The sale of their cotton and handicrafts sustained them."[46] Additionally, the name Combahee recalls Harriet Tubman's mobilization against the Confederacy and defense of the Combahee River Community in the Georgia Sea Islands and South Carolina. More than influential, Soul Fire calls itself kin to these communities and adapts their organizational patterns to their own circumstances. The better-known Combahee River Collective expressed their own remembrance of their history through a set of demands for a better future. Rather than work this out through claiming land, their statement imagines way of living that has inspired both Soul Fire Farm and the Austin Project's jazz aesthetic, which they model after the Combahee River Collective. The fact that a political organization could shape both a theater group in Texas and a farm in upstate New York proves how methods move between what we would consider wildly different disciplines, but what the people of Soul Fire or the Austin Project would consider the same path to social transformation: collaboration, obligation, intimacy, creativity, and the ability to tell one's own story.

If not always visible, the groups discussed here exist within a fluid network best described as the connective tissue of cultural work. Even if those stories are told in experimental ways, or on obsolete media, they offer what Vijay Iyer calls *traces of embodiment* of activist movements and emerge from communities sustained by labor-intensive carework.[47] The story of the civil rights movement, from the perspective of its cultural production, draws our focus to the interpersonal and community obligations that make up the aesthetics of social change. However, the Movement was a fractal of the larger organism of cultural work, which creates the conditions for emergence of community-based art/work and activates people to search for new, creative paths to social change. By tracing the aesthetics of obligation in cultural work, we witness the open channels and sonic resonances of the art of liberation in the United States. The civil rights movement offers a glimpse of this dialogue—dynamic suggestions and their responses—a fractal of a much larger whole.

Notes

Preface

1. Robin D. G. Kelley, *Freedom Dreams: The Black Radical Imagination* (New York: Penguin Random House, 2003), ix.

2. adrienne maree brown, *Emergent Strategy: Shaping Change, Shaping Worlds* (Chico, CA: AK Press, 2017), ix.

3. adrienne marie brown, *Holding Change: The Way of Emergent Strategy Facilitation and Mediation* (Chico, CA: AK Press, 2017), 19.

Introduction

1. Marcus Baram, *Gil Scott-Heron: Pieces of a Man* (New York: St. Martin's Press, 2014), 77.

2. See Leigh Raiford and Renee Romano, *The Civil Rights Movement in American Memory* (Athens: University of Georgia Press, 2006).

3. Ajay Heble, "'Why Can't We Go Somewhere There?' Sun Ra, Improvisation, and the Imagination of Future Possibilities," *Canadian Theatre Review* 143 (Summer 2010): 99.

4. Heble, "Why Can't We," 99.

5. Sharon Monteith, *SNCC's Stories: The African American Freedom Movement in the Civil Rights South* (Athens: University of Georgia Press, 2020), xix.

6. Kelley, *Freedom Dreams*, 11.

7. bell hooks, *Art on My Mind: Visual Politics* (New York: New Press, 1995), 9.

8. Toni Cade Bambara and Thabiti Lewis, "An Interview with Toni Cade Bambara: Kay Bonetti," in *Conversations with Toni Cade Bambara* (Jackson: University Press of Mississippi, 2012), 35.

9. Toni Cade Bambara, *Deep Sightings & Rescue Missions: Fiction Essays, and Conversations*, ed. Toni Morrison (New York: Penguin Random House, 1999), ix–x.

10. Bambara, *Deep Sightings*, ix–x.

11. David J. Elliott, Marissa Silverman, and Wayne D. Bowman, *Artistic Citizenship: Artistry, Social Responsibility, and Ethical Praxis* (New York: Oxford University Press 2016), 6.

12. Rúben A. Gaztambide-Fernández, "Why the Arts Don't Do Anything: Toward a New Vision for Cultural Production in Education," *Harvard Educational Review* 83, no. 1 (2013): 226.

13. Nato Thompson, *Seeing Power: Art and Activism in the 21st Century* (Brooklyn: Melville House, 2015), 19. Thompson's collection of terms exists outside the space of civil-rights-era cultural activism, both in his timeline of the mid-1990s and in the kinds of groups carrying out this art practice.

14. Lauren Berlant, "Introduction," in "Intimacy," special issue, *Critical Inquiry* 24, no. 2 (Winter 1998): 283.

15. Elliot, Silverman, and Bowman, *Artistic Citizenship*, 19.

16. brown, *Emergent Strategy*, 53.

17. brown, *Emergent Strategy*, 53.

18. brown, *Emergent Strategy*, 53.

19. Diana Taylor, *¡Presente! The Politics of Presence* (Durham: Duke University Press, 2020), 30.

20. Taylor, *¡Presente!*, 30.

21. Alice Lovelace, "Remembering Toni," *In Motion Magazine* (2014).

22. Jennifer Nash, *Black Feminism Reimagined: After Intersectionality* (Durham: Duke University Press, 2019), 113–15.

23. See chapter 8 in Charles Payne, *I've Got the Light of Freedom: The Organizing Tradition and the Mississippi Freedom Struggle* (Oakland: University of California Press, 2007), for a profile of SNCC workers in Mississippi, whom he observes as both "upwardly mobile" but also that "came from backgrounds very much like those of the people they were trying to organize" (237); and my discussion of Maria Varela's "Selma Literacy Program" in chapter 3, which details the difficulty of intraracial class prejudice. For this reason, historian Dave Struthers argues that there were "contested and uneven results" of "interracial organizing in a settler colonial society" and mobilizes the term "cultures of affinity" in his book *The World in a City: Multiethnic Radicalism in Early Twentieth-Century Los Angeles* (Champaign: University of Illinois Press, 2019), 6, that allowed for difference while working toward similar goals.

24. Asha Bhandary, *Freedom to Care: Liberalism, Dependency Care, and Culture* (New York: Routledge, 2020), 10.

25. brown, *Emergent Strategy*, 20.

26. brown, *Emergent Strategy*, 20.

27. James Smethurst, *Behold the Land: The Black Arts Movement in the South* (Chapel Hill: University of North Carolina Press, 2021), 1.

28. See Brian Benkhen, *The Struggle in Black and Brown: African American and Mexican American Relations during the Civil Rights Era* (Lincoln: University of Nebraska Press, 2012). The question of what constitutes the civil rights movement has long been debated by scholars, who argue over timelines, people involved, location, and so forth. See Sundiata Cha-Jua and Clarence Lang, "The 'Long Movement' as Vampire: Temporal and Spatial Fallacies in Recent Black Freedom Studies," *Journal of African American History* 92, no. 2 (Spring 2007).

29. Barbara Ransby, *Ella Baker and the Black Freedom Movement: A Radical Democratic Vision* (Chapel Hill: University of North Carolina Press, 2003), 310.

30. Angela J. Aguayo, *Documentary Resistance: Social Change and Participatory Media* (New York: Oxford University Press, 2019), 3.

31. Including, but not limited to, Faith S. Holsaert, Martha Prescod Norman Noonan, Judy Richardson, Betty Garman Robinson, Jean Smith Young, and Dorothy M. Zellner, eds., *Hands on the Freedom Plow: Personal Accounts by Women in SNCC* (Champaign: University of Illinois Press, 2010); Payne, *I've Got the Light of Freedom*; Clayborne Carson, David J. Garrow, Gerald R. Gill, Vincent Harding, and Darlene Clark Hine, eds., *The Eyes on the Prize Civil Rights Reader: Documents, Speeches, and Firsthand Accounts from the Black Freedom Struggle* (New York: Penguin, 1991); John Dittmer, *Local People: The Struggle for Civil Rights in Mississippi* (Champaign: University of Illinois Press, 1995).

32. Greta de Jong, *You Can't Eat Freedom: Southerners and Social Justice after the Civil Rights Movement* (Chapel Hill: University North Carolina Press, 2016), 3.

33. Alice Walker, "The Civil Rights Movement: What Good Was It?," *American Scholar*, Autumn 1967, reprinted on theamericanscholar.org, February 10, 2016.

34. Walker, "Civil Rights Movement."

35. bell hooks, *Outlaw Culture: Resisting Representations* (New York: Routledge, 2006), 239.

36. Elliot, Silverman, and Bowman, *Artistic Citizenship*, 3.

37. Thompson, *Seeing Power*, 17.

38. Fumi Okiji, *Jazz as Critique: Adorno and Black Expression Revisited* (Stanford: Stanford University Press, 2018), 3, 5.

39. Fred Moten, *In the Break: The Aesthetics of the Black Radical Tradition* (Minneapolis: University of Minnesota Press, 2003), 149.

40. See Amiri Baraka, "The Changing Same (R&B and New Black Music)," in *The LeRoi Jones/Amiri Baraka Reader*, ed. William J. Harris (New York: Thunder Mouth Press, 2000), and Robert G. O'Meally, Brent Hayes Edwards, and Farah Jasmine Griffin, *Uptown Conversation: The New Jazz Studies* (New York: Columbia University Press, 2004).

41. Monteith, *SNCC's Stories*, 23.

42. Smethurst, *Behold the Land*, 60.

43. James M. Harding and Cindy Rosenthal, eds., *Restaging the Sixties: Radical Theaters and Their Legacy* (Ann Arbor: University of Michigan Press, 2006).

44. Harding and Rosenthal, *Restaging the Sixties*, 28, emphasis in original.

45. Lorenzo Thomas, "Alea's Children: The Avant Garde on the Lower East Side, 1960–1970," *African American Review* 27, no. 4 (Winter 1993): 573.

46. Thomas, "Alea's Children," 573.

47. Thomas C. Dent, Gilbert Moses, and Richard Schechner, *The Free Southern Theater by the Free Southern Theater: A Documentary of the South's Radical Black Theater, with Journals, Letters, Poetry, Essays, and a Play Written by Those Who Built It* (New York: Bobbs-Merrill, 1969), 12.

48. David Fischlin, Ajay Heble, and George Lipsitz, *The Fierce Urgency of Now:*

Improvisation, Rights, and the Ethics of Cocreation (Durham: Duke University Press, 2013), xv.

49. Dan DiPiero, *Contingent Encounters: Improvisation in Music and Everyday Life* (Ann Arbor: University of Michigan Press, 2022) 15, emphasis in original.

50. Toni Cade Bambara, *The Salt Eaters* (New York: Knopf Doubleday), 1992, 262–63.

51. Bambara, *Salt Eaters*, 264.

52. Sarah Feinstein and David Rife, eds., *The Jazz Fiction Anthology* (Bloomington: Indiana University Press, 2009), ix.

53. Feinstein and Rife, *Jazz Fiction Anthology*, xvi.

54. Bambara, *Salt Eaters*, 264.

55. Bambara, *Salt Eaters*, 263.

56. Fischlin, Heble, and Lipsitz, *Fierce Urgency of Now*, xii.

57. DiPiero, *Contingent Encounters*, 34.

58. Amiri Baraka (Le Roi Jones), *Blues People: The Negro Experience in White America and the Music That Developed from It* (New York: Morrow Quill Paperbacks, 1963), 80.

59. See Tom Vitale's "The Story of Charlie Parker's 'Ko Ko,'" *NPR*, August 27, 2000.

60. They did, however, at one point try to budget for the rights to James Baldwin's *The Blues for Mr. Charlie*, but in their early days that put them in the red.

61. Okiji, *Jazz as Critique*, 9.

62. SNCC moved back and forth between these places, connecting these campaigns as two fronts of the same battle. See Benkhen's *Struggle in Black and Brown*.

63. Dolores Huerta, "Dolores Huerta Oral History," Farmworker Movement Documentation Project, UC San Diego, https://libraries.ucsd.edu/farmworkermovement/medias/oral-history/

64. This echoes Amiri Baraka's "changing same" in *Blues People*.

65. See William H. Lawson, *No Small Thing: The 1963 Mississippi Freedom Vote* (Jackson: University of Mississippi Press, 2018).

66. Richard Dyer, *Pastiche* (New York: Routledge, 2006), 2.

67. SNCC Legacy Project, https://sncclegacyproject.org/fannie-lou-hamer-declared-at-the-1964-democratic-national-convention-we-didnt-come-for-no-two-seats-when-all-of-us-is-tired/

68. Leon Hilton and Mariahdessa Ekere Tallie, "The Unwieldy Otherwise: Rethinking the Roots of Performance Studies in and through the Black Freedom Struggle," *Performance Matters* 8, no. 2 (2023).

69. Soyica Diggs Colbert, Douglas A. Jones, and Shane Vogel, eds., *Race and Performance after Repetition* (Durham: Duke University Press, 2020), 8.

70. Diggs Colbert, Jones, and Vogel, *Race and Performance*, 8.

71. This has long been central to the relationship between performance and activism, such as that reflected in the work of Augusto Boal's *Theater of the Oppressed* and Dwight Conquergood in "Health Theater in a Hmong Refugee Camp: Performance, Comunication, and Culture," who claimed, "For popular theater to work

effectively as a tool of critical awareness and empowerment for oppressed peoples it must be rooted in and begin with their cultural strengths" (Conquergood 181). Cultural activists of the civil rights movement exercised participatory democracy with less of a plan, learning as they practiced.

72. Daphne Brooks, *Bodies in Dissent: Spectacular Performances of Race and Freedom, 1850–1910* (Durham: Duke University Press, 2006), 5.

73. Brooks, *Bodies in Dissent*, 5.

74. Huerta, "Dolores Huerta Oral History."

75. Heble, "Why Can't We," 99.

76. Omi Osun Joni L. Jones, Lisa L. Moore, and Sharon Bridgforth, eds., *Experiments in a Jazz Aesthetic: Art, Activism, Academia, and the Austin Project* (Austin: University of Texas Press, 2010), 5.

Chapter 1

1. "Wynton Marsalis on Jazz as a Tool for Understanding Life," interview by Andrew Zuckerman for *Time Sensitive*, episode 55, November 12, 2021.

2. John O'Neal in "The Greatest Love," producer David Simon, et al., *Treme*, HBO, October 14, 2012.

3. Holland Carter, "A Broken City. A Tree. Evening," *New York Times*, December 2, 2007.

4. Dave Walker, "Wendell Pierce Explains 'Waiting for Godot,'" *Times-Picayune*, October 14, 2012.

5. Walker, "Wendell Pierce Explains 'Waiting for Godot.'"

6. "Creative Time Presents Paul Chan's Waiting for Godot in New Orleans: A Play in Two Acts. A Project in Two Parts," Creativetime.org, 2007.

7. John O'Neal, "Letter to Mary," Box 1, Fl. 6, John O'Neal Papers, Amistad Research Center.

8. "A Proposal in Cultural Affairs to National Education Television," March 4, 1970, Box 55, Fl. 28, The Free Southern Theater Papers, 7.

9. Marty Ardren, "Alternate ROOTS Memo," Box 51, Fl. 8, The Free Southern Theater Papers, Amistad Research Center.

10. Dent, Moses, and Schechner, *The Free Southern Theater by the Free Southern Theater*, 12.

11. Dent, "Evaluation," 5.

12. Dent, "Evaluation," 5.

13. Dent, Moses, and Schechner, *The Free Southern Theater by the Free Southern Theater*, 12.

14. "Letter from Neshoba Project, 1964." Box 101, Folder 5, The Free Southern Theater Records, 1960–1978, Amistad Research Center.

15. Roy Wilkins, "Interview with Roy Wilkins," in *Eyes on the Prize: America's Civil Rights Years 1954 to 1965*, *PBS*, 1987.

16. Julius B. Fleming Jr., *Black Patience: Performance, Civil Rights, and the Unfinished Project of Emancipation* (New York: NYU Press, 2022), 107.

17. Fleming, Jr., *Black Patience*, 108.

18. Doris Derby, "Personal Papers, Notes/Notebooks," Box 4, Doris A. Derby Papers.

19. Harding and Rosenthal, *Restaging the Sixties*, 18.

20. In one such example, members of the Ruleville, Mississippi White Citizens Council, deputized as forty armed local policemen, sat through a Free Southern Theater performance of *In White America* without violence. According to actor Murray Levy, the White Citizens Council spokesman claimed that "they were very impressed by the quality of acting . . . but naturally they couldn't accept the play's comments." A letter from performance scholar Erika Munk, who was at the event, describes the experience and states that the men were "unfriendly [*sic*], of course but not actively hostile . . . While it was impossible to tell from their faces whether these men were moved by what they saw, the fact that they stuck with it is a breakthrough—and that we were in no way harassed on our drive back to Ruleville after the show" ("Letter from Erika Monk," Box 101, Folder 4, The Free Southern Theater Records). Despite these minor miracles, the Free Southern Theater was harassed enough to relocate from Mississippi to New Orleans in order to "live like human beings and not be afraid all the time," as Denise Nicholas claims in Smethurst, *Behold*, 64.

21. Fleming, *Black Patience*, 91.

22. Smethurst, *Behold*, 75.

23. Smethurst, *Behold*, 67.

24. Dent, Moses, and Schechner, *The Free Southern Theater by the Free Southern Theater*, 158, emphasis mine.

25. Diana Taylor, *The Archive and the Repertoire: Performing Cultural Memory in the Americas* (Durham: Duke University Press, 2003), 129.

26. Smethurst, *Behold*, 67.

27. Smethurst, *Behold*, 67.

28. John O'Neal, "Unknown Correspondence," Box 1, Fl. 6, John O'Neal Papers, Amistad Research Center.

29. O'Neal, "Unknown."

30. O'Neal, "Unknown."

31. O'Neal, "Unknown."

32. John A. Williams, *The Man Who Cried I Am*, (New York: Abrams Press, [1967] 2004),

33. Kelley, *Freedom Dreams*, 24.

34. O'Meally, Edwards, and Griffin, *Uptown Conversation*, 2. See, for example, Krin Gabbard, ed., *Jazz among the Discourses* (Durham: Duke University Press, 1995); Scott Saul, *Freedom Is Freedom Ain't: Jazz and the Making of the Sixties* (Cambridge: Harvard University Press, 2003); and *The Jazz Cadences of American Culture*, ed. Robert O'Meally (New York: Columbia University Press, 1998).

35. O'Meally, Edwards, and Griffin, *Uptown Conversation*, 394.

36. O'Meally, Edwards, and Griffin, *Uptown Conversation*, 395.

37. Moten, *In the Break* 40.

38. Moten, *In the Break*, 41.

39. Daphne Brooks and José Muñoz, "Open Channels: Some Thoughts on Blackness, the Body, and Sound(ing) Women in the (Summer) Time of Trayvon," *Performance Research: A Journal of the Performing Arts* 19, no. 3 (2014): 64.

40. On African American cultural influence on Brecht and Reinhardt, see Carol Martin and Henry Bial, eds., *Brecht Sourcebook* (New York: Routledge, 2000), 2. I am also partial to Diana Taylor's rhetorical question on the use of Brecht in Latin American theater: "Why not do Brecht, still the most honored theatre practitioner in Latin America and, ironically, the world's greatest borrower?," in Taylor, *The Archive and the Repertoire*, 194.

41. Patrick Jarenwattananon, "Why Jazz Musicians Love 'The Rite of Spring,'" *NPR* 26 (May 2013).

42. Jarenwattananon, "Why Jazz Musicians Love 'The Rite of Spring.'"

43. James M. Harding, "From Cutting Edge to Rough Edges: On the Transnational Foundations of Avant-Garde Performance," in *Not the Other Avant-Garde*, ed. James M. Harding and John Rouse (Ann Arbor: University of Michigan Press, 2006), 24.

44. Brooks, "Open Channels," 66.

45. Samuel Beckett, *Waiting for Godot*, trans. Samuel Beckett (New York: Grove Press, 1954), 8.

46. Beckett, *Waiting for Godot*, 12.

47. Beckett, *Waiting for Godot*, 35.

48. Annemarie Bean, ed., *A Sourcebook of African-American Performance: Plays, People, Movements* (New York: Routledge, 1999), 108.

49. Beckett 19, *Waiting for Godot*, ellipses in original.

50. Bean, *Sourcebook of African-American Performance*, 106, ellipses in original.

51. Dent, Moses, and Schechner, *The Free Southern Theater by the Free Southern Theater*, 57.

52. Bean, *Sourcebook of African-American Performance* 68.

53. Beckett, *Waiting for Godot*, 21.

54. Beckett, *Waiting for Godot*, 32.

55. Beckett, *Waiting for Godot*, 23.

56. Beckett, *Waiting for Godot*, 34.

57. Susan King, "Spotlight: James Cromwell in 'Waiting for Godot,'" *Los Angeles Times*, March 28, 2012.

58. Dent, Moses, and Schechner, *The Free Southern Theater by the Free Southern Theater*, 54.

59. Beckett, *Waiting for Godot*, 20.

60. Beckett, *Waiting for Godot*, 27.

61. Beckett, *Waiting for Godot*, 29.

62. Sharon Stockard Martin, "Proper and Fine, Fanny [*sic*] Lou Hamer's Entourage," November 21, 1968, Box 76, Fl. 11, The Free Southern Theater Papers.

63. Stockard Martin, "Proper and Fine, Fanny [*sic*] Lou Hamer's Entourage," 9.

64. Free Southern Theater newsletter, April 1972, The Free Southern Theater Papers.

65. Harry J. Elam, *Taking It to the Streets: The Social Protest Theater of Luis Valdez* (Ann Arbor: University of Michigan Press, 2001), 17.

66. Elam, *Taking It to the Streets*, 79.

67. Elam, *Taking It to the Streets*, 23.

68. Ellen Louise Tripp, "Free Southern Theater: There Is Always a Message," PhD diss., University of North Carolina at Greensboro, 1986, 266.

69. Amiri Baraka (LeRoi Jones), "Slaveship" [*sic*] script, Box 78, Fl. 10, The Free Southern Theater Papers.

70. Baraka, "Slaveship," 17.

71. Baraka, "Slaveship," 17.

72. Elam, *Taking It to the Streets*, 13.

73. Tripp, "Free Southern Theater," 266.

74. Colbert, Jones, and Vogel, *Race and Performance after Repetition*, 16.

75. Colbert, Jones, and Vogel, *Race and Performance after Repetition*, 16.

76. Colbert, Jones, and Vogel, *Race and Performance after Repetition*, 10–11.

77. Colbert, Jones, and Vogel, *Race and Performance after Repetition*, 11.

78. Amiri Baraka, "The Revolutionary Theater," *Liberator*, July 1965, https://nationalhumanitiescenter.org/pds/maai3/protest/text12/barakatheatre.pdf

79. Richard Schechner, *Performance Theory* (London: Routledge, 2003), 79.

80. Colbert, Jones, and Vogel, *Race and Performance after Repetition*, 11.

81. Erika Fischer-Lichte, "Interweaving Cultures in Performance: Different States of Being In-Between," *Textures* (2010): 1.

82. Fischer-Lichte, "Interweaving Cultures in Performance," 16.

83. LeRoi Jones (Amiri Baraka), "The Revolutionary Theater" (1964), in *Home: Social Essays* (New York: Akashic Books, 2009), 236–41. For Antonin Artaud's "Theater of Cruelty," see Antonin Artaud, *The Theater and Its Double* (1964), trans. Victor Corti (London: Oneworld Classics, 2010).

84. For more on the "'community' and 'consciousness'" aesthetic in Black drama, see Abiodun Jeyifous, "Black Critics on Black Theater in America," in *The Theater of Black Americans Volume II: A Collection of Critical Essays*, ed. Erroll Hill (Englewood Cliffs, NJ: Prentice-Hall, 1980), 129–27. Ed Bullins rejected "white Anglo-Saxon Western art'" then claimed "'the Absurd people'" (xii–xiii) as an influence. Larry Neal, one of the major definers of the Black Aesthetic, claimed in his 1968 essay "The Black Arts Movement" that "the most 'important' plays come from Europe—Brecht, Weiss, and Ghelderode,'" before qualifying that "'even these have begun to run dry'" and calling for change (Bean, *Sourcebook of African-American Performance*, 60).

85. Harry J. Elam and David Krasner, *African American Performance and Theater History: A Critical Reader* (Oxford: Oxford University Press, 2001), 63.

86. Baraka, "Revolutionary Theater."

87. Smethurst, *The Black Arts Movement: Literary Nationalism in the 1960s and 1970s* (Chapel Hill: University of North Carolina Press, 2005), 351.

Chapter 2

1. Brian D. Behnken, ed., *Civil Rights and Beyond: African American and Latino/a Activism in the Twentieth-Century United States* (Athens: University of Georgia Press, 2016), 52.

Notes to Pages 56–65 · 183

2. Lauren Araiza, *To March for Others: The Black Freedom Struggle and the United Farm Workers* (University Park: University of Pennsylvania Press, 2013), 28.

3. Araiza, *To March for Others*, 8.

4. Behnken, *Struggle in Black and Brown*, 4.

5. Broyles-González, *El Teatro Campesino*, 33.

6. Broyles-González, *El Teatro Campesino*, 8. Multiple theatrical traditions converge in the *actos: carpas* or "tent shows" popular in Mexico and the Southwest, New Deal-era agit-prop, Soviet Blue Blouse theater, Bertolt Brecht's epic drama, and medieval morality plays.

7. Broyles-González, *El Teatro Campesino*, 225.

8. Broyles-González, *El Teatro Campesino*, 18.

9. Gillian Siddall and Ellen Waterman, *Negotiated Moments: Improvisation, Sound, and Subjectivity* (Durham: Duke University Press, 2016), 2.

10. Siddall and Waterman, *Negotiated Moments*, 18.

11. Shelley Snow, Shelley, Nicolò Francesco Bernardi, Nilufar Sabet-Kassouf, Daniel Moran, and Alexandre Lehmann, "Exploring the Experience and Effects of Vocal Toning." *Journal of Music Therapy* 55, no. 2 (2018): 222.

12. Luis Valdez, "Commentary of Luis Valdez: The Plan of Delano," Farmworker Movement Documentation Project, UC San Diego Library.

13. Broyles-González, *El Teatro Campesino*, 30.

14. "El Plan de Delano."

15. "El Plan de Delano."

16. Sharon Erickson Nepstad, *Catholic Social Activism* (New York: NYU Press, 2019), 41.

17. Kristy Nabhan-Warren, *Meatpacking America: How Migration, Work, and Faith Unite and Divide the Heartland* (Chapel Hill: University of North Carolina Press, 2021), 6.

18. Ana Louise Keating, "'I'm a Citizen of the Universe': Gloria Anzaldúa's Spiritual Activism as Catalyst for Social Change," *Feminist Studies* 34, nos. 1–2 (Spring and Summer 2008): 211.

19. Broyles-González, *El Teatro Campesino*, 70.

20. Mark Rifkin, *Beyond Settler Time: Temporal Sovereignty and Indigenous Self-Determination* (Durham: Duke University Press, 2017).

21. "El Plan de Delano."

22. See Robert Orsi's *The Madonna of 115th Street: Faith and Community in Italian Harlem* (New Haven: Yale University Press, 1988).

23. Elaine A. Peña, *Performing Piety: Making Space Sacred with the Virgin of Guadalupe* (Berkeley: University of California Press, 2011), 43.

24. Nepstad, *Catholic Social Activism*, 10.

25. Nepstad, *Catholic Social Activism*, 10.

26. Dylan A. T. Miner, *Creating Aztlán: Chicano Art, Indigenous Sovereignty, and Lowriding across Turtle Island* (Tucson: University of Arizona Press, 2014), 3.

27. Miner, *Creating Aztlán*, 26.

28. Miner, *Creating Aztlán*, 26.

29. Miner, *Creating Aztlán*, 29.

30. Gina Caison, *Red States: Indigeneity, Settler Colonialism, and Southern Studies* (Athens: University of Georgia Press, 2018), 23.

31. Caison, *Red States*, 66.

32. Juan Herrera, *Cartographic Memory: Social Movement Activism and the Production of Space* (Durham: Duke University Press, 2022), 6.

33. José Esteban Muñoz, *The Sense of Brown*, ed. Joshua Chambers-Letson and Tavia Nyong'o (Durham: Duke University Press, 2020), xxxiii.

34. Taylor, *The Archive and the Repertoire*, 126.

35. El Teatro Campesino, "Huelga," El Teatro Campesino Archives, Department of Special Collections, Donald C. Davidson Library, University of California, Santa Barbara, 1981.

36. brown, *Emergent Strategy*, 20.

37. José Esteban Muñoz, "Towards a Definition of the Brown Commons," LitHub, October 23, 2020.

38. Miner, *Creating Aztlán*, 30.

39. Jorge Huerta, "When Sleeping Giants Awaken: Chicano Theater in the 1960s," *Theatre Survey* 43, no. 1 (May 2002): 27.

40. Elam, *Taking It to the Streets*, 469.

41. Valdez, *Luis Valdez Early Works*, 28, emphasis in original.

42. Valdez, *Luis Valdez Early Works*, 32.

43. Keating, "I'm a Citizen of the Universe," 211.

44. Rick Fantasia and Kim Voss, *Hard Work: Remaking the American Labor Movement* (Berkeley: University of California Press, 2004), 127.

45. "Sunday Edition," Monterey: KMST, Ch. 46, 1981, Video Collection 024, El Teatro Campesino Archives, UC Santa Barbara.

46. "Sunday Edition."

Chapter 3

1. Today, Tuskegee University. Historically, Tuskegee holds a controversial position on civil rights because of the legacy of Booker T. Washington's gradualist approach to equal rights. Even though the Institute lobbied for rights during World War II and organized around voting registration before the 1960s, as Robert Norell argues, there was general disappointment with Tuskeegee's civil rights activism expressed by leaders of the Movement.

2. Dent, Moses, and Schechner, *The Free Southern Theater by the Free Southern Theater*, 149.

3. Dent, Moses, and Schechner, *The Free Southern Theater by the Free Southern Theater*, 149.

4. Gaztambide-Fernández, "Why the Arts Don't Do Anything," 225.

5. Gaztambide-Fernández, "Why the Arts Don't Do Anything," 218.

6. Jon N. Hale, *The Freedom Schools: Student Activists in the Mississippi Civil Rights Movement* (New York: Columbia University Press, 2016), 2. The education activism of the civil rights era has been overshadowed by the memory of desegregation of schools following in the wake of *Brown v. Board of Education* in 1954.

Notes to Pages 82–89 · 185

Images of Ruby Bridges, the Little Rock Nine, and James Meredith proliferate cultural memory. Even though highly publicized events projecting scenes of violence are the most dominant images of education activism, at the grassroots, organizers and activists poured endless hours and resources into establishing education programs across the South, such as Freedom Schools, literacy programs, and Head Start.

7. Hale, *Freedom Schools*, 3.

8. Maria Varela, "Selma Literacy Program," Maria Varela Papers, Wisconsin Historical Society.

9. Varela, "Selma Literacy Program."

10. Varela, "Selma Literacy Program."

11. Paulo Freire, *Pedagogy of Freedom: Ethics, Democracy, and Civic Courage*, trans. Patrick Clarke (New York: Rowman & Littlefield, 1998), 62–63, emphasis mine.

12. Freire, *Pedagogy of Freedom*, 81.

13. Varela, "Learning From Experience: Part 1," SNCC Digital Gateway.

14. Maria Varela, personal communication, September 5, 2023.

15. bell hooks, *Teaching Community: A Pedagogy of Hope* (New York: Routledge, 2004), 98.

16. John Dewey, *Art as Experience* (New York: Paragon Books, 1979), 9.

17. Dewey, *Art as Experience*, 3.

18. bell hooks, *Teaching to Transgress: Education as the Practice of Freedom* (New York: Routledge, 1994), 15

19. Freire, *Pedagogy of Freedom*, 25–26.

20. hooks, *Teaching Community*, 21.

21. hooks, *Teaching Community*, 21.

22. Freire, *Pedagogy of Freedom*, 30.

23. In collaboration with the farmworkers of El Teatro Campesino: Luis Valdez, *Luis Valdez Early Works: Actos, Bernabe and Pensamiento Serpentino* (Houston: Arte Publico Press, 1990), 18.

24. Valdez, *Luis Valdez Early Works*, 17.

25. Valdez, *Luis Valdez Early Works*, 23.

26. Valdez, *Luis Valdez Early Works*, 20–21.

27. Luis Valdez, "'Nine AM,' 019: KMST Nine A.M. next hit Show, Part I Monterey: KMST, Ch. 46, March 26, 1980," disk V1159, El Teatro Campesino Archives, University of California, Santa Barbara.

28. However, the audiences in rural Mississippi and California had little experience of theater, and differed from the audiences at the Baden-Baden festival and many other venues that received Brecht's work. Brecht and many of his experimental followers around the world tried in vain to close the gap between performer and spectator, something not easily accomplished within avant-garde theater, which, as Paul Mann argues, is continuously appropriated by bourgeois culture. Brecht complained about bourgeois productions of *The Threepenny Opera* in correspondence with Giorgio Strehler in *Collected Plays Two*, ed. John Willet and Ralph Manheim (New York: Bloomsbury, 2015), 320–23.

29. Mae M. Ngai, *Impossible Subjects: Illegal Aliens and the Making of Modern America* (Princeton: Princeton University Press, 2004), 95.

30. Ngai, *Impossible Subjects*, 4–5.

31. Ngai, *Impossible Subjects*, 8.

32. Brecht, *Brecht on Theater*, 128.

33. Gaztambide-Fernández, "Why the Arts Don't Do Anything," 227.

34. Bertolt Brecht, *Brecht on Theater: The Development of an Aesthetic*, trans. and ed. John Willet (London: Methuen Drama, 1990), 191.

35. Tom Prideaux, "A Loving Healing Kind of Theater," *Life*, September 16, 1966, 24.

36. hooks, *Teaching Community*, 21.

37. Brooks, *Bodies in Dissent*, 5.

38. Brooks, *Bodies in Dissent*, 5.

39. de Jong, *You Can't Eat Freedom*, 3.

40. Bertolt Brecht and Margarete Stefffin, "Señora Carrar's Rifles," in *Collected Plays 4* (London: Methuen Drama, 2003).

41. Varela, personal correspondence.

42. "Free Southern Theater Seeks to Build Negroes' Self-Esteem," *New York Times*, July 30, 1965), 15.

43. Brecht, "Organum," 35

44. Tom Prideaux, "A Loving Healing Kind of Theater," *Life*, September 16, 1966.

45. Dent, Moses, and Schechner, *The Free Southern Theater by the Free Southern Theater*, 5.

46. Varela, "Selma Literacy Project."

47. Bettina L. Love, *We Want to Do More Than Survive: Abolitionist Teaching and the Pursuit of Educational Freedom* (Boston: Beacon Press, 2019), 11.

48. Love, *We Want to Do More Than Survive*, 51.

Chapter 4

1. Toni Cade Bambara, *The Sea Birds Are Still Alive* (New York: Vintage Books, 1982), 12

2. Alice Walker, *The Color Purple* (New York: Washington Square Press, 1983), 60.

3. See Greta de Jong's *You Can't Eat Freedom*, chapter 4, and Jessica Gordon Nembhard's *Collective Courage: A History of African American Cooperative Economic Thought and Practice* (University Park: Penn State University Press, 2014), which discusses the Federation of Southern Cooperatives and the most famous cooperative: Fannie Lou Hamer's Freedom Farm. The Federation of Southern Cooperatives was founded in 1967 with 22 organizations across the South and had 130 members by the mid-'70s. Today it is called the FSC/Land Assistance Fund and boasts about 75 independent cooperatives and credit unions. At the time the FSC was founded, merely having NAACP membership was a basis for *denial for member-*

ship by white cooperative members. Even though images of the civil rights movement feature young college students protesting for a seat at the counter, less celebrated is how Black people in the South constantly organized around agriculture—a history that extends back to farming practices in Africa and has had a recent resurgence in social justice farming and foodways. For example, the US Department of Agriculture's "comprehensive" history of independent black farming in the US only mentions men like Father AJ Knight and Rev. Francis X. Walker in relation to cooperatives, excluding any and all women who organized and participated in these cooperatives, such as Derby.

4. Doris Derby, interview for *Newsfront*, January 13, 1969, Box 2, Fl. 4, Doris A. Derby Papers.

5. "Liberty House Brochure," Box 4, Fl. 2, Doris A. Derby Papers.

6. Jesse Morris, "Memo to All Workshops," Box 4, Doris A. Derby Papers. Morris writes that "Liberty House is in very bad financial shape" and apologizes for an anticipated six-week gap without purchasing of goods, which previously happened every two weeks. This meant over a month without pay, which would have been devastating to workers.

7. Cooperatives appear in many fictional accounts of social movements written by women of color. For example, Bambara's *The Salt Eaters* takes place within a cooperative, Academy of Seven Arts, that intersects cultural production with health care through traditional and alternative medicine. Similarly, in Ana Castillo's *So Far from God*, Sophia's movement for environmental justice includes starting a food and wool-making coop, inspired by a real cooperative in New Mexico.

8. James Smethurst, *Behold the Land: The Black Arts Movement in the South* (Chapel Hill: University of North Carolina Press, 2021), 65.

9. Anne Gessler, *Cooperatives in New Orleans: Collective Action and Urban Development* (Jackson: University Press of Mississippi, 2020).

10. Thomas DeFrantz, "To Make Black Bodies Strange: Social Critique in Concert Dance of the Black Arts Movement (1998)," in *A Sourcebook of African-American Performance: Plays, People, Movements*, ed. Annemarie Bean, 83–96 (New York: Routledge, 1999).

11. "Jimmy the Early Bird interviewing Doris Derby (Side A only)," AV1, Doris Adelaide Derby Papers 1960–1992, Stuart A. Rose Manuscript, Archives, and Rare Book Library, Emory University.

12. Robert Maslow, "More Liberty Houses?" Reprinted from *Manas Journal*, March 1, 1967, Box 4, Doris A. Derby Papers.

13. "Mt. Beulah Brochure," Poor People's Corporation, Box 3, Doris A. Derby Papers.

14. Greta de Jong elaborates on this: "The immediate purpose of these efforts was to assist people who had lost their homes and income. However, cooperatives were also a way for people to declare economic independence and facilitate the continuation of the freedom movement." De Jong, *You Can't Eat Freedom*, 89.

15. David A. Davis, *Driven to the Field: Sharecropping and Southern Literature* (Charlottesville: University of Virginia Press, 2023), 94.

16. Nembhard, *Collective Courage*, 1.

17. Nembhard, *Collective Courage*, 186.

18. Smethurst, *Behold*, 65, 51.

19. Doris Derby, "Jimmy the Early Bird."

20. Neil A. Maxwell, "Self-Help Struggle," *Wall Street Journal*, August 19, 1966, Doris A. Derby Papers.

21. "Eastland 'Praises' PPC," Poor People's Corporation Newsletter, n.d., Doris A. Derby Papers.

22. Interview with Doris Derby, *Newsfront*, June 13, 1969, Liberty House, Box 4, Doris A. Derby Papers.

23. "Lier Offers Self-Help," Liberty House Box 4, Doris A. Derby Papers.

24. Derby, "Jimmy the Early Bird."

25. The archive does not make it clear who these critics were. Historically, cooperatives have negotiated a difficult position within Marxist-derived political theory. Marx saw it as proof of social evolution away from capitalism, and Soviet Union leader Vladimir Lenin, in his 1923 article "On Cooperation," first published in *Pravda* no. 115–16 (1923), was in favor of cooperatives because they put organizational and political power into the hands of Soviet peasants. To make this function, he claimed "there is 'only' one thing we have left to do and that is to make our people so 'enlightened' that they understand all the advantages of everyone participating in the work of cooperatives, and organize this participation" and that this major political shift "cannot, in fact, be achieved without a cultural revolution." Lenin's paternalistic language and emphasis on enlightening workers draws attention to SNCC's anxiety over doing something similar and even echoes some of Hoffman's language over how cooperatives could liberate people. Even though cooperatives demanded shared ownership, the goal was still to create a surplus that could be divided among members and to build capital for the community. The term *self-help*, then, means both *self* and the *community* at the same time.

26. Abbott (Abbie) Hoffman, "The Crafts of Freedom," *Catholic Worker*, October–November 1966, Box 4, Doris A. Derby Papers.

27. Hoffman, "Crafts of Freedom."

28. Hoffman, "Crafts of Freedom."

29. bell hooks, *Sisters of the Yam: Black Women and Self-Recovery*, 2nd ed. (Cambridge: South End Press, 2005), 40.

30. Malcolm X, "Message to the Grassroots," http://www.csun.edu/~hcpas003/grassroots.html

31. Monica M. White, *Freedom Farmers: Agricultural Resistance and the Black Freedom Movement* (Chapel Hill: University of North Carolina Press, 2018), 5, 8–9.

32. White, *Freedom Farmers*, 4.

33. Ransby, 85.

34. Joanna Davis-McElligatt, "A Heritage Unique in the Ages: The Politics of Black Southern Womanhood in Anna Julia Cooper's A Voice from the South by a Black Woman from the South," in *A History of the Literature of the U.S. South*, ed. Harilaos Stecopoulos (Cambridge: Cambridge University Press, 2021), 203.

35. Anna Julia Cooper, "Colored women as wage earners. (Documents)," *Negro History Bulletin*, January-September 1996.

36. Cooper, "Colored women."

37. Davis-McElligatt, "Heritage Unique in the Ages," 207.

38. Anna Julia Cooper, *A Voice from the South* (New York: Negro Universities Press, 1969), 261.

39. Cooper, *A Voice*, 256.

40. Cooper, *A Voice*, 257, emphasis in original.

41. Cooper, *A Voice*, 32–33.

42. Saidiya Hartman, *Wayward Lives, Beautiful Experiments: Intimate Histories of Social Upheaval* (New York: Norton, 2019), 227–28, emphasis in original.

43. Patricia Turner, *Crafted Lives: Stories and Studies of African American Quilters* (Jackson: University of Mississippi Press, 2009), ix.

44. Joseph Mosnier and Doris Adelaide Derby and Civil Rights History Project, U.S., Doris Adelaide Derby oral history interview conducted by Joseph Mosnier in Atlanta, Georgia, March 26, 2011. Video. https://www.loc.gov/item/20156 69107/

45. Leigh Raiford, *Imprisoned in a Luminous Glare: Photography and the African American Freedom Struggle* (Chapel Hill: University of North Carolina Press, 2013).

46. Beverly Gordon, *Textiles: The Whole Story: Uses, Meanings, Significance* (London: Thames & Hudson, 2011), 26.

47. Gordon, *Textiles*, 74.

48. Turner, *Crafted Lives*, 180.

49. Turner, *Crafted Lives*, 134.

50. Turner, *Crafted Lives*, 133.

51. Alice Walker, "Everyday Use," *Harper's Magazine*, April 1973.

52. Riché Richardson, *Emancipation's Daughters: Reimagining Black Femininity and the National Body* (Durham: Duke University Press, 2021), 227.

53. Richardson, *Emancipation's Daughters*, 232.

54. Richardson, *Emancipation's Daughters*, 80.

55. Hartman, *Wayward Lives*, xiii.

56. Hartman, *Wayward Lives*, 17.

57. Hartman, *Wayward Lives*, 17.

58. Joseph Mosnier and Doris Adelaide Derby and Civil Rights History Project, U.S., Doris Adelaide Derby oral history interview conducted by Joseph Mosnier in Atlanta, Georgia, March 26, 2011. Video. https://www.loc.gov/item/20156 69107/

59. Frances Wegner, "Housewife Helps Others Help Themselves," *Long Island Press*, December 14, 1965, Doris A. Derby Papers.

60. Sara Ahmed, *Compliant!* (Durham: Duke University Press, 2021), 6.

61. "Poor People's Corporation Management Meeting, Minutes: December 20, 1969," Box 4, Liberty House, Doris A. Derby Papers.

62. "Poor People's Corporation Management Meeting."

63. Ahmed, *Compliant!*, 7.

64. Walker, *Color Purple*, 190–91.

65. Lauren Berlant, "Race, Gender, and Nation in 'The Color Purple,'" *Critical Inquiry* 14, no. 4 (Summer 1988): 858.

66. Berlant, "Race, Gender, and Nation," 858.

67. Walker, *Color Purple*, 123.

68. Varela, "Selma Literacy Program," Maria Varela Papers, Wisconsin Historical Society.

69. Karl Marx, "Wage Labor and Capital," in *The Marx-Engels Reader*, 2nd ed., ed. Robert Tucker (New York: Norton), 1978.

70. Marx, "Wage Labor and Capital," 204.

Chapter 5

1. West Batesville Farmer's Cooperative, *Something of Our Own* (Tougaloo: Flute Publications, 1966), 1.

2. Varela, "Learning from Experience: Part 2," SNCC Digital Gateway.

3. Monteith, *SNCC's Stories*, 23.

4. Monteith, *SNCC's Stories*, 23.

5. For more on how civil rights activists sought to improve daily life, see Greta de Jong's *You Can't Eat Freedom* (2016) and John Dittmer's *Local People* (1995).

6. Varela, personal correspondence.

7. See Allison Graham's description of the "civil rights genre" in "'We Ain't Doin' Civil Rights': The Life and Times of a Genre, as Told in *The Help*," *Southern Cultures* 20, no. 1 (Spring 2014), and Sharon Monteith's chapter, "Civil Rights Movement Film," in *The Cambridge Companion to American Civil Rights Literature*, ed. Julie Anderson (Cambridge: Cambridge University Press, 2015).

8. For example, see *Third World Newsreel: Reflections on Progressive Media since 1968*, ed. Cynthia Young, https://www.twn.org/Monograph/twn-monograph-20 18.pdf

9. Leigh Raiford, "'Come Let Us Build a New World Together': SNCC and Photography of the Civil Rights Movement," *American Quarterly* 59, no. 4 (2007): 1130.

10. Raiford, *Imprisoned in a Luminous Glare*, 3.

11. Nicole R. Fleetwood, *Troubling Vision: Performance, Visuality, and Blackness* (Chicago: University of Chicago Press, 2011), 13.

12. Fleetwood, *Troubling Vision*, 34.

13. Raiford, *Imprisoned*, 73.

14. Varela, personal correspondence.

15. Hayley O'Malley, "Another Cinema: James Baldwin's Search for a New Film Form," *James Baldwin Review* 7 (2021): 106.

16. Aguayo, *Documentary*, 3.

17. Varela, personal correspondence.

18. Aguayo, *Documentary Resistance*, 3, 7.

19. Or for that matter, its outpost in Iowa City, where Hans Breder institutionalized the form at the University of Iowa.

Notes to Pages 131–41 · 191

20. The main text for defining the artform is *Intermedia: Enacting the Liminal*, ed. Hans Breder and Klaus-Peter Busse (2005).

21. José Esteban Muñoz, *Cruising Utopia: The Then and There of Queer Futurity* (New York: NYU Press, 2009), 116.

22. Muñoz, *Cruising Utopia*, 116.

23. Taylor, *¡Presente!*.

24. The filmstrip projector made its way to SNCC as a tool of education that reflected the trend that brought projectors into classrooms between the 1930s and 1970s. In the 1960s, as the technology advanced and became more available, it was ubiquitous in classrooms across the US except in the rural South, where many one-room schoolhouses predominately in Black communities did not have access to this technology. These advances align the filmstrip projector with the rise of the educational industry, which promoted the use of technological media in the classroom. Like today, this included private partnerships with companies responsible for creating and installing objects like projectors into classrooms. Filmstrip projector companies would employ photographers to create content for the filmstrips and someone else to record an audio track on vinyl and later audiocassettes, creating a passive form of education where students could receive information from a machine. However, as Varela recalls, the advanced technology was not yet available to activists in the South.

25. West Batesville Farmer's Cooperative, *Something of Our Own*, 22.

26. Benjamin S. Child, *The Whole Machinery: The Rural Modern in Cultures of the U.S. South, 1890–1946* (Athens: University of Georgia Press, 2019), 13.

27. West Batesville Farmer's Cooperative, *Something of Our Own*, 33.

28. West Batesville Farmer's Cooperative, *Something of Our Own*, 27.

29. West Batesville Farmer's Cooperative, *Something of Our Own*, 30.

30. West Batesville Farmer's Cooperative, *Something of Our Own*, 32.

31. Leigh Anne Duck, "Commercial Counterhistory: Remapping the Movement in Lee Daniels' *The Butler*," *Journal of American Studies* 52, no. 2 (2018): 421.

32. *The Farm Workers' Strike*, Maria Varela, producer, photographs by George Ballis, Flute Productions, 17.

33. *The Farm Workers' Strike*, 17.

34. *The Farm Workers' Strike*, 27.

35. Chrissie Iles and Whitney Museum of American Art, *Into the Light: The Projected Image in American Art, 1964–1977* (New York: Whitney Museum of American Art, 2001), 41.

36. Aguayo, *Documentary Resistance*, ix.

37. Varela, "Learning from Experience," part 4. Varela also states, "We assumed school leaders would let the local movement people use school projectors. Many did not. This is ultimately why the books were much more useful and more widely distributed. SNCC organizers took the books to all the communities where they worked. The SNCC and CORE networks distributed the books."

38. According to Varela, because of the high value attributed to books in the Black Belt South, Hamer "wanted a more well rounded version of her life in print." After Hamer's death, her friends encouraged Varela to make the book available

online and you can find it at https://snccdigital.org/wp-content/themes/sncc/flipb ooks/mev_hamer_updated_2018/index.html?swipeboxvideo=1#page/1

39. Geer Morton, "Prospectus: Southern Media, Inc.: documentary films for the rural south, a self-help project" 1967, Southern Media, Box 3, Fl. 17, Doris A. Derby Papers, 1.

40. Lary Rand, "Goals and Purposes," Southern Media, Box 3, Fl. 17, Doris A. Derby Papers, 1.

41. Morton, "Prospectus: Southern Media, Inc.," 13.

42. Rand, "Goals and Purposes," 3.

43. Varela, "Jane Stembridge." Jane Stembridge, a white woman lesbian and southerner, was active as a SNCC staff member and literary activist in the Movement. She withdrew from SNCC in protest of their homophobic treatment of Bayard Rustin.

44. Bambara, *The Sea Birds Are Still Alive*, 5.

45. *Furrows* is available in open access on the Civil Rights Movement Veterans Archive website: https://www.crmvet.org/poetry/pcobb_furrows-r5.pdf

46. Varela, personal correspondence.

47. Cobb, *Furrows*, 1.

48. Riché Richardson, *Emancipation's Daughters: Reimagining Black Femininity and the National Body* (Durham: Duke University Press, 2021), 227.

49. Cobb, *Furrows*, 38.

50. Cobb, *Furrows*, 38 and 41.

51. Cobb, *Furrows*, 38.

52. Tavia Amolo Nyong'o, *Afro-Fabulations: The Queer Drama of Black Life* (New York: NYU Press, 2019), 51.

53. Nyong'o, *Afro-Fabulations*, 49.

54. Cobb, *Furrows*, 39.

55. Taylor, *¡Presente!*, 2.

56. "A Proposal in Cultural Affairs to National Education Television," March 4, 1970, Box 55, Fl. 28, The Free Southern Theater Papers, 13, 14, 15.

57. "A Proposal," 15.

58. "A Proposal," 13.

59. The Free Southern Theater, "Nation Time Begins October 11th-10 P.M.," *FST Newsletter* 1, no. 3 (October 1972).

60. The Free Southern Theater, "Nation Time Begins."

61. "Summary of Discussion in Meetings of FST Production Staff Group" 1973, Box 54, Fl. 27, The Free Southern Theater Papers.

62. "Summary of Discussion," 3, 4.

63. "African Slave Trade to the Civil War," *Nation Time*, The Free Southern Theater, December 20, 1974, Audiovisual Materials, The Free Southern Theater Papers.

64. William Rouselle, "'Nation Time' Returns for Third Season," The Free Southern Theater, Box 50, Fl. 27, The Free Southern Theater Papers.

65. "African Slave Trade."

66. "African Slave Trade."

67. "African Slave Trade."

68. Tina Post, *Deadpan: The Aesthetics of Black Inexpression* (New York: NYU Press, 2023), 3, 12.

69. Colbert, Jones, and Vogel, *Race and Performance after Repetition*, 8.

70. "African Slave Track."

71. "Nation Time Cancellation: Public Television in Whose Interest?," Box 50, Fl. 27, The Free Southern Theater Papers, 1.

72. "Nation Time Cancellation," 2.

Conclusion

1. Jeanette Winterson, *Art Objects: Essays on Ecstasy and Effrontery* (New York: Knopf, 1996), 12.

2. This name comes from a poster of the event found in the Free Southern Theater archives, but other versions of the title exist, including "The Funeral of the Free Southern Theater, a Valediction without Mourning."

3. John O'Neal, "'The Performance Festival', FST Conference-Report on the FST Project /Outline, 1985," Box 28, Folder 4, The John O'Neal Papers, Amistad Research Center, Tulane University Libraries, New Orleans, LA.

4. brown, *Emergent Strategy*, 131.

5. Brooks and José Muñoz. "Open Channels," 63.

6. Brooks and Muñoz, "Open Channels," 64.

7. Christina Sharpe, *In the Wake: On Blackness and Being* (Durham: Duke University Press, 2016).

8. In Lawrence Weschler's *Everything That Rises: A Book of Convergences* (San Francisco: McSweeney's, 2006), he makes the case for visual convergences across art history.

9. Smethurst, *Behold the Land*, 181.

10. Smethurst, *Behold the Land*, 181.

11. John O'Neal, "Story Circle Methodology," Junebug Productions, https://www.junebugproductions.org/story-circle

12. Jones, Moore, and Bridgforth, *Experiments in a Jazz Aesthetic*, 5.

13. Jones, Moore, and Bridgforth, 5.

14. Jones, Moore, and Bridgforth, 15–16, 6.

15. Jones, Moore, and Bridgforth, 16.

16. Jones, Moore, and Bridgforth, 7.

17. Jones, Moore, and Bridgforth, 273.

18. Jones, Moore, and Bridgforth, 9.

19. Dent, Moses, and Schechner, *The Free Southern Theater by the Free Southern Theater*, 12.

20. Virginia Grise and Irma Mayorga, *The Panza Monologues*, 2nd ed. (Austin: University of Texas Press, 2014), 15.

21. Grise and Mayorga, *Panza Monologues*, 49.

22. Grise and Mayorga, *Panza Monologues*, 16.

23. Grise and Mayorga, *Panza Monologues*, 16.

24. Grise and Mayorga, *Panza Monologues*, 13.

25. Broyles-González, *El Teatro Campesino*, 22.

26. My observations come from a live performance I attended at the University of Mississippi in 2014.

27. Grise and Mayorga, *Panza Monologues*, 26.

28. Grise and Mayorga, *Panza Monologues*, 17, 22.

29. Grise and Mayorga, *Panza Monologues*, 62.

30. Grise and Mayorga, *Panza Monologues*, 87.

31. Grise and Mayorga, *Panza Monologues*, 87.

32. Okiji, *Jazz as Critique*, 29.

33. Okiji, *Jazz as Critique*, 29.

34. Grise and Mayorga, *Panza Monologues*, 74.

35. Grise and Mayorga, *Panza Monologues*, 81.

36. Grise and Mayorga, *Panza Monologues*, xi.

37. Grise and Mayorga, *Panza Monologues*, 43.

38. Mayorga and Grise, *Panza Monologues*, xi.

39. Appalshop, "Our Mission," https://appalshop.org/pdf/Appalshop%20Mission%20Statement%20Text.pdf

40. Leah Penniman, *Farming While Black: Soul Fire Farm's Practical Guide to Liberation on the Land* (White River Junction, Vt.: Chelsea Green Publishing, 2018), 27.

41. Penniman, *Farming While Black*, 8.

42. Penniman, *Farming While Black*, 67.

43. Penniman, *Farming While Black*, 69.

44. soulfirefarm, "Our Ancestral Farming Practices," Instagram and Facebook, July 19, 2023.

45. Mumu Fresh aka Maimouna Youssef, "Reparations," *Vintage Babies II: Queen of Culture*, June 18, 2021.

46. Penniman, *Farming While Black*, 15.

47. O'Meally, Edwards, and Griffin, *Uptown Conversation*, 395.

Bibliography

Aguayo, Angela J. *Documentary Resistance: Social Change and Participatory Media.* New York: Oxford University Press, 2019.

Ahmed, Sara. *Compliant!* Durham: Duke University Press, 2021.

Appalshop. "Our Mission." Appalshop.org. https://appalshop.org/pdf/Appalshop%20Mission%20Statement%20Text.pdf

Araiza, Lauren. *To March for Others: The Black Freedom Struggle and the United Farm Workers.* University Park: University of Pennsylvania Press, 2013.

Bambara, Toni Cade. *Deep Sightings & Rescue Missions: Fiction Essays, and Conversations*, edited by Toni Morrison. New York: Penguin Random House, 1999.

Bambara, Toni Cade. "An Interview with Toni Cade Bambara: Kay Bonetti." In *Conversations with Toni Cade Bambara*, edited by Thabiti Lewis. Jackson: University Press of Mississippi, 2012.

Bambara, Toni Cade. *The Salt Eaters.* New York: Vintage Books, 1982.

Bambara, Toni Cade. *The Sea Birds Are Still Alive.* New York: Vintage Books, 1982.

Baraka, Amiri (LeRoi Jones). *Blues People: The Negro Experience in White America and the Music That Developed from It.* New York: Morrow Quill Paperbacks, 1963.

Baraka, Amiri (LeRoi Jones). "The Changing Same (R&B and New Black Music)." In *The LeRoi Jones/Amiri Baraka Reader*, edited by William J. Harris, 186–92. New York: Thunder's Mouth Press, 2000.

Baraka, Amiri. *Home: Social Essays.* New York: Akashic Books, 2009.

Baraka, Amiri (LeRoi Jones). "Slaveship" [*sic*] script, Box 78, Fl.10, The Free Southern Theater Papers. Amistad Research Center. New Orleans, LA.

Baram, Marcus. *Gil Scott-Heron: Pieces of a Man.* New York: St. Martin's Press, 2014.

Bean, Annemarie, ed. *A Sourcebook of African-American Performance: Plays, People, Movements.* New York: Routledge, 1999.

Beckett, Samuel. *Waiting for Godot.* Translated by Samuel Beckett. New York: Grove Press, 1954.

Behnken, Brian D., ed. *Civil Rights and Beyond: African American and Latino/a Activism in the Twentieth-Century United States.* Athens: University of Georgia Press, 2016.

Behnken, Brian D., ed. *The Struggle in Black and Brown: African American and Mexican American Relations during the Civil Rights Era*. Lincoln: University of Nebraska Press, 2012.

Berlant, Lauren. Introduction to "Intimacy," special issue, *Critical Inquiry* 24, no. 2 (Winter 1998): 281–88.

Berlant, Lauren. "Race, Gender, and Nation in 'The Color Purple.'" *Critical Inquiry* 14, no. 4 (Summer 1988): 831–59.

Bhandary, Asha. *Freedom to Care: Liberalism, Dependency Care, and Culture*. New York Routledge, 2020.

Bial, Henry, and Carol Martin, eds. *Brecht Sourcebook*. New York: Routledge, 2000.

Boal, Augusto. *Theater of the Oppressed*. Translated by Charles A. McBride, Maria-Odilia Leal McBride, and Emily Fryer. London: Pluto Press, 1979.

Brecht, Bertolt. *Brecht on Theater: The Development of an Aesthetic*. Translated and edited by John Willett. London: Methuen Drama, 1990.

Brecht, Bertolt. *Collected Plays Two*. Edited by John Willett and Ralph Manheim. New York: Bloomsbury, 2015.

Brecht, Bertolt, and Margarete Steffin. "Señora Carrar's Rifles." In *Collected Plays Four*. London: Methuen Drama, 2003.

Brooks, Daphne. *Bodies in Dissent: Spectacular Performances of Race and Freedom, 1850–1910*. Durham: Duke University Press, 2006.

Brooks, Daphne A., and José Muñoz. "Open Channels: Some Thoughts on Blackness, the Body, and Sound(ing) Women in the (Summer) Time of Trayvon." *Performance Research: A Journal of the Performing Arts* 19, no. 3 (2014): 62–68.

brown, adrienne maree. *Emergent Strategy: Shaping Change, Shaping Worlds*. Chico, CA: AK Press, 2017.

brown, adrienne maree. *Holding Change: The Way of Emergent Strategy Facilitation and Mediation*. Chico, CA: AK Press, 2017.

Broyles-González, Yolanda. *El Teatro Campesino: Theater in the Chicano Movement*. Austin: University of Texas Press, 1994.

Bullins, Ed. "The So-Called Western Avant-Garde." In *Twelve Plays & Selected Writings*, edited by Mike Sell. Ann Arbor: University of Michigan Press, 2006.

Caison, Gina. *Red States: Indigeneity, Settler Colonialism, and Southern Studies*. Athens: University of Georgia Press, 2018.

Carson, Clayborne, David J. Garrow, Gerald R. Gill, Vincent Harding, and Darlene Clark Hine, eds. *The Eyes on the Prize Civil Rights Reader: Documents, Speeches, and Firsthand Accounts from the Black Freedom Struggle*. New York: Penguin, 1991.

Cha-Jua, Sundiata, and Clarence Lang. "The 'Long Movement' as Vampire: Temporal and Spatial Fallacies in Recent Black Freedom Studies." *Journal of African American History* 92, no. 2 (Spring 2007): 265–88.

Child, Benjamin S. *The Whole Machinery: The Rural Modern in Cultures of the U.S. South, 1890–1946*. Athens: University of Georgia Press, 2019.

Cobb, Charlie. *Furrows*. Jackson, MS: Flute Publications, 1967. https://www.crmvet.org/poetry/pcobb_furrows-r5.pdf

Colbert, Soyica Diggs, Douglas A. Jones, and Shane Vogel, eds. *Race and Performance after Repetition*. Durham: Duke University Press, 2020.

Conquergood, Dwight. "Health Theater in a Hmong Refugee Camp: Performance, Comunication, and Culture." *TDR* 32, no. 3 (Autumn 1988): 174–208.

Cooper, Anna Julia. "Colored women as wage earners. (Documents)." *Negro History Bulletin*, January –September 1996, 33+ pages. Gale Academic OneFile, https://go.gale.com/ps/i.do?p=AONE&u=googlescholar&id=GALE|A83667145&v=2.1&it=r&sid=bookmarkAONE&asid=90cc52cc

Cooper, Anna Julia. *A Voice from the South*. New York: Negro Universities Press, 1969.

"Creative Time Presents Paul Chan's Waiting for Godot in New Orleans: A Play in Two Acts. A Project in Two Parts." *Creativetime.org*, 2007. https://creativeti me.org/programs/archive/2007/chan/welcome.html

Davis, David A. *Driven to the Field: Sharecropping and Southern Literature*. Charlottesville: University of Virginia Press, 2023.

Davis-McElligatt, Joanna. "A Heritage Unique in the Ages: The Politics of Black Southern Womanhood in Anna Julia Cooper's A Voice from the South by a Black Woman from the South." In *A History of the Literature of the U.S. South*, edited by Harilaos Stecopoulos. Cambridge: Cambridge University Press, 2021.

DeFrantz, Thomas. "To Make Black Bodies Strange: Social Critique in Concert Dance of the Black Arts Movement (1998)." In *A Sourcebook of African-American Performance: Plays, People, Movements*, edited by Annemarie Bean, 83–96. New York: Routledge, 1999.

de Jong, Greta. *You Can't Eat Freedom: Southerners and Social Justice after the Civil Rights Movement*. Chapel Hill: University of North Carolina Press, 2016.

Dent, Thomas C., and Richard Schechner. *The Free Southern Theater by the Free Southern Theater: A Documentary of the South's Radical Black Theater, with Journals, Letters, Poetry, Essays, and a Play Written by Those Who Built It*. New York: Bobbs-Merrill, 1969.

D'Erasmo, Stacey. *The Art of Intimacy: The Space Between*. Minneapolis: Graywolf Press, 2013.

Derby, Doris Adelaide. Doris Adelaide Derby Papers, 1960–1992. Manuscript Collection No. 935. Stuart A. Rose Manuscripts, Archives, and Rare Book Library. Emory University, Atlanta, GA.

Dewey, John. *Art as Experience*. New York: Paragon Books, 1979.

DiPiero, Dan. *Contingent Encounters: Improvisation in Music and Everyday Life*. Ann Arbor: University of Michigan Press, 2022.

Dittmer, John. *Local People: The Struggle for Civil Rights in Mississippi*. Champaign: University of Illinois Press, 1995.

Duck, Leigh Anne. "Commercial Counterhistory: Remapping the Movement in Lee Daniels' The Butler." *Journal of American Studies* 52, no. 2 (2018): 418–46.

Dyer, Richard. *Pastiche*. New York: Routledge, 2006.

Elam, Harry J. *Taking It to the Streets: The Social Protest Theater of Luis Valdez*. Ann Arbor: University of Michigan Press, 2001.

Elam, Harry J., and David Krasner. *African American Performance and Theater History: A Critical Reader*. Oxford: Oxford University Press, 2001.

Elliott, David J., Marissa Silverman, and Wayne D. Bowman, eds. *Artistic Citizen-*

ship: Artistry, Social Responsibility, and Ethical Praxis. New York: Oxford University Press, 2016.

El Teatro Campesino, CEMA 5. El Teatro Campesino Archives. Donald C. Davidson Library, University of California at Santa Barbara, CA.

Fantasia, Rick, and Kim Voss. *Hard Work: Remaking the American Labor Movement.* Berkeley: University of California Press, 2004.

The Farm Worker's Strike. Maria Varela, producer, photographs by George Ballis. Tougaloo, MS: Flute Productions.

Feinstein, Sarah, and David Rife, eds. *The Jazz Fiction Anthology.* Bloomington: Indiana University Press, 2009.

Fischer-Lichte, Erika. "Interweaving Cultures in Performance: Different States of Being In-Between." *Textures* (2010): 1–17.

Fischlin, David, Ajay Heble, and George Lipsitz. *The Fierce Urgency of Now: Improvisation, Rights, and the Ethics of Cocreation.* Durham: Duke University Press, 2013.

Fleetwood, Nicole R. *Troubling Vision: Performance, Visuality, and Blackness.* Chicago: University of Chicago Press, 2011.

Fleming, Julius B., Jr. *Black Patience: Performance, Civil Rights, and the Unfinished Project of Emancipation.* New York: NYU Press, 2022.

Free Southern Theater. Records, 158, The Free Southern Theater Papers. Amistad Research Center, New Orleans.

"Free Southern Theater Seeks to Build Negroes' Self-Esteem." *New York Times,* July 30, 1965, 15.

Freire, Paulo. *Pedagogy of Freedom: Ethics, Democracy, and Civic Courage.* Translated by Patrick Clarke. Lanham, MD: Rowman & Littlefield, 1998.

Gabbard, Krin, ed. *Jazz among the Discourses.* Durham: Duke University Press, 1995.

Gaztambide-Fernández, Rúben A. "Why the Arts Don't Do Anything: Toward a New Vision for Cultural Production in Education." *Harvard Educational Review* 83, no. 1 (2013): 211–37.

Gessler, Anne. *Cooperatives in New Orleans: Collective Action and Urban Development.* Jackson: University Press of Mississippi, 2020.

"Gilbert Moses and Richard Murphy." Interview with Robert Penn Warren, Tape 1, *Who Speaks for the Negro? An Archival Collection,* Vanderbilt University. https:// whospeaks.library.vanderbilt.edu/interview/gilbert-moses-and-richard-mu rphy

Gordon, Beverly. *Textiles: The Whole Story: Uses, Meanings, Significance.* London: Thames & Hudson, 2011.

"The Greatest Love." Produced by David Simon, et al. *Treme.* HBO, October 14, 2012.

Grise, Virginia, and Irma Mayorga. *The Panza Monologues.* 2nd ed. Austin: University of Texas Press, 2014.

Hale, John N. *The Freedom Schools: Student Activists in the Mississippi Civil Rights Movement.* New York: Columbia University Press, 2016.

Harding, James M. "From Cutting Edge to Rough Edges: On the Transnational

Foundations of Avant-Garde Performance." In *Not the Other Avant-Garde*, edited by James M. Harding and John Rouse, 18–40. Ann Arbor: University of Michigan Press, 2006.

Harding, James M., and Cindy Rosenthal, eds. *Restaging the Sixties; Radical Theaters and Their Legacy*. Ann Arbor: University of Michigan Press, 2006.

Hartman, Saidiya. *Wayward Lives, Beautiful Experiments: Intimate Histories of Social Upheaval*. New York: W. W. Norton, 2019.

Heble, Ajay. "'Why Can't We Go Somewhere There?' Sun Ra, Improvisation, and the Imagination of Future Possibilities." *Canadian Theatre Review* 143 (Summer 2010): 98–100.

Herrera, Juan. *Cartographic Memory: Social Movement Activism and the Production of Space*. Durham: Duke University Press, 2022.

Hilton, Leon, and Mariahdessa Ekere Tallie. "The Unwieldy Otherwise: Rethinking the Roots of Performance Studies in and through the Black Freedom Struggle." *Performance Matters* 8, no. 2 (2023).

Holsaert, Faith S., Martha Prescod Norman Noonan, Judy Richardson, Betty Garman Robinson, Jean Smith Young, and Dorothy M. Zellner, eds. *Hands on the Freedom Plow: Personal Accounts by Women in SNCC*. Champaign: University of Illinois Press, 2010.

hooks, bell. *Art on My Mind: Visual Politics*. New York: New Press, 1995.

hooks, bell. *Feminist Theory: From Margin to Center*. Boston: South End Press, 1984.

hooks, bell. *Outlaw Culture: Resisting Representations*. New York: Routledge, (1994) 2006.

hooks, bell. *Sisters of the Yam: Black Women and Self-Recovery*. 2nd ed. Cambridge, MA: South End Press, 2005.

hooks, bell. *Teaching Community: A Pedagogy of Hope*. New York: Routledge, 2004.

hooks, bell. *Teaching to Transgress: Education as the Practice of Freedom*. New York: Routledge, 1994.

Huerta, Dolores. "Dolores Huerta Oral History." Farmworker Movement Documentation Project, UC San Diego. https://libraries.ucsd.edu/farmworkermove ment/medias/oral-history/

Huerta, Jorge. "When Sleeping Giants Awaken: Chicano Theater in the 1960s." *Theatre Survey* 43, no. 1 (May 2002).

Iles, Chrissie, and Whitney Museum of American Art. *Into the Light: the Projected Image in American Art, 1964–1977*. New York: Whitney Museum of American Art, 2001.

Jarenwattananon, Patrick. "Why Jazz Musicians Love 'The Rite of Spring.'" *NPR*, May 26, 2013.

Jones, LeRoi (Amiri Baraka). *Blues People: Negro Music in White America*. New York: Morrow Quill, 1963.

Jones, Omi Osun Joni L., Lisa L. Moore, and Sharon Bridgforth. *Experiments in a Jazz Aesthetic: Art, Activism, Academia, and the Austin Project*. Austin: University of Texas Press, 2010.

Keating, Ana Louise. "'I'm a Citizen of the Universe': Gloria Anzaldúa's Spiritual

Activism as Catalyst for Social Change." *Feminist Studies* 34, nos. 1–2 (Spring and Summer 2008): 53–69.

Kelley, Robin D. G. *Freedom Dreams: The Black Radical Imagination*. New York: Penguin Random House, 2003.

King, Susan. "Spotlight: James Cromwell in 'Waiting for Godot.'" *Los Angeles Times*, March 28, 2012.

Lenin, Vladimir. "On Cooperation." *Pravda*, nos. 115–16, May 26–27, 1923, reprinted in https://www.marxists.org/archive/lenin/works/1923/jan/06.htm

Love, Bettina L. *We Want to Do More Than Survive: Abolitionist Teaching and the Pursuit of Educational Freedom*. Boston: Beacon Press, 2019.

Lovelace, Alice. "Remembering Toni." *Feminist Wire*. November 21, 2014. https://thefeministwire.com/2014/11/revolutionary-love/

Martin, Carol, and Henry Bial, eds. *Brecht Sourcebook*. New York: Routledge, 2000.

Marsalis, Wynton. "Wynton Marsalis on Jazz as a Tool for Understanding Life." Interview with Andrew Zuckerman for *Time Sensitive*, podcast episode 55, November 12, 2021.

Marx, Karl. "Wage Labor and Capital." In *The Marx-Engels Reader*, 2nd ed., edited by Robert Tucker. New York: W.W. Norton, 1978.

Miner, Dylan A. T. *Creating Aztlán: Chicano Art, Indigenous Sovereignty, and Low-riding across Turtle Island*. Tucson: University of Arizona Press, 2014.

Monteith, Sharon. *SNCC's Stories: The African American Freedom Movement in the Civil Rights South*. Athens: University of Georgia Press, 2020.

Mosnier, Joseph, Doris Adelaide Derby, and Civil Rights History Project, U.S. "Doris Adelaide Derby Oral History Interview Conducted by Joseph Mosnier in Atlanta, Georgia." April 26, 2011. Video. https://www.loc.gov/item/2015669107/

Moten, Fred. *In the Break: The Aesthetics of the Black Radical Tradition*. Minneapolis: University of Minnesota Press, 2003.

Mumu Fresh, aka Maimouna Youssef. "Reparations." *Vintage Babies II: Queen of Culture*, June 18, 2021.

Muñoz, José Esteban. *Cruising Utopia: The Then and There of Queer Futurity*. New York: NYU Press, 2009.

Muñoz, José Esteban. *The Sense of Brown*. Edited by Joshua Chambers-Letson and Tavia Nyong'o. Durham: Duke University Press, 2020.

Muñoz, José Esteban. "Towards a Definition of the Brown Commons." *LitHub*, October 23, 2020.

Nabhan-Warren, Kristy. *Meatpacking America: How Migration, Work, and Faith Unite and Divide the Heartland*. Chapel Hill: University of North Carolina Press, 2021.

Nash, Jennifer. *Black Feminism Reimagined: After Intersectionality*. Durham: Duke University Press 2019.

Neal, Larry. "The Black Arts Movement." *Drama Review* (Summer 1968).

Nembhard, Jessica Gordon. *Collective Courage: A History of African American Cooperative Economic Thought and Practice*. University Park: Pennsylvania State University Press, 2014.

Nepstad, Sharon Erickson. *Catholic Social Activism.* New York: NYU Press, 2019.

Ngai, Mae M. *Impossible Subjects: Illegal Aliens and the Making of Modern America.* Princeton: Princeton University Press, 2004.

Nyong'o, Tavia Amolo. *Afro-Fabulations: The Queer Drama of Black Life.* New York: NYU Press, 2019.

Okiji, Fumi. *Jazz as Critique: Adorno and Black Expression Revisited.* Stanford: Stanford University Press, 2018.

O'Malley, Hayley. "Another Cinema: James Baldwin's Search for a New Film Form." *James Baldwin Review* 7 (2021): 90–114.

O'Meally, Robert G., Brent Hayes Edwards, and Farah Jasmine Griffin, eds. *Uptown Conversation: The New Jazz Studies.* New York: Columbia University Press, 2004.

O'Neal, John. "Story Circle Methodology." Junebug Productions. https://www.jun ebugproductions.org/story-circle

Payne, Charles. *I've Got the Light of Freedom: The Organizing Tradition and the Mississippi Freedom Struggle.* Oakland: University of California Press, 2007.

Peña, Elaine A. *Performing Piety: Making Space Sacred with the Virgin of Guadalupe.* Berkeley: University of California Press, 2011.

Penniman, Leah. *Farming While Black: Soul Fire Farm's Practical Guide to Liberation on the Land.* White River Junction, VT: Chelsea Green, 2018.

Prideaux, Tom. "A Loving Healing Kind of Theater." *Life,* September 16, 1966.

Raiford, Leigh. "'Come Let Us Build a New World Together': SNCC and Photography of the Civil Rights Movement." *American Quarterly* 59, no. 4 (2007): 1129–57.

Raiford, Leigh. *Imprisoned in a Luminous Glare: Photography and the African American Freedom Struggle.* Chapel Hill: University of North Carolina Press, 2013.

Ransby, Barbara. *Ella Baker and the Black Freedom Movement: A Radical Democratic Vision.* Chapel Hill: University of North Carolina Press, 2003.

Reed, T. V. *The Art of Protest: Culture and Activism from the Civil Rights Movement to the Present.* 2nd ed. Minneapolis: University of Minnesota Press, 2019.

Richardson, Riché. *Emancipation's Daughters: Reimagining Black Femininity and the National Body.* Durham: Duke University Press, 2021.

Rifkin, Mark. *Beyond Settler Time: Temporal Sovereignty and Indigenous Self-Determination.* Durham: Duke University Press, 2017.

Schechner, Richard. *Performance Theory.* London: Routledge, 2003.

Sharpe, Christina. *In the Wake: On Blackness and Being.* Durham: Duke University Press, 2016.

Siddall, Gillian, and Ellen Waterman. *Negotiated Moments: Improvisation, Sound, and Subjectivity.* Durham: Duke University Press, 2016.

Smethurst, James. *Behold the Land: The Black Arts Movement in the South.* Chapel Hill: University of North Carolina Press, 2021.

Smethurst, James. "The Black Arts Movement and Historically Black Colleges and Universities." In *New Thoughts on the Black Arts Movement,* edited by Lisa Gail Collins and Margo Natalie Crawford, 75–91. New Brunswick, NJ: Rutgers University Press, 2006.

Smethurst, James. *The Black Arts Movement: Literary Nationalism in the 1960s and 1970s*. Chapel Hill: University of North Carolina Press, 2005.

Smethurst, James. "Black Arts South: Rethinking New Orleans and the Black Arts Movement in the Wake of Hurricane Katrina." In *Radicalism in the South since Reconstruction*, edited by Chris Green, Rachel Rubin, and James Smethurst, 129–48. New York: Palgrave Macmillan, 2006.

Snow, Shelley, Nicolò Francesco Bernardi, Nilufar Sabet-Kassouf, Daniel Moran, and Alexandre Lehmann. "Exploring the Experience and Effects of Vocal Toning." *Journal of Music Therapy* 55, no. 2 (2018): 221–50.

Soul Fire Farm. "Our Ancestral Farming Practices." Instagram and Facebook. Reel. July 19, 2023.

Struthers, David M. *The World in a City: Multiethnic Radicalism in Early Twentieth-Century Los Angeles*. Champaign: University of Illinois Press, 2019.

Taylor, Diana. *The Archive and the Repertoire: Performing Cultural Memory in the Americas*. Durham: Duke University Press, 2003.

Taylor, Diana. *¡Presente! The Politics of Presence*. Durham: Duke University Press, 2020.

Thomas, Lorenzo. "Alea's Children: The Avant Garde on the Lower East Side, 1960–1970." *African American Review* 27, no. 4 (Winter 1993): 573–78.

Thompson, Nato. *Seeing Power: Art and Activism in the 21st Century*. Brooklyn: Melville House, 2015.

Tripp, Ellen Louise. "Free Southern Theater: There Is Always a Message." PhD diss., University of North Carolina at Greensboro, 1986.

Turner, Patricia. *Crafted Lives: Stories and Studies of African American Quilters*. Jackson: University of Mississippi Press, 2009.

Valdez, Luis. "Commentary of Luis Valdez: The Plan of Delano." Farmworker Movement Documentation Project, UC San Diego Library. https://libraries.ucsd.edu/farmworkermovement/essays/essays/Plan%20of%20Delano.pdf

Valdez, Luis. *Luis Valdez Early Works: Actos, Bernabe, and Pensamiento Serpentino*. Houston: Arte Publico Press, 1990.

Varela, Maria. "Jane Stembridge: A SNCC Origin Story." *crmvet.org*, 2021. https://www.crmvet.org/comm/janestem.htm

Varela, Maria. "Learning from Experience: Maria Varela's Perspective, SNCC Field Secretary, 1963–1967." SNCC Digital Gateway. https://snccdigital.org/our-voices/learning-from-experience/part-1/

Varela, Maria. Personal correspondence. September 5, 2023.

Varela, Maria. "Selma Literacy Program." *Papers, 1964–1966*. University of Wisconsin-Madison, Madison.

Walker, Alice. "The Civil Rights Movement: What Good Was It?" *American Scholar*, Autumn 1967, reprinted on theamericanscholar.org, February 10, 2016.

Walker, Alice. *The Color Purple*. New York: Washington Square Press, 1983.

Walker, Alice. "Everyday Use." *Harper's Magazine*, April 1973. https://harpers.org/archive/1973/04/everyday-use/

Bibliography · 203

Walker, Dave. "Wendell Pierce Explains 'Waiting for Godot.'" *Times-Picayune*, October 14, 2012.

West Batesville Farmer's Cooperative. *Something of Our Own*. Maria Varela, producer. Tougaloo, MS: Flute Productions, 1966.

White, Monica M. *Freedom Farmers: Agricultural Resistance and the Black Freedom Movement*. Chapel Hill: University of North Carolina Press, 2018.

Wilkins, Roy. "Interview with Roy Wilkins." *Eyes on the Prize: America's Civil Rights Years 1954 to 1965*. *PBS*, 1987.

Williams, John A. *The Man Who Cried I Am*. New York: Abrams Press, (1967) 2004.

X, Malcolm. "(1963) Malcom X, 'Message to the Grass Roots,'" Black Past. https://www.blackpast.org/african-american-history/speeches-african-american-history/1963-malcolm-x-message-grassroots//

Ybarra-Frausto, Tomas. "Rasquachismo: A Chicano Sensibility." 1989. Documents of Latin American and Latino Art, International Center for the Arts of the Americas at the Museum of Fine Arts in Houston. https://icaa.mfah.org/s/en/item/845510#?c=&m=&s=&cv=1&xywh=-1354%2C368%2C4363%2C2442

Index

abolitionism, 100–101
access
  art and, 141
  to citizenship, 75, 90
  education and, 52, 80
  farming and, 138–39
  food and, 163
  to land ownership, 92
  to literacy, 113
  sound truck and, 143
  technology and, 191n24
  to theater, 15
activism
  Chicanx, 66
  as collaboration, 22
  complexity of, 120
  creativity and, 25, 67
  improvisation and, 1–2, 16
  interpurpose, 141, 151, 154
  jazz consciousness and, 17
  love and, 7
  performance and, 178n71
  plays as, 29
  See also spiritual activism
activist theater
  civil rights movement and, 22
  dislocation and, 93–94
  performance studies and, 19–25
  propaganda and, 85
  See also El Teatro Campesino; Free
    Southern Theater;

actos, of El Teatro Campesino
  aesthetics of obligation in, 60
  artistic expression of, 61
  audience and, 89
  carpa theater and, 58
  community and, 56
  contrafact and, 75
  cultural activism and, 75
  cultural memory and, 166
  early, 23
  as essentialism critique, 71
  Huerta on, 73
  identity and, 66–67, 91
  improvisation and, 58–59, 66, 70, 89
  influences on, 58, 183n6
  labor reform and, 54
  participatory toning and, 23, 59
  spirituality and, 60
  See also specific actos
Adorno, Theodor, 13, 14
aesthetics of obligation, 157, 173
  in *actos* of El Teatro Campesino, 60
  artistic citizenship and, 5
  Bambara and, 4–5, 169
  community and, 81, 154
  in filmmaking, 169
  in Free Southern Theater, 28, 35
  improvisation and, 17
  interpurpose art and, 132
  intimacy and, 24, 104
  jazz aesthetic and, 35

aesthetics of obligation (*continued*)
  Liberty House and, 104
  Morrison on, 5
  poetry and, 143
  in El Teatro Campesino, 60
Africa, textiles and, 115–17
African American plays, 30
"African Slave Trade to the Civil War,"
  148, 149
Afro-alienation acts, 21, 94
agency
  of Black women, 111
  farmworkers' movement and, 131
  improvisation and, 99
  participatory toning and, 59
  relationality and, 86
agricultural labor
  citizenship and, 76
  poetry and, 145
  racial identity and, 90–91
agricultural time, capitalism and, 66
agriculture
  artistic expression and activism in,
    168–73
  Black, 145
  natural world and, 73
  See also farmworkers' movement;
    food
aid and assistance, in civil rights movement, 94
alienation, 112, 124–25
Alternate ROOTS, 29, 157
alternative seasonal calendar (Lent), 73
American protest art, Free Southern
  Theater and, 31–35
Anderson, Madeline, 169
Anzaldúa, Gloria, 62, 162
Appalshop, 169
archival textiles. *See* textiles
archive, cultural activism and, 3
art
  access and, 141
  civil rights movement and role of, 4
  debate on politics and, 4, 13

Dewey on objects of, 84
education and role of, 5
Free Southern Theater and American protest, 31–35
jazz and experimental, 13–15
See also creativity; intermedia; interpurpose art
art activism
  civil rights movement and, xviii, 2
  cultural memory and, 13
  as education, 82–86
  history of, 13
  philosophy and, 13
artistic citizenship, aesthetics of obligation and, 5
artistic experimentation
  civil rights movement and, xvii
  cultural activism and, 85
  jazz and, 13–15
artistic expression, 4
  of actos of El Teatro Campesino, 61
  agricultural activism and, 168–73
  social movements and, 13, 14
arts organizations, civil rights movement and, 25
Ashé Cultural Arts Center, xv, xvii
audience
  actos of El Teatro Campesino and, 89
  of Austin Project, 160, 164
  in California, 185n28
  communication and, 57
  community and, 168
  cultural worker and, 141
  education and, 85–86
  of farmworkers' movement, 67, 73, 89
  of Free Southern Theater, 33–34, 37,
    40, 42, 85, 94–95
  of *Governor Brown*, 69–70
  learning of, 78
  of *The Lesson*, 80–81
  of *The Panza Monologues*, 167–68
  presence of elsewhere and, 24, 86, 98
  racism and, 37
  relajo, 33

relationality of, 95
in rural Mississippi, 185n28
of *Slave Ship*, 50–51
television, 149
of theater, 33–34
Austin Project, 25
audience of, 160, 164
Finding Voice circle and, 158
influences on, 159
jazz aesthetic and, 157–61, 172–73
social transformation and, 160, 173
authorship, 113
autonomy
Black, 108–9, 171–72
in Black feminism, 102
media, 130
Poor People's Corporation and
economic, 110
unions and, 134
avant-garde
Black Arts, 46–51, 53
cultural production and forms of, 15
Free Southern Theater and, 32–33
jazz and, 14
social relations and, 15
theater, 185n28
Azteca Theater, 68

Baden-Baden festival, 185n28
The Baden-Baden Lesson on Consent
(Brecht), 24, 93
Baker, Ella, xvii–xviii, 9–10, 111
Baldwin, James, 17
The Ballad of Sexual Dependency
(Goldin), 140
Ballis, George, *138*, 139
Bambara, Toni Cade
aesthetics of obligation and, 4–5, 169
on community organizing, 7
"The Organizer's Wife," 101, 105, 143,
147
on revolution, 4
The Salt Eaters, 16–17, 187n7
See also aesthetics of obligation

Baraka, Amiri, xvii
Blues People, 18
"The Revolutionary Theater," 53
See also Slave Ship
beautiful experiments, 113
Beckett, Samuel. *See Waiting for Godot*
Berlant, Lauren
on *The Color Purple*, 123
on intimacy, 6
Beyoncé, 117
Black Aesthetic, 53, 182n84
Black agriculture, 145
Black Arts avant-garde, 46–51, 53
Black Arts Movement, civil rights
movement and, 9
Black autonomy, 108–9, 171–72
Black bodies, violence against, 130
Black cooperatives, 107
See also cooperative movement; craft
cooperatives
Black cultural expression, 130
Black dance, 155
Black feminism
autonomy in, 102
craft cooperatives and, 113
economic reform and, 24
economic theory of, 102
intimacy-making and, 104
tradition of, 7
Black freedom struggle, 56, 129
Black independent media, 169–70
Black liberation, 171
Black liberation theater, 28
Black Lives Matter protests, 154–55
Black migration, 108
Black militancy, 97–98
blackness, Brooks on, 37
Black ownership, 137
Black Panthers, 145
Black performance, embodiment and,
94
Black Scholar, 151
Black sharecroppers, 102
Black southern identity, 133

Black visual culture, 130
Black women
  agency of, 111
  civil rights movement and, 102
  See also Black feminism
BLKARTSOUTH (arts program), 53,
  104, 148, 157
Blues People (Baraka), 18
Boal, Augusto, 178n71
bodies
  cultural memory and, 168
  image of, 162–63
  violence against Black, 130
  white supremacy and standards of,
    161–62
  See also embodiment
Bracero Program, 10, 90, 135
Brecht, Bertold, 15
  The Baden-Baden Lesson on Consent,
    24, 93
  followers of, 185n28
  Free Southern Theater and ideas of,
    32
  language and, 52
  Latin American theater and, 181n40
  presence of elsewhere, Free Southern
    Theater and theater of, 93–99
  "A Short Organum for the Theater,"
    91–92
broadcasting community, with *Nation
  Time*, 147–52
Brooks, Daphne, 37, 94, 154
brown, adrienne maree, 6, 7, 152, 154
Brownness, 66, 71
Brown v. Board of Education (1954),
  184n6
Bullins, Ed, 53, 182n84
business, love and, 105
Butler, Octavia, 170

call-and-response, 23, 70
camera, 130
capitalism, 36, 94, 109
  agricultural time and, 66

Poor People's Corporation and, 105
  utopian, 123
  white supremacy and, 137–38
Carmichael, Stokely, 97
carpa theater, 58
Castillo, Ana, 187n7
Catholicism
  alternative seasonal calendar of, 72
  Americanness and, 64
  El Teatro Campesino use of conver-
    sion methods of, 67
  farmworkers' movement and, 60,
    62–63
  iconography of, 70
  inclusivity and, 62, 64–65
  indigenous temporality and, 63
  La quinta temporada, labor and, 71–75
  social movements and, 64
  symbolism of, 60
  unions and, 63–64
Celie (character), 123–24
Chan, Paul, 27–28
Charleston Hospital Workers' Strike,
  169
Chavez, Cesar, 76
"Cherokee," 18, 30
Chicanx activism, 66
Chicanx identity, 70–71, 90, 162
Child Development Group of Mississippi, 82
children, labor of, 138–39
Chumacero, Olivia, 164
citizenship
  access to, 75, 90
  aesthetics of obligation and artistic, 5
  agricultural labor and, 76
  labor and conditions of, 23
  racism and, 5
civil disobedience, 155, 156
civil participation, 158
Civil Rights Act (1964), 105
civil rights movement
  activist theater and, 22
  aid and assistance in, 94

art activism and, xviii, 2
art and, 4
artistic experimentation and, xvii
arts organizations and, 25
Ashé Cultural Arts Center timeline
 of, xvii
Black Arts Movement and, 9
Black women and, 102
celebrations of, 12
community and, 5–6
cooperative ownership and, 105
creativity in, 19
cultural activism and history of, 8–13
cultural memory of, 3, 11, 115, 147
cultural production and, 173
defining scope of, 175n28
education and, 82, 83
farmworkers' movement and, 10
Free Southern Theater and, 45
grassroots elements of, 11
integration and, 80
intermedia and, 133
intimacy and, 13, 25
media poetics of, 143–47
narratives of, 27
participatory democracy and, 179n71
photography, 130
Slave Ship and, 48
Tuskagee University and, 184n1
violence of, 40
Walker, A., on, 12–13
"The Civil Rights Movement," 12–13
civil rights organizations, 94
civil rights workers, murders of, 12, 31
class prejudice, communication and, 83
Cobb, Charlie, 25, 129, 133, 143–47, 152
collaboration, 117
 activism as, 22
 in cooperative movement, self-
  expression and, 104–5
 Hamer on, 141
 intermedia and, 131–32
 technology and, 137
 See also intimacy-making

collective, storytelling and, 157
collective creativity, 102
 See also cooperative movement
The Color Purple (Walker, A.), 105
 Berlant on, 123
 cooperative movement and, 121–22
 cultural nationalism in, 123
 intimacy and, 121–25
Combahee River Collective, 172–73
commitment to witnessing, 132, 147
communication
 audience and, 57
 barriers of, 83
 class prejudice and, 83
 jazz improvisation and nonverbal, 36
 performance as, 78
communism, 70, 105, 108, 188n25
community
 actos of El Teatro Campesino and, 56
 aesthetics of obligation and, 81, 154
 audience and, 168
 Bambara on organizing, 7
 civil rights movement and, 5–6
 cooperatives and, 101–2
 cultural activism and, 12
 El Teatro Campesino and, 61
 Free Southern Theater and, 28, 33
 intimacy-making and, 5–6
 Nation Time and broadcasting,
  147–52
 participatory democracy and, 10
 self and, 6, 86
 to self-expression, right of, 5
 social wealth and, 112
 theater and, 21
Conquergood, Dwight, 178n71
contrafact
 actos of El Teatro Campesino and, 75
 creativity and, 18
 cultural activism and, 18
 El Teatro Campesino and, 19, 68
 ethnography and, 165
 European theater and, 18–19
 Free Southern Theater and, 39, 155

contrafact (*continued*)
   in *Governor Brown*, 68
   jazz and, 104–5
   jazz methodology, improvisation
     and, 16–19, 22–23, 160
   "KoKo" as, 18
   resourcefulness and, 21
Cooper, Anna Julia, 100, 111, 124–25
cooperative labor, 125
Cooperative League of the USA, 141
cooperative movement
   Black autonomy in, 108–9
   civil rights movement and owner-
     ship in, 105
   collaboration and self-expression in,
     104–5
   The Color Purple and, 121–22
   communism and, 108, 188n25
   community and, 101–2
   creativity and, 102
   Eastland on, 108
   economics of, 136–37, 187n14
   Hoffman on, 109
   labor organizing and, 129
   Maslow on, 109
   Poor People's Corporation meeting
     by Derby, *120*, 121
   SNCC and, 109
   social movements and, 187n7
   white supremacy and, 134
   See also craft cooperatives; *specific*
     cooperatives
Council of Federated Organizations,
   19–20
Cox, Ida, 16
craft cooperatives, 102
   Black feminism and, 113
   creativity and, 110
   Liberty House and, 102–3
   textiles and, 113
   women sewing by Derby, *119*
   See also Liberty House
Creating Aztlan (Miner), 65
creativity, 156, 173

activism and, 25, 67
   in civil rights movement, 19
   contrafact and, 18
   cooperative movement and, 102
   craft cooperatives and, 110
   cultural activism and, 5
   cultural workers and, 1–2
   education and, 91–92, 100
   of farm workers, 56
   improvisation and, 141
   jazz aesthetic and, 156, 159
   repurposing and, 139
   resourcefulness and, 18
   SNCC and, 10
   sustainability and, 171
   unions and, 76
cultural activism
   actos of El Teatro Campesino and, 75
   archive and, 3
   artistic experimentation and, 85
   civil rights movement history and,
     8–13
   community and, 12
   contrafact and, 18
   creativity and, 5
   education activism and, 23–34
   future of, 154
   improvisation and, 1–2, 16
   pedagogical experimentation and, 85
   performance collectives and, xv
   possibilities of, 126–27
   racism, performance and, 95–96
cultural borrowing, by Free Southern
   Theater, 38
   See also contrafact
cultural memory
   actos of El Teatro Campesino and,
     166
   art activism and, 13
   bodies and, 168
   of civil rights movement, 3, 11, 115,
     147
   of education activism, 185n6
   filmstrips and, 130

cultural nationalism, 123
cultural production, 5
  avant-garde forms and, 15
  civil rights movement and, 173
  as protest, 28
  queer, 131
cultural stereotypes, 70–71
cultural workers, 154
  audience and, 141
  creativity and, 1–2
  definition of, 147
  role of, 147
  See cultural activist
Cunningham, Ezra, 96

daily lives, racism and, 100
dance, 155
Deacons for Defense, 44
defamiliarization, 21
  El Teatro Campesino and, 99
  Free Southern Theater and, 99
  of racism conditions, 94
Delano grape strike and boycott. *See* farmworkers' movement
Delano strike, 55
Delta Ministry of the National Council of Churches, 142
Dent, Tom, xv, 48
Derby, Doris, xvii
  cooperative women sewing by, *119*
  Head Start workshop, *gele* wrapping, *114*, 115–17
  on Liberty House, 107
  Poor People's Corporation cooperative meeting by, *120*, 121
  Slave Ship production photos, *47*, *49*, *51*
  on theater, 11
  Walker, A., and, 122
  See also Southern Media
Dewey, John, 84
dislocation
  activist theater and, 93–94
  El Teatro Campesino and, 99

Free Southern Theater and, 99
  hooks on, 24, 86, 93–94
  racism and, 95, 98
documentary forms, 169
Does Man Help Man, 92, 93, 95, 98
domestic labor, 100, 104, 106–7, 111, 124
Don Coyote (character), 74
Douglass, Frederick, 149
dreamwork, xvii–xviii

Eastland, James O., 108
economic reform, 24, 134
economics
  of cooperative movement, 136–37, 187n14
  racism and, 106
  in *Something of Our Own*, 137
economic theory, of Black feminism, 102
education
  access and, 52, 80
  art activism as, 82–86
  arts role in, 5
  audience and, 85–86
  civil rights movement and, 82, 83
  creativity and, 91–92, 100
  El Teatro Campesino and, 81
  Free Southern Theater and, 81
  hooks on racism in, 84
  inequality and, 82
  The Lesson and, 82–83
  performance and, 99
  plays and, 81–82
  SNCC and, 84
  white supremacy and, 24, 80
education activism
  Brown v. Board of Education and, 184n6
  cultural activism and, 23–34
  cultural memory of, 185n6
elections, performativity of, 20
El Plan de Delano, 59, 66
elsewhere. *See* presence of elsewhere

El Teatro Campesino, 2, 9
  aesthetics of obligation in, 60
  Catholicism conversion methods
    used by, 67
  community and, 61
  contrafact and, 19, 68
  cultural stereotypes mocked by,
    70–71
  defamiliarization and, 99
  dislocation and, 99
  Las dos caras del Patroncito produc-
    tion by, 24, 86, *87*, 88–93
  education and, 81
  Free Southern Theater similarity
    with, 57
  Governor Brown production by, 23,
    61, *69*
  humor in, 60, 88–89
  identity and, 66–67
  inclusivity in, 58
  labor organizing of, 60, 76–77
  La quinta temporada production by,
    71, 72, 73–75
  medieval morality plays and, 61,
    67–68, 73
  origin of, 11
  participatory democracy embodied
    by, 58–59
  performance methodology of, 75
  protest aesthetics and, 19, 60–61
  protest and, 77
  racial identity and, 66–67
  rasquachismo, 60, 68
  social transformation and, 60
  spirituality of, 60–61
  stock characters in, 15, 73–74
  success of, 57–58
  Valdez directorship of, 166
  Los vendidos production by, 70–71
  See also actos, of El Teatro
    Campesino
embodiment
  Black performance and, 94
  traces of, 36, 173

emergence, regeneration and, 153–57
Emergent Strategy (brown), 6–7, 152, 154
English language, 88–89
Ensler, V (Eve), 162
equal pay, 111
equal rights, 129, 184n1
essentialism, 71
estrangement, intimacy-making and, 6
ethnography, contrafact and, 165
European theater, contrafact and, 18–19
everyday life, musical improvisation
    and, 16
"Everyday Use," 116
everyday use, archival textiles and
    performances of, 113–21
experimental art, jazz and, 13–15
exploitative labor, 73, 106, 125
Eyes on the Prize, 169

farming, 187n3
  access and, 138–39
  indigenous methods of, 170–71
Farming While Black, 170, 172
farm machinery, *136*
farm workers, creativity of, 56
farmworkers' movement, 11
  agency and, 131
  audience of, 67, 73, 89
  Black freedom struggle and, 56
  Catholicism and, 60, 62–63
  civil rights movement and, 10
  El Plan de Delano, 59
  exploitation and, 73
  faith-based work approach of, 62
  forgiveness as tool of, 63
  identity and, 90
  learning-plays as aesthetic in, 89
  march to Sacramento, 55–56
  organization of, 55
  paternalism and patriarchal attitudes
    in, 71
  performances of, 65–66
  process-oriented approach to, 71
  relationality in, 86–87

Index · 213

self-reflection of, 63
SNCC and, 56–57
spiritual activism of, 62–64
unions and, 75–76
See also Governor Brown; El Teatro
  Campesino
Farm Worker's Strike, 127–28, 134, 137,
  138, 139
fatphobia, 167
Federal Theater Project, 15
Federation of Southern Cooperatives,
  102, 127, 170, 186n3
feminism. *See* Black feminism
filmmaking, aesthetics of obligation
  in, 169
filmstrips, 126–28
  cultural memory and, 130
  intermedia and SNCC, 131–41, 172,
    191n24
  production of, 141
  projectors and, 139–41, 191n24
  repurposing in, 139
  storytelling in, 139
  of Varela, 141–42
  See also specific films
finances
  of Free Southern Theater, 38–39
  intimacy and, 123
  of Liberty House, 103–4, 187n6
Finding Voice circle, 158–59, 166
Fleming, Julius B., Jr., 32
Fletcher, Bob, 144, 145
Flute Publications, 133, 141
Fluxus, 140
food
  access and, 163
  cultivation, 110
  diet, 167
  health and, 163–64, 167
  justice, media experimentation and,
    168–73
  love and, 167
"Formation," 117
Forti, Simone, 139–40

freedom
  Black struggle for, 56, 129
  improvisation and, 17–18
  Liberty House and, 105–13
  Poor People's Corporation and,
    105–13
Freedom Farm, 107, 110, 170
Freedom Quilting Bee, 102, 113
Freedom Rides, 12
Freedom Schools, 82
Freedom Summer, 12, 20
Free Southern Theater, xv, 2
  aesthetics of obligation in, 28, 35
  alienation of actors in, 98
  American protest art and, 31–35
  audience of, 33–34, 37, 40, 42, 85,
    94–95
  avant-garde and, 32–33
  The Baden-Baden Lesson on Consent
    production by, 93
  BLKARTSOUTH and, 53, 104, 148,
    157
  Brechtian theater, presence of else-
    where and, 93–99
  Brecht ideas and, 32
  civil rights movement and, 45
  community and, 28, 33
  contrafact and, 39, 155
  cultural borrowing by, 38
  cultural history of, 54
  "death" of, 153
  defamiliarization and, 99
  dislocation and, 99
  Does Man Help Man production by,
    92, 93, 95, 98
  education and, 81
  El Teatro Campesino similarity
    with, 57
  European theater and, 19
  final performance of, 8, 9
  finances of, 38–39
  formation of, 11
  funding of, 82
  harassment of, 180n20

Free Southern Theater (*continued*)
  ideological struggles of, 31
  improvisation and aesthetics of, 33
  integration of cast at, 79
  intimacy-making and, 33
  jazz aesthetic of, 30, 33, 35, 157
  learning-plays of, 93–94
  The Lesson production by, 24, 33, 79, 80
  lineage of, 158
  location requests for tour of, 31
  Nation Time, 24, 129, 133, 147–52
  newsletter of, 149
  performance studies and, 21, 52
  performance theory and, 52
  plantation geography and, 32
  Proper and Fine production by, 29, 44–46
  racial identity and, 37
  repertoire of, 34
  The Rifles of Señora Carrar production by, 24, *95*, 96–98
  royalties of, 38
  segregation and, 31
  set design of, 33
  Slave Ship production by, 22, 23, 29, 30, 46, *47*, 48–51
  sponsorships of, 35
  theater of, 42
  theater traditions of, 32
  A Valediction Without Mourning production by, 153–54, 155
  voter registration and, 31
  Waiting for Godot production by, 27–29, 34–35, 39, *41*, 43–44, 150–51
  In White America production by, 180n20
  workshops of, 35
The Free Southern Theater by the Free Southern Theater, 29, 31, 81
Freire, Paulo, 83
Fresh, Mumu, 172
fully human life, 124
Furrows (Cobb), 25, 129, 133, 143–47, 152

gele wrapping, Head Start workshop on, *114*, 115–17
Genet, Jean, 38
genres, improvisation and crossing of, 2
gestures of protest, 155
Ghana, 171
Goldin, Nan, 140
Governor Brown, 61
  audience of, 69–70
  contrafact in, 68
  El Teatro Campesino production of, 23, *69*, 156
  improvisation and, 67–71
  language in, 23
  participatory toning in, 69–70
  visual jazz and, 23
Governor Brown (character), 70
Graham, Dan, 139–40
Grand Marie Vegetable Cooperative, 142
grape boycott, 22
"The Greatest Love," 26–27
Great Migration, 136
Grise, Virginia, 25, 157, 161–68

Hamer, Fanny Lou, 45–46
  autobiography of, 141
  on collaboration, 141
  Freedom Farm, 107, 110, 170
  on MFDP, 20
happenings, 22
Harlem Renaissance, 155
Harlem Workshop, 106
Hartman, Saidiya, 113, 118
hatred, intimacy and, 44
Head Start, 82, 105, *114*, 115–17, 143, 185n6
health, food and, 163–64, 167
"Health Theater in a Hmong Refugee Camp.," 178n71
Heron, Gil Scott, 2–3
Highlander Research and Education Center (Highlander Folk School), 14–15, 35, 133, 157–58

Index · 215

Hinton, Rufus, 145
Hoffman, Abbie, 109
hooks, bell
    on dislocation, 24, 86, 93–94
    on integration stresses, 109–10
    on love, 13
    on racism in education, 84
    on revolution, 4
    on self-actualization of teachers, 85
    Sisters of the Yam, 109–10
    Teaching Community, 84, 100
    on white supremacy, 100
Huerta, Jorge, 73
humanism, 100
humor, 60, 88–89, 163

I Am Somebody, 169
identity
    actos of El Teatro Campesino and,
        66–67, 91
    Black southern, 133
    Brownness, 66, 71
    Chicanx, 70–71, 90, 162
    El Teatro Campesino and, 66–67
    farmworkers' movement and, 90
    improvisation and, 59
    performance and, 74
    shared, 132
identity formation, 94, 117
immigration law, 90
improvisation
    activism and, 1–2, 16
    actos of El Teatro Campesino and,
        58–59, 66, 70, 89
    aesthetics of obligation and, 17
    agency and, 99
    in *carpa* theater, 58
    creativity and, 141
    cultural activism and, 1–2, 16
    everyday life and musical, 16
    freedom and, 17–18
    Free Southern Theater aesthetics
        and, 33
    genre crossing in, 2

    Governor Brown and, 67–71
    identity and, 59
    inclusivity of, 77
    jazz methodology, contrafact and,
        16–19, 22–23, 160
    nonverbal communication and jazz,
        36
    relationality of, 36
    of Sun Ra, 3
    visual jazz and aesthetics of, 35–4
        6
    in *Waiting for Godot*, 37–38
    See also participatory toning
inclusivity
    Catholicism and, 62, 64–65
    in El Teatro Campesino, 58
    of improvisation, 77
    politics of, 64–65
    religion and, 62, 64–65
    unions and, 23
indigenous communities, Liberty
    House and, 103
indigenous farming methods, 170–71
indigenous mobility, 68
indigenous resistance, 73
indigenous temporality
    Catholicism and, 63
    La quinta temporada and, 71
    peregrinación and, 62–67
    spiralic time, 66, 73
    tribalography of, 65, 66, 73
indigenous thought, religion and, 65
indigenous worldviews, 78
industrial labor, 112
inequality
    of artistic exchange, 38
    education and, 82
    social, 82, 156
"In Furrows of the World," 144–45
integration, 42, 105
    civil rights movement and, 80
    Free Southern Theater cast, 79
    hooks on stresses of, 109–10
interdisciplinarity, 132

intermedia, 127
  in art history, 131
  civil rights movement and, 133
  collaboration and, 131–32
  definition of, 25
  intimacy-making and, 133
  performance and, 132
  SNCC filmstrips and, 131–41, 172,
    191n24
  storytelling, 129, 132
interpurpose activism, 141, 151, 154
interpurpose art
  aesthetics of obligation and, 132
  Morrison and, 154
interracial relationships, 39
intimacy, 100
  aesthetics of obligation and, 24, 104
  Berlant on, 6
  between women, 116–17
  civil rights movement and, 13, 25
  finances and, 123
  hatred and, 44
  social change and, 70
  textiles and, 115
  transformational healing and, 75
intimacy-making
  Black feminism and, 104
  community and, 5–6
  estrangement and, 6
  Free Southern Theater and, 33
  intermedia and, 133
  learning-play and, 24
  in *La quinta temporada*, 75
  at Liberty House, 104
  love and, 7
  privacy and, 160
  storytelling and, 7–8
  theater and, 57
  women and, 112–13
In White America, 180n20
Ionesco, Eugene, 24, 33
  See also The Lesson
I Play Flute (Stembridge), 133
Iyer, Vijay, 36, 173

Jacklyn Early (character), 80–81
jazz
  by Adorno, dismissal of, 14
  avant-garde and, 14
  consciousness, activism and, 17
  contrafact and, 104–5
  experimental art and, 13–15
  as language, 17
  Marsalis on, 26
  musicians, Baraka on, 18
  nonmusical media and, 14
  participatory democracy and, 36
  repurposing and, 18, 156
  revolution and, 3
  Stravinsky and, 38–39
  theater and, 30, 159–60
  in writing, 36
  writing, Baldwin on, 17
  See also improvisation; visual jazz
jazz aesthetic
  aesthetics of obligation and, 35
  Austin Project and, 157–61, 172–73
  creativity and, 156, 159
  of Free Southern Theater, 30, 33, 35,
    157
jazz methodology
  contrafact, improvisation and, 16–19,
    22–23, 160
  as new idiom for theater, 16
  The Panza Monologues and, 167
Johnson, Patrick E., 164
Jones, LeRoi. *See* Baraka, Amiri
joy, 117
Judson Dance Theater, 140
Junebug Productions, 157–58

Karamu House Theater, 35
Katrina (hurricane), xvi, 26
King, Martin Luther, Jr., 50, 76, 170
"KoKo," 18, 30
Ku Klux Klan, 31, 97

labor
  camp, *138, 139*

changing nature of, 75–78
Chicanx identity and, 90
children and, 138–39
citizenship conditions and, 23
cooperative, 125
Cooper on, 111
domestic, 100, 104, 106–7, 111, 124
exploitative, 73, 106, 125
industrial, 112
La quinta temporada, Catholicism
 and, 71–75
movement, 10, 75–76, 90
race and, 90
reform, *actos* of El Teatro Campesino
 and, 54
rights, 76
of women, 120
See also agricultural labor
labor organizing
cooperative movement and, 129
creative approach to, 77
of El Teatro Campesino, 60, 76–77
land ownership, 109
access to, 92
X, Malcolm, on, 110
language
Brecht and, 52
Chavez on, 76
English, 88–89
in *Governor Brown*, 23
jazz as, 17
praxis and, 6
Spanish, 88
theater and, 52, 88
language-play, 58
La quinta temporada
Catholicism, labor and, 71–75
Don Coyote, 74
indigenous temporality and, 71
intimacy-making in, 75
personification in, 73–74
spiritual activism and, 73
El Teatro Campesino production of,
 71, *72*, 73–75

Las dos caras del Patroncito (The Two
 Faces of the Boss), 24, 86, *87*, 88–93
La Virgen de Guadalupe, 64
learning, of audience, 78
"Learning from Experience," 191n37
learning-plays (*Lehrstücke*)
farmworkers' movement and aesthetic of, 89
of Free Southern Theater, 93–94
intimacy-making and, 24
Lehrstücke. See learning-plays
Lenin, Vladimir, 188n25
The Lesson (Ionesco)
audience of, 80–81
education and, 82–83
Free Southern Theater production
 of, 24, 33, 79, *80*
Jacklyn Early, 80–81
Liberty House, 2, 24
aesthetics of obligation and, 104
craft cooperatives and, 102–3
as cultural center, 103
Derby on, 107
economy of, 105–7
finances of, 103–4, 187n6
freedom and, 105–13
Greenwich Village store of, 103,
 105–6
indigenous communities and, 103
intimacy-making at, 104
organizational structure of, 121
Lira, Augustin, 68–69, 70, 166
literacy
access to, 113
alternative forms of, 142
programs, 185n6
SNCC initiatives for adult, 128
theater and, 52
See also Selma Literacy Project
lived religion, 64, 71
Los vendidos (The Sellouts), 70–71
love, 170
activism and, 7
business and, 105

love (*continued*)
  food and, 167
  hooks on, 13
  intimacy-making and, 7
  material concerns and, 13
  social change and, 7
Love, Bettina, 100
lynching, 135

The Man Who Cried I Am (Williams), 36
the March. *See* farmworkers' movement
Marsalis, Wynton, 26
Martin, Sharon Stockard, 29, 44–45
Marx, Karl, 124–25, 188n25
Marxist theater, 67
Maslow, Ellen, 109
Mayorga, Irma, 25, 157, 161–68
media
  autonomy, 130
  Black independent, 169–70
  as distraction, 2–3
  experimentation, 57, 130, 168–73
  food justice and experimental, 168–73
  jazz and nonmusical, 14
  participatory culture of, 10
  poetics of civil rights movement, 143–47
  See also intermedia
medieval morality plays, 61, 67–68, 73
Meridian (Walker, A.), 122
minstrelsy, 42, 43, 151
missionaries, 67–68
Mississippi Freedom Democratic Party (MFDP), 20
Mississippi Freedom Vote (1963), 19–20, 21
mobility
  indigenous, 68
  of outdoor performances, 60
  peregrinación and, 66
Moraga, Cherríe, 162
Morris, Jesse, 141–42
Morrison, Toni

on aesthetics of obligation, 5
on art and politics debate, 4
interpurpose art and, 132
Moses, Gil, xv, 29, 44
  See also Slave Ship
The Movement, 12, 56–57
Mr. Smith (character), 94
Muñoz, José Esteban, 25, 66, 71, 131–32
musical improvisation. *See* improvisation
"My Sister's Panza," 167

National Educational Television, 148
National Farm Workers Association (NFWA), 9, 55
National Labor Relations Act, 63, 76
National Student Association, 84
Nation Time, 24, 129, 133, 147–52
natural world, agriculture and, 73
Neal, Larry, 53, 182n84
New Orleans
  Ninth Ward, 27
  Urban Bush Women performance in, *xvi*
  See also Free Southern Theater; Katrina
NFWA. *See* National Farm Workers Association
Ninth Ward, 27
Nkombo, 148, 157
non-iconicity, 130
nonverbal communication, jazz improvisation and, 36
nonviolence, 97
nonviolent protest, 44
nourishment, 170
"Now's the Time," 16–17
Nyang'o, Tavia, 146

"On Cooperation," 188n25
O'Neal, John, 27
oral tradition, 58, 127

"The Organizer's Wife," 101, 105, 143, 147
Outside people, 83

"Panza Girl Manifesto," 167
The Panza Monologues (Grise & Mayorga), 25, 157, 161–68
Parable of the Sower, 170
Parker, Charlie, 36
  "KoKo," 18, 30
  "Now's the Time," 16–17
participatory commons, 10, 131
participatory democracy
  civil rights movement and, 179n71
  community and, 10
  definition of, 10
  El Teatro Campesino embodiment of, 58–59
  jazz and, 36
  power relations and, 110
  relationality and, 85
participatory instruction, 131
participatory media culture, 10
participatory toning, 58
  actos of El Teatro Campesino and, 23, 59
  agency and, 59
  call-and-response in, 70
  in *Governor Brown*, 69–70
  transformational healing and, 59
paternalism, 71, 83, 188n25
patriarchy, 71
Patroncito (character), 88, 92
pedagogical activism, 82
pedagogical experimentation, cultural activism and, 85
Pedagogy of Freedom (Freire), 83
Pedagogy of the Oppressed (Freire), 83
peregrinación (pilgrimage), 23, 55–56
  indigenous temporality and, 62–67
  mobility and, 66
  See also farmworkers' movement
performance
  activism and, 178n71

collectives, cultural activism and, xv
  as communication, 78
  education and, 99
  embodiment and Black, 94
  of everyday use, archival textiles and, 113–21
  of farmworkers' movement, 65–66
  of Free Southern Theater, final, 8, 9
  identity and, 74
  intermedia and, 132
  methodology of El Teatro Campesino, 75
  mobility of outdoor, 60
  multiplicity of meaning communicated through, xvi
  propaganda and, 22
  protest and, 77
  racism, cultural activism and, 95–96
  resonance of *Slave Ship*, 51
  techniques, appropriation of, 38
  theory, Free Southern Theater and, 52
  transformation and, 21–22
  Urban Bush Women New Orleans, *xvi*
performance studies
  activist theater and, 19–25
  Free Southern Theater and, 21, 52
  relationality and, 20–21
personification, in *La quinta temporada*, 73–74
philosophy, art activism and, 13
photography
  civil rights movement, 130
  SNCC, 25, 129, 135, 142, 143–47, 168–69
  subjects of, 146
pilgrimage. *See peregrinación*
Plain Truth, 148
plantations
  conditions of, 107
  geography, Free Southern Theater and, 32

plays
  as activism, 29
  African American, 30
  education and, 81–82
  medieval morality, 61, 67–68, 73
  See also learning-plays; theater;
    specific plays
Plessy, Homer, xvi
poetry
  aesthetics of obligation and, 143
  agricultural labor and, 145
  revolution and, 143–47
politics
  debate on art and, 4, 13
  of inclusivity, 64–65
  relationality and, 57
  religion and, 63
Poor People's Corporation, 24, 102–3,
    157
  capitalism and, 105
  cooperative meeting by Derby, *120*
  economic autonomy and, 110
  freedom and, 105–13
  organizational structure of, 121
  Training Center, 106
"Pour a Little Honey in My Tea," 164
power relations, participatory democ-
    racy and, 110
praxis, 6, 100
Preacher (character), 49
presence of elsewhere
  audience and, 24, 86, 98
  Free Southern Theater, Brechtian
    theater and, 93–99
  racism and, 86
privacy, intimacy-making and, 160
projectors, 1, 96, 126–27, 139–41, 191n24
propaganda, 99
  activist theater and, 85
  performance and, 22
Proper and Fine, 29, 44–46
protests
  aesthetics, El Teatro Campesino and,
    19, 60–61

art, Free Southern Theater and
  American, 31–35
Black Lives Matter, 154–55
cultural production as, 28
El Teatro Campesino and, 77
gestures of, 155
performance and, 77
SNCC and, 44
See also nonviolent protest

queer cultural production, 131
queer family-making, 125
quilting, 115
  in "Everyday Use," 116
  studies, 116
  Walker, A., and, 118
  See also textiles

race
  labor and, 90
  relations, 37, 40, 42
racial formation, 130
racial identity
  agricultural labor and, 90–91
  El Teatro Campesino and, 66–67
  Free Southern Theater and, 37
  labor movement and, 90
racial solidarity, *Las dos caras del
    Patroncito* and, 86, *87*, 88–93
racism, 90
  absurdity of, 42, 44, 163
  audience and, 37
  citizenship and, 5
  daily lives and, 100
  defamiliarization of conditions of,
    94
  dislocation and, 95, 98
  economics and, 106
  in education, hooks on, 84
  performance, cultural activism and,
    95–96
  presence of elsewhere and, 86
  as systemic, 1, 139
  voter registration and, 20

white supremacy and, 81
in workplace, 109–10, 113
rasquache, 68
rasquachismo, 60, 68
Reconstruction, 135
regeneration, emergence and, 153–57
Reinhardt, Max, 38
relajo, 33, 163
relationality
   agency and, 86
   of audience, 95
   brown on, 6
   in farmworkers' movement, 86–87
   as fractal, 6, 85
   of improvisation, 36
   modes of, 128
   participatory democracy and, 85
   performance studies and, 20–21
   politics and, 57
   in social movements, 85–86
religion
   inclusivity and, 62, 64–65
   indigenous thought and, 65
   lived, 64, 71
   missionaries, 67–68
   politics and, 63
   unions and, 62
   See also Catholicism; spiritual activism
reparations, 112, 171–72
"Reparations," 172
representation, 130
repurposing
   creativity and, 139
   in filmstrips, 139
   jazz and, 18, 156
   technology, 24–25, 137
   See also contrafact
resilience, 139, 154
resourcefulness
   contrafact and, 21
   creativity and, 18
   social inequality and, 156

revolution
   Bambara on, 4
   definitions of, 66
   as fractal, 10
   hooks on, 4
   jazz and, 3
   poetry and, 143–47
   X, Malcolm, on, 110
"The Revolutionary Theater," 53
"The Revolution Will Not Be Televised.," 2–3
Richardson, Riché, 116–17, 123
The Rifles of Señora Carrar, 24, *95*, 96–98
right to complexity, 99–100
Rouselle, Bill, 148–50
royalties, 18, 38
rural modernity, 135

The Salt Eaters (Bambara), 16–17, 187n7
Schechner, Richard, 51–52
seasons, 74
segregation, Free Southern Theater and, 31
self
   actualization, 85, 125
   brown on, 7
   community and, 6, 86
   defense, 97, 98
   healing, social transformation and, 75
   help, 103–5, 107–9, 111, 188n25
   reflection of farmworkers' movement, 63
   sufficiency, 108
self-expression
   community and right to, 5
   in cooperative movement, collaboration and, 104–5
   See also artistic expression
Selma Literacy Project, 83, 85–86, 99, 124, 176n23
set classroom time, 86
set design
   of Free Southern Theater, 33
   of *Slave Ship*, 48

sewing, 105, 106, *119*, 122, 124
sex workers, 140
sharecropping, 106, 107
"A Short Organum for the Theater,"
    91–92
Shuffle Along, 38
Shug Avery (character), 122
Sisters of the Yam (hooks), 109–10
16th Street Baptist Church bombing,
    50
slavery, 43
    "African Slave Trade to the Civil
        War," 148, 149
    aftermath of, 112
    history of, 40, 117
    "What to a Slave Is the Fourth of
        July," 149
    white supremacist tactics of, 134
Slave Ship (Baraka), xvii
    audience of, 50–51
    Black Arts avant-garde and, 46–51
    civil rights movement and, 48
    Derby production photos of, *47, 49,*
        51
    Free Southern Theater production
        of, 22, 23, 29, 30, 46, *47*, 48–51
    lighting and visibility in, 48–49
    performance resonance of, 51
    Preacher's speech in, 49
    script of, 46, 51
    set design of, 48
slideshows, of SNCC, 140
SNCC. *See* Student Nonviolent Coor-
    dinating Committee
social change, 131
    intimacy and, 70
    love and, 7
social inequality, 82, 156
social justice, 1, 56, 65, 99–100, 127, 156
social movements, 1
    artistic expression and, 13, 14
    Catholicism and, 64
    cooperative movement and, 187n7
    hierarchy within, 85

interior dynamics of, 4, 129
    relationality in, 85–86
    space and, 66
social norms, theater and resistance to,
    14–15
social relations, avant-garde and, 15
social stratification, 106–7
social transformation, 159
    Austin Project and, 160, 173
    El Teatro Campesino and, 60
    self-healing and, 75
social wealth, 111–12, 124–25
So Far from God (Castillo), 187n7
solidarity
    commitment to witnessing, 132, 147
    Las dos caras del Patroncito and racial,
        86, *87,* 88–93
    scope of, 86
    Taylor on, 132
    unions and, 75, 91
Something of Our Own, 127, *128,* 133–35
    economics in, 137
    farm machinery in, *136*
    Fletcher and, 145
    Goldin and, 140
Soul Fire Farm, 25, 169–73
sound, Urban Bush Women use of, xvi
sound truck, access and, 143
Southern Black Cultural Alliance, 157
Southern Christian Leadership Con-
    ference, 49
Southern Media, 24–25, 141–43
space, social movements and, 66
Spanish Civil War, 96
Spanish language, 88
spiralic time, of indigenous temporality,
    66, 73
spiritual activism, 23, 59
    of farmworkers' movement, 62–64
    La quinta temporada and, 73
spirituality
    actos of El Teatro Campesino and,
        60
    of El Teatro Campesino, 60–61

Spoken Word Orchestra, 160
"Starred-Dark Night," 145
Stembridge, Jane, 133
stock characters, in El Teatro
    Campesino, 15, 73–74
Story Circles, xv, 158, 160
storytelling
    collective and, 157
    in filmstrips, 139
    intermedia, 129, 132
    intimacy-making and, 7–8
    of SNCC, 141
    tribalography and, 73
Stravinsky, Igor, 38–39
Student Nonviolent Coordinating
    Committee (SNCC), 126–27
    adult literacy initiatives of, 128
    Baker and, 9–10, 111
    cooperative movement and, 109
    creativity and, 10
    education and, 84
    expansion of, 56
    farmworkers' movement and, 56–57
    Flute Publications of, 133, 141
    formation of, 9
    intermedia and filmstrips of, 131–41,
        172, 191n24
    photography, 25, 129, 135, 142, 143–47,
        168–69
    protest and, 44
    slideshows of, 140
    storytelling of, 141
    technology and, 137
    values of, 134
    workers of, 175n23
    See also The Movement
Sun Ra, improvisation of, 3
sustainability, 170–71

Taft-Hartley Act (1947), 76
Taylor, Diana, 132, 147
teachers, hooks on self-actualization
    of, 85
Teaching Community (hooks), 84, 100

teaching plays. *See* learning-plays
technology
    access and, 191n24
    collaboration and, 137
    farm machinery, *136*
    projectors, 1, 126–27, 139–41, 191n24
    repurposing, 24–25, 137
    SNCC and, 137
television, 147–52
textiles
    Africa and, 115–17
    craft cooperatives and, 113
    gele wrapping, Head Start workshop
        on, *114*, 115–17
    intimacy and, 115
    narratives of, 113
    performances of everyday use and
        archival, 113–21
    See also craft cooperatives; sewing
theater
    access to, 15
    audience, 33–34
    Black liberation, 28
    Brecht and Latin American, 181n40
    carpa, 58
    community and, 21
    Derby on, 11
    Federal Theater Project, 15
    intimacy-making and, 57
    jazz and, 30, 159–60
    jazz methodology as new idiom for,
        16
    language and, 52, 88
    literacy and, 52
    oral tradition in, 58
    social norms resistance and, 14–15
    See also activist theater; European
        theater; Free Southern Theater; El
        Teatro Campesino
Theater of the Oppressed (Boal), 178n71
This Bridge Called My Back (Anzaldúa
    & Moraga), 162
"The Ties That Bind," 118, 123
toning. *See* participatory toning

traces of embodiment, 36, 173
transformation, performance and, 21–22
transformational healing
  intimacy and, 75
  participatory toning and, 59
Treme, 26–27, 54
tribalography, 65, 66, 73
Tubman, Harriet, 101, 172
Tuskagee University, 184n1
The Two Faces of the Boss. See Las dos caras del Patroncito

UFW strike. *See* farmworkers' movement
unemployment, 102
unfinished projects, 141–43, of Southern Media
unions
  autonomy and, 134
  Catholicism and, 63–64
  creativity and, 76
  farmworkers' movement and, 75–76
  inclusivity and, 23
  mobilization of, 71
  religion and, 62
  solidarity and, 75, 91
  Taft-Hartley Act, 76
United Farm Workers, 134
unreal time, 37
Urban Bush Women, xv, *xvi*

The Vagina Monologues (Ensler), 162
Valdez, Luis, 88, 92, 166
A Valediction Without Mourning, 153–54, 155
Varela, Maria, 83–84, 97, 114, 115, 116, 118, 191n37
  filmstrips of, 141–42
  Selma Literacy Program report by, 124
  Something of Our Own okra image by, *128*
violence
  against Black bodies, 130
  of civil rights movement, 40

visual jazz
  definition of, 37
  Governor Brown and, 23
  improvisation aesthetics and, 35–46
  process, 38
  See also contrafact; Free Southern Theater
Vitale-Penniman, Neshima, 170–71
voter registration, 4, 11–12, 44, 184n1
  Free Southern Theater and, 31
  racism and, 20

Waiting for Godot (Beckett), 26
  Free Southern Theater production of, 27–29, 34–35, 39, *41*, 43–44, 150–51
  improvisation in, 37–38
  Martin's adaptation of, 29, 44–45
  script of, 41
Walker, Alice
  on civil rights movement, 12–13
  Derby and, 122
  "Everyday Use," 116
  Meridian, 122
  quilting and, 118
  See also The Color Purple
Walker, Bill, 142
Wall of Truth, 142
Washington, Booker T., 184n1
Wayward Lives, Beautiful Experiments (Hartman), 113
"We Shall Overcome," 45
West Batesville Farmer's Cooperative, 126
"What to a Slave Is the Fourth of July," 149
White Citizens Council, 56, 180n20
white supremacy
  body standards and, 161–62
  capitalism and, 137–38
  cooperative movement and, 134
  education and, 24, 80
  hooks on, 100
  internalization of, 84

racism and, 81
slavery and tactics of, 134
"Wild Women Don't Have the Blues,"
16
Williams, Jeannette, 149–50
Williams, John A., 36
Winterson, Jeanette, 153, 156
women
intimacy between, 116–17
intimacy-making and, 112–13
labor of, 120
sewing by Derby, cooperative, *119*
See also Black women
workplace, racism in, 109–10, 113
writing, jazz in, 36
WYES television station, 147–52

X, Malcolm, 110, 170

Young Negroes Cooperative League,
111